In memory of a
holiday spent in Cranleigh

To Alice
From Auntie Pcy.

The County Books Series
GENERAL EDITOR: ERIAN VESEY-FITZGERALD

SURREY

THE COUNTY BOOKS SERIES

FOLLOWING ARE THE FIRST TWENTY
VOLUMES IN ORDER OF PUBLICATION

Sussex	*Esther Meynell*
Surrey	*Eric Parker*
Somerset . . .	*M. Lovett Turner*
Lowlands of Scotland .	*George Blake*
Kent . . .	*Richard Church*
Cornwall	*Claude Berry*
Devonshire . . .	*D. St. Leger Gordon*
Staffordshire . . .	*Phil Drabble*
Worcestershire . . .	*L. T. C. Rolt*
Shropshire	*Edmund Vale*
Dorset	*Eric Benfield*
Derbyshire . . .	*Crichton Porteous*
Yorkshire—East Riding	
	John Fairfax-Blakeborough
Gloucestershire . . .	*Kenneth Hare*
Herefordshire . .	*H. L. V. Fletcher*
Cheshire	*F. H. Crossley*
Cambridgeshire and Huntingdonshire	
	E. A. R. Ennion
Hampshire and Isle of Wight	
	Brian Vesey-FitzGerald
Isle of Man . . .	*Canon E. H. Stenning*
Essex . . .	*C. Henry Warren*

PLEASE WRITE TO THE PUBLISHERS
FOR FULL DESCRIPTIVE PROSPECTUS

SURREY

by

ERIC PARKER

Illustrated and with a Map

London
Robert Hale Limited
18 Bedford Square WC1

First published September 1947
Second impression November 1947

PRINTED IN GREAT BRITAIN
BY WESTERN PRINTING SERVICES LTD., BRISTOL

CONTENTS

Chapter		page
I	BROOKLANDS	1
II	SURREY SOILS	10
III	LAKES AND PONDS	18
IV.	ANCIENT CAMPS	33
V.	INDUSTRIES	45
	Iron—Glass—Gunpowder—Cloth—Leather—Pottery: Ancient, Modern	
VI.	ROADS	80
	Stane Street to Bypasses—East and West—Byways—Smugglers' Path	
VII.	THE PILGRIMS' WAY	94
VIII.	CHANGES	105
	The Fold Country—Leatherhead Mill Pool—Vine Cottage	
IX.	FIELDS YESTERDAY AND TO-DAY	113
X.	IN THE WOODS	120
XI.	AN OLD FARM ACCOUNT BOOK	137
XII.	WOMEN'S INSTITUTES	150
XIII.	FALLOW DEER TO FROGS	157
XIV.	BIRDS IN GARDEN AND WILD	174
XV.	INSECTS IN A GARDEN	200
XVI.	FOLK LORE	213
XVII.	THREE MUSEUMS	224
XVIII.	TALK WITH A COUNTRYMAN	232
XIX.	GRASSHOPPERS AND SCHOOL CRICKET	245

ILLUSTRATIONS

1	The Old Mill, Cobham	*frontispiece*
		facing page
2	The old Coaching-yard, Guildford	16
3	An old corner of Lingfield	17
4	The dining-room at the Hautboy Hotel, Ockham	32
5	The Parish Church, Farnham	32
6	Old cottages facing the River Wey, Eashing	33
7	View of the Thames, Richmond Terrace	33
8	March sunshine, Coldharbour	48
9	The Tower, Leith Hill	48
10	Castle Mill, Dorking, with Box Hill behind	49
11	The Church, Windlesham	49
12	Waverley Abbey, near Farnham	64
13	An inn yard, Farnham	65
14	Castle Street, Farnham	80
15	A corner in Albury below Newlands Corner	81
16	Pilgrims' Way, looking east from St. Martha's	96
17	Chancel of Compton Church	96
18	Abbot's Hospital, Guildford	97
19	Abinger Hammer	97
20	Mill on the Mole, Leatherhead	112
21	The New Cathedral, Guildford (*Detail Work by the late Eric Gill*)	112
22	Guildford Grammar School	113
23	Ewhurst, from Pitch Hill	113
24	Autumn in a Surrey beech-wood—Leith Hill	128
25	Harvest at Gatton	128
26	Richmond Bridge	129
27	On the North Downs: chalk pit near Ockley	129
28	Pyrford Mill on the River Wey, near Ripley	144
29	On the Wey Canal, Byfleet	145
30	The King's Stone, Kingston-on-Thames	160
31	Walton-on-Thames	161
32	Bridge over the River Wey, Tilford	176
33	Friday Street	176
34	North Downs, looking to Ranmore	177
35	Ockley	177
36	Box Hill	192

vii

ILLUSTRATIONS

facing page

37 Almshouses from the porch of Godstone Church   192
38 Brewer Street, Bletchingley   193
39 A Thames-side path, Ham   193
40 Whitgift's Hospital, Croydon   208
41 Shere   208
42 Old houses in Shere   209
43 Looking over the Devil's Punch Bowl, near Hind-
    head   209
44 Old water-mill at Elstead   224
45 Castle Gate, Guildford   224
46 Mediæval doorway in Quarry Street, Guildford   225
47 Through the lychgate at Shalford   225
48 Colley Hill, Reigate   240
49 Wolsey's Tower, on the banks of the Mole, Esher
    Place   241
    Folding Map   *at end*

ACKNOWLEDGMENTS

The Illustrations above, numbered 2, 5, 6, 11, 14, 15, 17, 18, 19, 21, 22, 30, 42, 44, 45, 46 are reproduced from photographs by Mr Reece Winstone, A.R.P.S., of Bristol; 1, 24, 26, 39 by Mr A. K. Rittener of Teddington; 3, 8, 47 by Mr E. W. Tattersall of St. Albans; 12, 49 by Mr T. Edmondson of Folkestone; 4, 40 by Humphrey and Vera Joel of Radlett; 13 by Mr E. C. Griffith of Farnham; 41 by Aerofilms of London. The remaining 20 are reproduced from photographs supplied by Mr Will F. Taylor of Reigate.

Chapter I

BROOKLANDS

THE sun is shining on a lawn that lies under trees. Three of the trees are always in my mind when I think of that sunshine, and first of them a chestnut, not because of its size or any beauty beyond that of others, but because its crimson and orange blossoms reminded me when I first saw it of a chestnut on a lawn I knew when I was a child in Hertfordshire—a chestnut neighbouring a swing and a tiny stream wandering through fields to the road.

A cherry tree is next in my mind which through fifty weeks of the year stood as cherry trees stand in flower gardens, with no separate graces of foliage or shape, but which in each returning May spread a transparency of white flowers alive with bees, so that you looked to a deeper blue in the sunlight beyond. Laurence Binyon once, I remember, coming suddenly into the garden to that cherry tree, exclaimed and was silent, and as I think back through the years to its white flowers, all the garden is warm again.

And third is an apple tree, a little tree at the side of the lawn under which I used to sit and write. It is a tree, too, which belongs certainly to this book, for under it I wrote many pages of *Highways and Byways in Surrey*, when I was walking day after day through its fields and roads, and writing the next day of what I had learnt and found. But I remember it for two other reasons. I used to hang coco-nuts sawn in halves to its branches, with the idea, when I first hung them up, of attracting nuthatches and tits, and it was on a nut hanging there that one morning I saw a sudden flash of red and black and white, a greater spotted woodpecker come to feed. I had never before been able to watch a spotted woodpecker so close to me, nor did I know that a woodpecker would hop about a lawn and hammer hazel nuts to pieces in an oak paling, as I used to watch that woodpecker from a window hammering them. But it was not only woodpeckers that the nuts attracted. There was a red

squirrel. He was a wild squirrel who was first attracted, I
think, by the sawn coco-nuts, but who one day, when I was
writing under the apple tree, dropped from its boughs on to
my knee and so to the ground in the most natural way in the
world, and later became so tame that he would come in at the
window of my study and sit beside me eating nuts out of a
bowl. He belongs to my happiest memories of those Weybridge days—just a wild red squirrel. I doubt if another
exists in Surrey to-day. The American invader from Woburn
has taken his place and to-day all the squirrels in Surrey are
grey.

One more memory goes with that apple tree, of days of
high summer. It is mingled of scent and sound, for it belongs
to the time when the Spanish chestnuts of Oatlands Park were
in flower, and the scent came on the wind to me as I wrote
on the lawn—a scent of cricket matches on the ground in the
Park, but of games at Lord's, too, because of that time of
the year. But the scent goes with a sound which is also of that
particular place in the month of July; the music of the post-
horn that was blown from the Brighton coach travelling on
the road by the park day after day, the coach with its four
horses and its driver in his tall white hat, in an hour of quiet
midsummer.

Those were the days when I first came to know Surrey,
and my knowledge began at Weybridge. It was a Surrey
different from the Surrey of to-day, and if you are to choose
in the whole country a single area of, say, ten square miles
to sum up the changes that have marked its history and its
countryside during the present century, I suppose that you
could find nowhere a greater difference from the past than
here above the banks of the Wey. You may see from the railway most of the change. When I first came to Weybridge in
1902, you could take a boat on the river not far from the
parish church and row up from the Thames under banks of
sallow and comfrey for mile after mile past Byfleet and
Wisley Church by Newark Priory to Woking and beyond.
When you came near to what was then Brooklands meadow,
you passed under the railway bridge and rowed on the little
stream with the pines of St. George's Hill on one side and
on the other the orchids and cowslips of wood and field. It

was a stretch of virgin river of the South Country, and if there was anywhere in Surrey where on an April morning you could count on hearing snipe drumming and green plover calling above their nests, it was along those few miles of stream. I have never been nearer the Surrey of centuries past than there.

And then, in 1907, came the change. As I look back, I think first of the change that has come to the river, for it was the river that I knew best, and no boat goes on it to-day. But the great change that came to the shape and look of the countryside was in the destruction of trees and fields which came with the making of Brooklands motor race-course. For a man of middle age to-day, gazing from the train at that great cement-rimmed saucer, with its race stands, its hangars and its sewage works, it needs some imagination to picture pine woods sloping down to the stream in place of the tiers of the stand, and open fields instead of corrugated iron and arrangements for disposal of drainage. Perhaps I may be forgiven for reprinting some lines I wrote at the time :

By Brooklands hill but since a year
    Untrod the meadows lay,
Unspanned through musk and meadowsweet
    Ran olive-bright the Wey.

Blackbirds about that wind and wild
    Carolled a roguish choir,
From willow green to willow grey
    Kingfishers shot sapphire !

There gay and far the Surrey sun
    Spread cowslips far and gay,
Lit wide the orchid's purple flame,
    The white fire of the may;

And thither stole a happy boat
    To hear the ringdoves coo,
To mark again the drumming snipe
    Zigzag the April blue;

3

To watch the darting dragon-flies
Live pine-needles a-wing—
O Brooklands meadow, there we knew
You first knew all the spring!

And then—the change! Spade, engine, pick,
The gangers' myriad Hun,
A thousand branches' banished shade,
Flat glare of sand and sun.

From pine and stream to steam and stone,
From peace to din and pain,
From old unused to new unuse,
But never Wey again!

That was the beginning of the Surrey of to-day; the Surrey in which cars have displaced broughams, by-passes run from county to county where lanes loitered from village to farm, and planes roaring overhead shut out the song of larks. Brooklands meadow became hemmed in by a race-course, and within a few months was to see the first flight of aeroplanes from a levelled stretch of fields—we called it an aerodrome then—in the south of England.

But even as the pine trees fell and the cement hardened, there came the touch of a hand from the past. Under the steel of the ganger lay in the sun a contrast of other metal. I quote from the terse report of the Keeper of Coins and Medals of the British Museum, Sir George Hill:

"On Whitsun Monday, May 20th, 1907, the workmen engaged in making the Brooklands Motor-Track discovered, about two feet six inches below the surface, and broke with the pick, an earthenware jar containing a number of large coins. The exact number will probably never be known, for there was a scramble for the contents of the jar. The find comprised, so far as I have been able to ascertain, sixty-eight coins, which were seized by the coroner, under the impression that they were treasure-trove. I have seen sixty-four of these; the remaining four are, I believe, in the possession of the coroner and the local inspector of police, as mementos of the discovery. . . . Seventy-two were shown at the British Museum by two persons soon after the discovery was made.

4

Two others were mentioned by one of these persons as having been sold by him to someone else. But there were doubtless many more in the original treasure."

And so we are left guessing; but admiring, too, the Keeper's report for what it does not say. "The coins that I have seen," the report goes on, "amounting to 137, are all of the so-called middle-brass kind," that is, they belong to a period of coinage following the year A.D. 296. They are stamped with effigies of the Emperors Diocletian, Maximilian, Galerius and Constantius, and sixty of them were presented to the British Museum by the owner of the land, Mr Locke-King, who retained four for himself. Who retained the other seventy-odd, besides the "many more in the original treasure" we do not learn, and are left picturing the scene of the scramble.

And so Roman coins linked the past with the betting-ring of bookmakers that followed motor-racing on the track, which began in the summer. I have before me the prospectus —it is a six-page document printed on the finest paper—of the first meeting. It is headed "Brooklands Automobile Racing Club; Licensed to hold Motor Race Meetings by the Automobile Club of Great Britain and Ireland," and following the Nomination Circular and various printed regulations comes the list of officials :

"Stewards—The Earl of Dudley, G.C.V.O., Colonel H. G. Holden, The Earl of Lonsdale. Judge—W. C. Manning, Esq. Deputy-Judge—A. S. Manning, Esq. Starter—Hugh Owen, Esq. Clerk of the Scales—A. S. Manning, Esq. Deputy-Clerk of the Scales—W. E. Bushby, Esq. Clerk of the Course and Racing Manager—E. de Rodakowski, Esq."

Next, in red ink :

"The following Races will be run on the Brooklands Course on Saturday, July 7th, 1907. They close and name to the Secretary, the Brooklands Automobile Racing Club, Carlton House, Regent Street, London, S.W., by 12 o'clock mid-day, on June 25th, 1907."

And then comes the list of races, six in number :

"*The Horsley Plate* of 300 sov. (The nominator of the winner to receive 250 sov., and the nominator of the second 50 sov.) For motor-cars propelled by internal combustion engines only, of a cylinder dimension of 60 to under 85. Weight 3,000 lb. About three miles. Entrance : 15 sov.

"*The Gottlieb Daimler Memorial Plate* of 650 sov. (The nominator of the winner to receive 500 sov., and the nominator of the second 150 sov.) For motor-cars propelled by means of internal combustion engines only, of a cylinder dimension 120 to under 155. Weight 3,000 lb. About fifteen miles. Entrance : 30 sov. p.p.

"*The Byfleet Plate* of 550 sov. (The nominator of the winner to receive 450 sov., and the nominator of the second 100 sov.) For motor-cars propelled by means of internal combustion engines only, of a cylinder dimension of 110 to under 135. Weight 3,000 lb. About ten miles. Entrance : 25 sov. p.p.

"*The Stephenson Plate* of 300 sov. (The nominator of the winner to receive 200 sov., and the nominator of the second 100 sov.) For motor-cars of a price not less than £600, and not exceeding £700. Weight 3,500 lb. About six miles. Entrance : 25 sov. p.p.

"*The First Montagu Cup* of 2,100 sov. (A Cup value 200 sov., and the remainder in specie. The nominator of the winner to receive the Cup and 1,400 sov., the nominator of the second to receive 400 sov., and the nominator of the third 100 sov.) For motor-cars propelled by means of internal combustion engines only of a cylinder dimension 155 to under 235. Weight 2,600 lb. About thirty miles. Entrance 500 sov. p.p.

"*The Marcel Renault Memorial Plate* of 550 sov. (The nominator of the winner to receive 400 sov., the nominator of the second 100 sov., and the nominator of the third 50 sov.) For motor-cars propelled by means of internal combustion engines only, of a cylinder dimension 85 to under 110. Weight 3,000 lb. About twelve miles. Entrance : 25 sov."

It all reads strangely enough to-day, modelled in its verbiage on the phraseology and conditions of horse-racing. And that meeting in the summer of 1907 echoed on cement what began on green turf in the days of Eclipse; we read of races for so many "hundred sov." and we listened to the strident clamour of the betting ring on slopes which a few months before had heard nothing louder than the wind in pine trees above the Wey.

6

But greater changes were to come. Two years later, to Brooklands meadow that was came what was not so much a development as a surprise. On 18, 19 and 20 October 1909, the first flying meeting held in this country took place at . Blackpool; this was followed by a meeting at Brooklands on October 28, 29 and 30. It must have been arranged at short notice, for in the *Field* I can find no preliminary notice of the date; but people came down from London in numbers, in spite of the weather which was showery. I kept a copy of the card of the meeting, a twenty-page brochure on glazed paper with a cover printed in light blue with an illustration of "the celebrated aviator Paulhan" seated in the chair of his machine, a fragile-looking affair open to the air. On the opening page are the names of the committee of twenty responsible for the meeting, among them the Earl of Lonsdale, president; Lord Montagu of Beaulieu, vice-president; the Duke of Beaufort, Viscount Churchill, the Earl of Dudley, the Earl of Essex, Lord Northcliffe, the Earl of Sefton, Prince Francis of Teck, and the Duke of Westminster.

"It has been during the last two years"—so runs the text of the brochure—"that the art of flying has developed so phenomenally," and during those two years "it is the French who have provided the largest proportion of modern aviators." So we are introduced to Paulhan, "more phenomenal than the rest," and his biplane, so called

"because it is constructed with two superimposed planes or 'decks' on the lower of which is situated the pilot's seat. These 'decks' are not flat, but cambered in a peculiar manner, so as to sweep the air downwards as they are driven broadside on through it. It is the reaction derived from this downward sweeping of the air—analogous to the recoil of a gun—which sustains the machine in flight, and unless sufficient velocity is maintained, it is impossible for the flyer to rise."

Thus were the elements of the art of flying explained to Weybridge, and so we come to the flyer himself:

"Watching him on his machine aloft it is difficult to follow what he does to keep it so steadily in flight. Calmly he sits in the little low-backed seat, holding the lever in one hand, while the other commonly clasps in easy attitude one of the uprights of his machine; he is the impersonation of confidence.

7

As he turns about a mark post it is possible to see the rudder move upon its pivot, a manœuvre which he has accomplished by pressing upon one end of the crossbar with his foot. Then if the machine cants a little, he corrects it by pushing the lever in his right hand sideways, or if the flyer is not quite on an even keel he will move the same lever to and fro, and so dip or tilt the 'elevator' according as the head of the machine is too high or too low. Simple as these manœuvres are to describe they require practice to be carried out with just that nicety which alone will keep the flyer from lurching to the ground. Especially in windy weather is great skill necessary, and Paulhan has a reputation for flying in breezes which keep most experts in their hangars."

That was in 1909, and those were the beginnings of the change in the outlook on everyday life in England which began at Brooklands. Where the change was leading we did not yet see. I look back through the files of the *Field* to find on 4 February 1911, after a caution to British makers of flying-machines as to the competition of the French, who "will strain every nerve to win the Gordon-Bennett trophy and the *Daily Mail* £10,000 prize," the following :

"Londoners seem scarcely to be aware of the splendid exhibition of flying that can be seen any fine day at Brooklands, and they appear also to imagine that if the weather be dull or foggy in town it is the same everywhere else. By the way, it might be well for the Brooklands authorities to arrange to have displayed in some conspicuous position at Waterloo Station, and somewhere in the West-end also, daily statements as to the weather at Weybridge. Often when it is dull in London it is sunny and warm there, although such a little way out. Saturdays are the busiest flying days, of course, but Brooklands is well worth visiting on other days in the week. There are about forty sheds and about fifty machines in the aerodrome. Some of the aviators are quite brilliant flyers, and the Brooklands centre has peculiar interest on account of the variety of types of aeroplanes at work. Frenchmen and Englishmen and ladies can be seen flying and learning to fly, and passenger flights are common. Flights can be booked beforehand in London if desired."

Memories of those flights are still in my mind. You can

book a flight for yourself, in imagination, by looking through the pages of the *Field* or other illustrated papers of the time, and can guess what it was like to sit on a plain open chair, so to speak, high above the motor race-course and feel the wind over face, body and legs under the wings of those queer naked skeletons of machines.

So came and went 1911 for Surrey and England, and three years later fell the greatest change of all.

CHAPTER II

SURREY SOILS

IN its name Surrey holds its distinction. It is not called after its people, nor does it tell you its place. It is not to be found by the map, as is Northumberland or Westmorland, nor by the men who live in it, as Norfolk and Suffolk, Essex and Kent. Surrey is a name of two words, *Suth* and *rige* or *rice*, the realm of the South; you find *rice* in our word bishopric, and Suthrige is the diocese, the place of dwelling apart, in the south. Surrey is the kingdom south of the Thames.

That is Surrey's only natural boundary, the Thames. East lies Kent, the country of the Cantii, south lies Sussex, west Wessex, three separate peoples. And perhaps it was the countryside itself which divided the peoples from one another, the men of Sussex as the tribe which lived between what is still to-day forest to the north, the marshland of Kent and the forest of Hampshire. In the country north of the forest of Sussex the people had their camps along the high ridge which holds Hascombe, Holmbury and Anstiebury, and their high ground ran out to where now stands Farnham to the far west, and Hindhead looking down on Hampshire and Sussex.

> The Wey, that Taffy called Wagai
> Was more than six times bigger then . . .

and the forests were deeper and the ramparts of the hill camps higher. But the people were of the same bent and outlook; Surrey to them was a kingdom, as it is to-day a realm of itself, a part of the countryside whole and secure, from the quiet fields by its riversides in the north through the pines and junipers, the sand and heather of its middle ridge, to the oaks and primroses of its Wealden clay in the south. It is a kingdom of southern England self-contained.

Surrey divides itself geologically into five parts, distinguished by soil and products. You may pass through the main part of them in a day's walking, north to south, and watch the change of field and hill, trees and heather, but I like, too, to follow the lie of soils on a map, and I know no more delightful hour of its kind with a book than to open the *Victoria History of the County of Surrey* at its geological map, to show you at a glance—but you will look longer than that—the features of the countryside south of the Thames.

To take the five districts in order. Along the valley of the Thames, travelling east from the border of Kent, lies a belt of the London Clay. This belt, some ten miles deep north and south from Southwark to Croydon, or from Kew to Epsom, narrows gradually from Esher past Church Cobham, Ockham and Ripley to Stoke by Guildford, and then tapers out by Aldershot into Hampshire. North of this narrowing strip, which towards the west is no more than two miles wide, lies the broad area of the Bagshot Beds. In the Bagshot Beds, a region of hill and upland of thirsty sands, lie St. George's Hill, Esher Common, Cobham Ridges, St. Anne's Hill, and Bagshot Heath—summed up, perhaps, as regards the possibilities of farming and crops by the rifle ranges of Bisley.

Next we come to the main feature of the Surrey landscape, the great chalk ridge that runs east and west from Tatsfield on the Kent border, Caterham Common, Coulsdon, Banstead, and Epsom Downs, Box Hill, Merrow Down by Guildford, past Guildford to the Hog's Back that drops down to Farnham on the extreme west. If any feature of the country south of the Thames might seem at first thought to form a natural boundary, it is this chalk ridge, but the early Britons looked at it from a different point of view. They thought of the long line of height as a stretch along which they could see to right and left and know where they were going. It is their old road, their high way, and we who walk along it to-day see the England they saw.

South of the great chalk ridge and roughly parallel to it lies what to some of us at all events is the most interesting country in Surrey, the Lower Greensand. On the southern edge of the chalk, from Titsey, past Gatton, towards St. Catherine's Hill and past Farnham into Hampshire runs an ever-narrowing strip of the Upper Greensand, and all along this strip of Upper Greensand runs a band, also narrowing

from east to west, of the Gault. Both these clayey soils are
rich ground, as you may see from the hop gardens by and
beyond Farnham, but they are narrow, and it is to the south
that you come to the Surrey alike of the fruit grower, the
farmer, the gardener and the artist, the varied stretch
through Oxted, Reigate, Dorking, Abinger, Godalming and
Thursley to Hindhead itself. It is a noticeable contrast of the
two ranges of high ground that the chalk range gets gradually higher towards the east of the county, while the Greensand tends, with here and there an outstanding eminence, to
become higher towards the west. Thus the Downs above
Albury rise to 600 ft., north of Reigate to 767 ft., north of
Blechingley to 775 ft., finally above Limpsfield to 876 ft., the
highest point in the range. On the Greensand the tendency
runs from Tilburstow Hill, which is less than 600 ft., higher
and higher, with Leith Hill the topmost point in Surrey,
967 ft., towards Hindhead, which is the great jutting but-
tress of the west, 894 ft. above sea level.

All these Greensand heights look out over the Wealden
Clay. This is the soil of the main part of the country along
the Sussex border, with a few square miles in the extreme
south-eastern corner, south of Lingfield, which cuts into the
Hastings Beds of Sussex and Kent. This strip of Wealden
Clay, some five miles deep on the east and west, with an
extreme depth of seven miles in the middle between Betchworth to the north and Rusper just in Sussex to the south,
contains ironstone in places, as does the Greensand. We shall
come to iron among the Surrey industries, but the time has
not yet arrived when, as H. E. Malden suggests in his
History of Surrey, ironstone "which gave once an active industry to the county, may again alter its character from a
farming and residential to a mining and manufacturing district, should the search for Wealden Coal be completely
successful." To-day in the Greensand we turn up ironstone
with the plough and the spade, but its best use, as I sometimes guess, may yet prove to be road-metal.

There is no sharper contrast of soils than from the chalk
of the great east-to-west ridge, through the light earth of
the Greensand, to the heavy clay of the Weald. If I were to
choose one single spot to show to a stranger the difference, it

would be a wide field nobly named Hundred Acre, which lies within a mile of the "single spot beloved over all" where I have spent the main part of my life.

I remember the field years ago, when I first looked at an old map and picked out the names of the fields near it, some of them easy to understand, others belonging to memories long gone—Poor Field, Great Bettams, Crowledge Field, Smallberries, Ten Acre, Feathercombe. That was before the war of 1914, when it was a wide plain of rough, wild grass. I doubt if it had ever been ploughed; it was bare downland without a building near. To-day, of course, the farm tractor passes and repasses over it, dust following the engine's hum, and corn springs in rows a little comfortlessly in the sun. But Hundred Acre it remains in village thought and talk, and it is a name with its own meaning, in its vastness and loneliness, for the countryside round. On the dividing line between the two separate soils of the South Country, the sand with its heather and pine, and the solid clay of the Weald, it belongs to neither and to both. How sharply differing those soils may be I realized on the day when first I climbed the sharp south side of Hundred Acre, up from the clay into the sand. You may count the crowded contours on the map, where a quarter of an inch of flat paper means hundreds of feet rising from primroses and wayside pools to whortleberry and ling.

And it is in such a soil as that of Hundred Acre, and the fields that lie along the strip of Surrey between the chalk ridge to the north, and the clay of the Weald, that you find the link that binds north and south—a farmer's link, lime. For sand and clay alike, lime for centuries has been the fertilizer. How great the need for lime, and how high its value in simpler days gone by, you may reckon by the size of the great chalk pits along the ridge, for example, white in the sun for miles to the south. And for other evidence of what must have been not only a big Surrey industry but part and parcel of the year's work of every farmer of this section of the county, there are the limekilns themselves, solidly built structures, still to be found more or less in the state in which they were last used. Of those the site of which I know myself, the most perfect lies just to the south of Hambledon

churchyard. It is covered with soil and brambles, but its
general shape and construction are easy to see.

It is a structure mainly consisting of a wall of stone and a
bank of earth. From the rough farm path outside the churchyard it looks exactly like a miniature tunnel. The tunnel
entrance is in the middle of a wall nine feet high in the centre,
sloping gradually down to the ground eight yards on each
side. The wall is of bargate stone, here and there patched
with ironstone, and the tunnel arch is of three concentric half-
circles of brick, one behind the other, the diameter of the
arch measuring three feet. The tunnel goes back, roofed with
brick five feet into a big mound of earth, hollowed in the
middle, and into this middle hollow the fuel must have been
placed with the lime to be burnt. In the old days I imagine
the smoke from the furnace must have been a familiar sight
to church-goers at Hambledon's church, St. Peter's : to-day
the mound of the kiln, shaded by elms, is covered with ivy,
dog's mercury and celandines, fit covering for the grave of
an industry past and gone.

Although the industry of converting chalk into lime and
cement is an old one, oddly enough we have very little evidence of the working of the lime kilns in early days. John
Aubrey, who was born in 1626, and spent many years in
putting together notes for his *Perambulation of Surrey*, which
was afterwards included in Richard Rawlinson's *Natural
History and Antiquities of Surrey* (published in 1719, after
Aubrey's death in 1697), evidently could get hold of no dates
as to lime-burning. He tells us that workmen grubbing an old
dead oak at Smallfield, to make room for a lime kiln, found
one ready-made to their hands with lime stones in it, which
had been disused beyond the memory of man. Tradition is
equally vague. Mr Montague Giuseppi, writing in the
Victoria History of the county, quotes a friend, Mr George
Clinch, on the point :

"There is a tradition which may have more of fact for its
basis than have the generality of traditions, that the extensive
chalk pit near the railway station at Sutton was dug mainly
when St. Paul's Cathedral was being built by Wren, the chalk
being burnt for the lime employed for the mortar being used
in that church."

If tradition speaks truly, then, that chalk pit was dug towards the end of the seventeenth century. A later historian, James Malcolm, in his *Compendium of Modern History principally written during a Survey of Surrey,* writing of the quarries in Surrey in 1805, says that the best limestone pits in the county, if not in England, were at Dorking, and that the stone burnt into lime at Dorking was sought after by every mason and bricklayer in London. With the Dorking lime were built the West India Docks and the docks at Wapping.

All along the chalk ridge at this period lime-burning went on, the best quality stone being reckoned to be that at Denbies, and next that at Merstham, Sutton and Carshalton. Guildford chalk was considered to be inferior. Six kilns were worked at Denbies; six loads of chalk went to a kiln, and the price of the six loads was from fifteen shillings to twenty-one shillings. But lime itself was far more expensive. The price of a kiln of lime, Malcolm tells us, at a distance of seven to twelve miles from the chalk pit, was from £10 to £14 or £15, the difference between prices of chalk and lime being partly due to the cost of fuel and carriage.

Not all the old lime kilns are so plain to view to-day as the kiln next the churchyard at Hambledon. There is one at the foot of Hydons Ball to the south, and if Hundred Acre was ever ploughed in the old days, I imagine that the lime burned in the Hydons Ball kiln was used there. To-day you can find the kiln and see the shape of the entrance, with part of the stone and brick work, but most of it is buried.

A third kiln lies on the western slopes of Hydons Ball, within a few yards of a right-of-way leading east and west. Nothing can be seen of the kiln itself, except a deep hollow in the hillside, but the right-of-way passes close enough to the mouth to have made passers-by, you would think, uncomfortably hot. But that suggests the question, How did the right-of-way come into existence? There is nothing to-day at either end of it to suggest that any traveller would need to get from here to there. Were those who made the path just travelling to and from the kiln? That is a theory which would fit in with other facts of history. Soon after I came to live on the flank of Hydons Ball, I was given by a friend an old map of the fields in the neighbourhood. This map, dated 1845, drawn and coloured by hand, shows an old road running from buildings named Green's Farm, across two fields marked "arable" (one of them to-day hazel coppice), direct to the kiln. Another old road approaches and passes the kiln, running roughly north and south, so that the kiln lies at the juncture of four cross-roads. None of these roads can be seen to-day, lying as they do under what are to-day plain plough and woodland. But years ago, I was told, you could still see in hot weather the track of one of those old roads to the kiln, crossing a field named on the map Great Bettams. I would like to think that that quaint name should not perish as have the old roads.

I shall always remember the way in which I accidentally discovered this kiln at the old cross-roads. Very soon after I and my family had come to live in the house which has been my home for most of my life in Surrey, we had as our guest Leonard Huxley, whom I had come to know through working in the office of the *Cornhill Magazine*, which was then edited by my friend Reginald Smith. On a day in 1910 Huxley and I were returning from a walk over Hydons Ball, and I pointed out to him a spot near the juncture of the four cross-roads, of whose existence I then knew nothing, which apparently consisted of solid chalk. The path itself, and the ground on each side of it, seemed to be made of chalk. He was a man of wide general knowledge, and had lived in Surrey for years—his wife had founded a girls' school, Prior's Field, near Godalming, whose pupils have thought with gratitude of her ever since—and I supposed vaguely that he might have an answer to what looked an odd riddle—chalk in a district of sand. But he was puzzled. "An outcrop of chalk —an outcrop of chalk?" he repeated, and it was not until weeks afterwards that I found in spilt cartloads of chalk for burning an answer to the riddle.

But those cross-roads, those four old roads, two of them to-day invisible, meeting by that hidden kiln—I have often thought they might be marked on the map with a cross all to themselves. For they stand at the meeting-place of differing soils and of things old and new. A dozen yards to the north of the kiln, where chalk has been piled on sand, is a

16

patch of loam carpeted with primroses. A hundred yards to the south, running east and west through my garden, is a long, deep strip of clay. Another hundred yards or so to the south of the strip of clay you have only to dig down in the sand to come upon bargate stone, of a quality to build houses with, or for that matter rock gardens. Alongside of the clay lie strata of ironstone, and to ironstone, and Surrey's industry of iron, we come elsewhere. And running right up to the kiln, and past it, is what I have sometimes thought may be the rampart of an ancient camp—perhaps the camp of "Hydon's Top"—the subject of the old rhyme I have quoted in another chapter.

An old corner of Lingfield

CHAPTER III

LAKES AND PONDS

I HAVE often had in mind an imagined book of a river; of the kind of book which a man might write who should spend day after day, year in year out, on the banks of a single stream and should watch it and think of it as a man would live with a friend. I have thought of a book such as might be written of a salmon river in Scotland, a river which a man had seen in days of February, high and flooding by banks of blue-shadowed snow, and in August low and clear under fern and heather; or trout water such as George Dewar knew, writing of the little Pang and its June wild roses, or of a river in wild country, like the Irish Lee loved by Francis Mahony, within sound of the Shandon bells. And I have thought, dreaming still of the weather and the skies I have known over lakes and rivers, that a man might write a book of his own on so small and common a thing as a pond.

Perhaps small is not a right word to use, for a pond can be little or big, as insignificant as a village pond or as wide and windswept as the stretches of water we call lakes in Sussex and ponds in Surrey. And I write here, of course, of Surrey ponds, of which I know something and wish I knew more, for I live on a hill, and to know a pond thoroughly you must work by day and sleep by night on its level. But I have had the good fortune through many years to be near enough to ponds of different sizes to be able to watch the bird life on them through the seasons, if not day by day, at least on many days; and looking back on years gone, and forward to the hope of days to come, I find two thoughts uppermost. One is that Surrey, at the opening of the war of 1939, was richer in the bird life of her waters than at any time in living memory; and the other that though, as I write, the war has done infinite harm in destruction of bird life, there is still hope of return to happier and easier days.

First, then, for a comparison of the past with what, for

the moment, we may consider the present. Take the conditions of days when Sir John Bucknill was writing his *Birds of Surrey*, published in 1900. He was surveying the bird life of the county as it had been chronicled during the last half of the nineteenth century, that is, roughly, of conditions as they existed from a hundred up to fifty years ago. That was a period before the Wild Birds Protection Acts of the 'eighties and 'nineties had had time to become effective; when the possibilities of photography, in studying the natural history of birds, had hardly begun to be realized; and when the first idea in the mind of an observer, if he wished to establish the identity of a bird, was to shoot it. I do not attempt here, of course, a list of birds which became rare, or perhaps extinct, in Surrey, during the period preceding the Wild Birds Protection Acts. But here are a few records of the occurrence of visitors and residents, rare or local, which witness the attitude of the public at large, during these nineteenth-century decades, towards bird observation in Surrey.

"*Cormorant.* On 12 September 1884, an immature specimen was killed on a pond near Witley, and 'A Son of the Marshes' mentions an adult male obtained in Surrey in August 1894 (*In the Green Leaf*, pp. 178–9). It has also been shot at Poynter's, near Cobham. . . . In the autumn of 1899 one was observed and remained for several days on Frensham Great Pond.

"*Bittern.* In the winter of 1890–1 seven were killed in the frost at Godalming. In the same year a fine male was killed on Epsom Common. In 1893 another was shot on the Thames at Apps Court. On 9 January 1895 a female was killed at Weybridge. . . . In certain suitable seasons (adds Bucknill) it is probable that a few visit us, but generally speaking it may be considered as a distinct rarity, and, as such, deserves every possible protection.

"*Grey Phalarope.* The year 1866 was remarkable for the numbers of this species which appeared in Great Britain. Mr J. Gurney, jun., who published a pamphlet dealing with the 1866 immigration, mentions several shot in the county; one near Aldershot, 8 September; three at Tilford, Millcourt, and Farnham respectively, which were placed on 22 and 24 September in the hands of Mr Mansell of Farnham, for preservation; one on the Thames, close to Waterloo Bridge, near the wharves, and one at Frensham Pond on 30 September. Since that time one was shot on the reservoir at Barnes at the end of October 1870 (another great Phalarope year), and recorded in the *Field* (5 November 1870, p. 338); another whilst swimming on a brook near Redhill by a Mr Andrew Marriage, 16 October 1877, and I have myself (writes Bucknill) seen a specimen in winter plumage, which was obtained at Sutton about 1884.

"On 25 October 1891, one was shot at West Molesey by a Mr T. Taylor. Another in winter plumage was obtained near Cranleigh some years ago, and Mr Hook mentions the occurrence of a specimen about 1895 near Frensham. It has also been obtained at Poynter's, near Cobham.

"*Green Sandpiper*. In Surrey the Green Sandpiper is a spring and autumn migrant, but is much less abundant than the Common Sandpiper. It has been killed and observed on many occasions during the last few years in Surrey (i.e. previous to 1900); on the Mole, Wey, Thames, and many of the smaller streams as well as on the larger ponds and lakes, and sometimes on the rough moorland.

"*Common Sandpiper*. 'A Son of the Marshes' states that it has nested within a few miles of his residence (Dorking) on the River Mole, and Mr Streatfield found two young birds a few days old and a nest on Little Frensham Pond, in 1896. Generally speaking, all along the Mole and Wey, it may usually be seen in May and August, and on the Wandle and Thames is also constantly observed, whilst by many of the larger sheets of water it is, though less often, frequently noticed at the same seasons. I have records of specimens shot and seen in all parts of the county.

"*Redshank*. An occasional visitor on migration. . . . I have notes of its occasional occurrence on Frensham Pond. There is a specimen preserved in the hotel at that lake, shot there in September of 1893; and two were shot at Mitcham, by Mr Felton, in the autumn of 1895.

"*Greenshank*. A casual visitor of some rarity. . . . In the winter of 1891, the Rev W. Basset, of Frimley, shot a specimen on the Blackwater Brook, near that place. Mr Bryan Hook has one in his collection from Frensham Pond; and on

11 September 1893, on the edge of the Little Pond, Messrs
S. A. Davies and Robertson, of Godalming, observed a single
bird feeding, which, though very wary, they were able to
identify without doubt. A specimen (possibly the same bird)
was also seen about the same time on the Great Pond. In the
autumn of 1895 one was killed by Mr Felton at Mitcham.

"*Curlew.* An occasional visitor. . . . Though it is quite
possible that it may have bred in the county—there being
many suitable localities—I am unaware of any definite record
of its having done so.

"In 1893, on 13 May, Mr B. B. Gough, heard several
after dark, whistling overhead on Wray Common, Reigate.
In the same year during the whole of the summer a pair were
noticed near Frensham, which probably had a nest on the
moor. Early in October 1894 a flock of five or six were seen
on Epsom Downs by Dr Daniel; one was seen calling over
Munstead Woods, near Godalming, in November of the
same year; and 'A Son of the Marshes' mentions a pond near
Boxhill occasionally visited by this species (*On Surrey Hills*,
p. 83).

"*Great Northern Diver.* As a casual visitor, this fine
species has occurred in Surrey on a few occasions, Frensham
Pond supplying nearly all the examples. . . . A specimen in
immature plumage weighing eight pounds was shot on Frensham Pond at the end of 1869. It was preserved by Mr
Mansell, of Farnham, and recorded in the *Field*, 8 January
1870. In 1885, an immature specimen was shot on the same
pond, and is now preserved in the hotel.

"*Black-throated Diver.* On 26 March 1881, a specimen
was shot at West Molesey, and a single specimen has been
shot at Poynter's, near Cobham.

"*Red-throated Diver.* A gentleman, writing in the *Field*,
19 March 1892, records a bird of this species which fre-
quented a pond near Cobham in February 1892 for several
days in extremely severe weather. It kept a piece of water
free from ice by its active swimming."

These are short extracts from a comprehensive book of 374
pages, which may be said to embody the substance of all
recorded observation of birds in Surrey during the nineteenth
century. During the latter half of Queen Victoria's reign,

with the passing of the Wild Birds Protection Acts of 1881 onwards, the attitude of the public in general towards birds, their interest and value, was gradually changing; but there was much that needed change. Sir John Bucknill was an enthusiastic observer and lover of birds, but he seems to accept as a natural course of events—at all events, he makes no protest in recording it—the callous and senseless shooting of rare birds. He accepts the phraseology of the period; a bird is shot and sent to So-and-so "for preservation"; birds are observed and "obtained" here and there. I may quote, finally, a passage relating to that most interesting bird, the Great Crested Grebe, which illustrates through Sir John's pen the surroundings and atmosphere in which bird observation in the later years of the nineteenth century was carried on :

"This fine and handsome species was, at the beginning of the century, a resident on probably all of the large sheets of water in the rural districts of the county, particularly those of the western portion, where it could breed without being much disturbed. At the present day, however, it is almost entirely an occasional visitor, its breeding attempts in Surrey having recently been, as far as I am aware, attended with success in five places only, of which, for obvious reasons, I do not intend to give more information than is advisable.

"It is, however, most pleasing to know that this splendid species has not yet been quite exterminated in the county, and the localities being carefully guarded and well looked after will all, no doubt, become its regular home. Many reasons have contributed to its almost complete local extinction— gunners, increase of building, and the facilities for travel, which bring a large number of persons to the neighbourhood of what were once almost inaccessible places, have all had their share; but I have little doubt that any person carefully preserving a large sheet of water in a suitable neighbourhood could induce this species to frequent its precincts; its presence would well repay a little trouble, as it is a most graceful and lovely object.

"In writing of it now, it must generally be regarded as an occasional visitor, and in looking over a list of occurrences in and near the county it would seem that those which

22

appear in Surrey as a rule follow the course of the Thames, from the waters of which it has frequently been recorded. From the Thames it has passed up the Wey and Mole, and thence to our inland waters."

Sir John Bucknill, I think, must have been attracted more than commonly by the Great Grebe, if we may judge from the space—three full pages—which he devotes to records of its occurrence. Here are the later entries :

"In 1877, on 26 October, a specimen was shot at West Molesey on the Thames. In the winter of 1883 or 1884 one was observed between Charing Cross and Waterloo Bridges ! and recorded in the *Field* by Mr S. R. Glynn (11 May 1889), both these latter examples being interesting as showing how the inland specimens probably come from that river. Mr Swann states that it has been seen once or twice in the early 'nineties on the ponds in Richmond Park, and it has frequently been observed on Virginia Water in recent years.

"In 1890 I saw a specimen at a pond in the neighbourhood of Hindhead in summer, where I should imagine it may have been nesting. In 1896, on 3 February, a specimen was shot at Gatton Park by the head keeper of Mr J. J. Colman, and was noticed in the *Surrey Mirror* of 7 February 1896; and in 1897 a pair brought off their young in the county, the nest being visited by more than one ornithologist of repute. In 1899 it nested on one of the western lakes, and also on a southern sheet of water, and in the spring of the same year a male took up its quarters on the Penn Ponds in Richmond Park. It was eventually joined by a female, and the pair nested and brought off two or three young birds. (See the *Field*, 29 April and 15 July 1889.) Mr Felton, in the spring of the same year, saw a single bird on the Putney reservoir.

"It must not be thought [writes Sir John in conclusion] from the comparative paucity of this list that it represents in any way the number of birds that have visited the county in recent years. It must be remembered that inland it frequents only the largest and quietest sheets of water, and keeps to the middle, being far more often observed by people who do not know what it is, than shot, and for this reason it is difficult to obtain definite records of its occurrence. Frensham, where it can be sometimes seen, and where three were observed, and one immature bird shot in 1897, and other ponds, no doubt, hold it safely on many occasions, and if it were to be unmolested it would no doubt soon re-establish itself in several suitable places."

I have quoted Sir John Bucknill here somewhat at length, because I think he gives a very fair idea of the conditions in which rare birds were observed, and if seen by the wrong type of observer, shot, in days of the last century. I believe these conditions have now altered for the better. It is not now the first reaction of the observer, suddenly catching sight of a rare bird, to get a gun and shoot it. The sportsman who to-day should shoot a rare bird at sight would not write to the *Field* about it; he would probably be prosecuted, and certainly execrated, if his name were known. True, to-day there still lingers another danger to the life of rare birds, not from the man with a gun, but from the egg-collector. It is still possible, or it was possible in years just preceding the war, for a man who has broken the law in taking the eggs of birds protected by Act of Parliament to exhibit in public his collection of eggs, and to do so with impunity. For weeks together, in a series of articles published during the autumn and winter of 1934, the *Field* drew attention to the activities and methods of collectors, and to the open way in which they could defy the law. The exposure had its effect, as letters to the *Field* clearly showed, but you do not easily cure the twist of mind of a collector of eggshells, and for years to come, doubtless, it will be necessary to guard in every way possible the nests of birds, such as the great crested grebe, which can only be attracted to our inland waters by peace and quiet.

Of those waters which during the present century became the recognized home of breeding birds of which the great crested grebe is the most interesting example, Frensham Pond is the chief. It is, or rather was, the largest stretch of water in Surrey, stretching for eighty acres and more through hills of sand and heather. Here, as you may learn from Sir John Bucknill, watchers in the past have caught sight of visitors as different in habit and size as the great northern diver and the gently confident grey phalarope, have seen graceful sandpipers flit and settle, have heard the haunting lament of redshank; and here too, in years between the wars of later days, have known that besides unnumbered moorhen and coot we could count on the dark outlines of tufted duck and the bright heads of mallard and pochard in winter sunshine; above all, that here we might hope to watch through hours of April the new and separate sight, unlike in its detail that of any bird in all Great Britain, of the courtship of the great crested grebe.

It was here, by the Frensham Ponds, that Julian Huxley first watched that courtship. He was to add greatly to his knowledge, and to that of all students of bird habits, in later days at Aldbury in Hertfordshire, where he spent many morning hours with notebook and telescope on the bank of the Tring reservoirs. But it was by the quiet acres of Frensham Great Pond that he was first attracted by the sight of the birds with their ruffs and ear-tufts, their gleaming underparts and their strange preenings and head-shakings, and if it was at Tring that he made his series of note-takings into a serious contribution to post-Darwinian theories of sexual selection, it was by the heather and sand of those then unspoiled Surrey waters that he chronicled in his mind, if not yet in papers of the Zoological Society, the tiny detail of the great crested grebes' ceremonies and display.

Those records belong to days before the First Great War. We other folk who watched birds in those quiet days did not guess what the future had in store for us, for the Surrey homes of ourselves and the wild creatures who lived with us. We had no vision in those days of other flights over Surrey heather than those of the wild fowl who were so natural to the places we knew; we never thought of wings hideous in light and dark that were to bring horror with them and fear of knowledge of the Surrey we lived in. Who would have guessed that Englishmen were to blot Surrey lakes out of existence and spread the stain of weed and root in place of water that had reflected the stars? But the water had shown foreign eyes where they travelled high in air over the dwellings of birds and men; so the light that shone from sun and moon was to be taken out of maps that guided an enemy. In the early months of the Second German War Frensham Great Pond was drained, and Virginia Water was emptied : they were the water-marks that told the way to Windsor.

Yet, even in those months of fear, and of the new ways of safeguarding a countryside in darkness, was there any mind among the thinkers of defence which foresaw the change defence was making? Did any one of those who drained the depths of Frensham Pond know that he was planting a valley of trees? I doubt if to any of those who watched the first lessening of those broad acres, who saw the rim of mud creep out wider from surrounding reeds and sedges as the water poured through the sluices, there was present the vision of years to come. Few, indeed, of us to whom Frensham Pond had become permanently a part of living Surrey, gave even a passing thought to the channels through which the Wey's tiny tributary fed its great neighbour. We had been thinking all our lives of a noble level edged by reeds and sallows, of punts which took us on happy afternoon voyages, of moorhens paddling in and out of sedges and calling screwy greetings to their mates, and coots in wind-ruffled waves suddenly vanishing and suddenly there again in the wind, above all of grebes in their brown tippets posing to each other with their queer, ear-like crests—it was all part of a sight of every day for those who cared to look for it in the heather of West Surrey.

And then . . . one day I heard that Frensham Great Pond had been drained, to prevent enemy aeroplanes from using its bright surface as a guide. And on 27 October 1943, a day to be marked with a grey stone for the sudden sadness it brought to those who loved those broad waters, I went, with a friend who knew the pond as well as I did, to look at it. And when we came by the familiar roads to its side and stood to gaze, as I had supposed we should, over a hollow of mud, I could not at first understand what I saw.

Frensham Pond was not there. In the place of its water was a birch wood, acres of saplings crowded as thick as broadcast corn, every height from a few inches to eight or ten feet. It was a growth incredible; I had not guessed—had any one guessed?—what could be the usurping strength, given fit soil in which the tiny, air-borne, voracious atoms could plant themselves, of seedling birches. And to Nature's sudden seizure of opportunity man had added his own touch of purposed deformation and careless litter. All along the side nearest the road, where water used to lap on sand under ling and gorse, with bell-heather miles away to the horizon, were trenches and parapets cut and dug and channelled by lorries, dry desert menacing with broken bottles. That surface used to be the floor of a swimming-pool. I walked across it, past a sheet-iron notice to bathers getting out of their depth—*Danger*. There, under a clump of stunted rushes, I picked up a woolly bear caterpillar.

That was the autumn of the fourth year of war. And because the jungle of birches in place of the level water was so unexpected by myself, and, as I reasoned, probably unexpected by those who had drained the pond, I tried to see whether something could not be done, before the birches had grasped the floor too tightly, to get the pond back again. But how? Cutting, burning? Either seemed hopeless over eighty acres. I thought of a bulldozer, wondering if army minds would think so too. At all events, an article published in the *Guardian* brought me a letter from a valued correspondent in which I learnt for the first time that Virginia Water had been reduced by alder seedlings to the same state as Frensham, and a letter hospitably printed by *The Times* was followed by an article by their naturalist correspondent, who evidently had shared my own pre-war visions of bird life.

"If one identifies correctly," he wrote, "the lakes (or large ponds) in mind, it is indeed essential that they be restored as soon as possible to their pre-war condition, so that the great crested grebes may once more mirror the gleaming whiteness of their satin breasts in the blue waters and delight beholders with their courtship courtesies, bill to bill, prick ears bent forward, so making their thin stripy faces, backed by the magnificence of black and chestnut ruffles, more intelligently dog-like than ever."

But he had been more fortunate than I, for all that I had been able to see had been jungle, while he, in the wrecked lake he had visited, had found water running through mud, with birds in the mud :

"Yet the drained ponds are not without their interest, indeed their fascination, for the naturalist. A tiny stream still flows through a desert of dried mud, and in the morass along the course peewits and redshanks hide their young in June, the first-named parents wailing overhead, the redshanks crying 'Tuke, tuke,' as they perch, red-legged, on stumps or piles. Not far away, growing vigorously on dried mud, the spiky-leaved blue spiderwort makes its exotic appearance, having migrated out of what was once a tea-house garden on to what was once a pond."

Happily Virginia Water came back. From the same friend who first told me of the alders which had taken the place of shadowed depths and windy ripples, a letter reached me in February 1945—telling me that the lake was "almost normal" and the water birds back in force. "It must be nearly a year since they allowed the water in again. Of course some of the trees come above the surface, but I suppose they will gradually die. During the frost they made skating rather dangerous; I mean when going backwards, so I didn't put my skates on!"

That last sentence filled a bird-watcher junior in years with envy. I cannot think of a parallel sequence of experience—to have watched birds through a long series of years over a large lake, to have seen the lake emptied, then changed into a wood, filled with water again, frozen over, offering the chance of skating, and then with its birds back again—it is a lustrum without its like.

To the records of rare birds at Virginia Water I can add that of a visitor distinguished with only a few lines by Bucknill. For myself, my efforts at identification fill me with humility. It was on a day in February 1937, and I was walking by the banks of the lake with two companions of many winter hours. We saw the usual duck which we expected, mallard, tufted and so on, and watched a pleasant gathering, too, in an alder tree of some thirty small birds, which in the winter light were at first difficult to pick out—a mixed company of siskins, linnets and goldfinches. And suddenly we saw, beyond a number of coot, a bird which dived. When it came up it was a long way off, and before I could sight it properly it dived again. It came up again, far away, and we timed the dive—fifty-five seconds. It was extremely difficult to get the glasses on it, for there was a ripple on the water, and the bird might come up anywhere. It was grebe-like in its movements, but looked bigger than a grebe. I thought of the divers, but I was at a loss. I carried in my mind the coloured illustrations in Gould's unmatched *Birds of Great Britain*, but it would not fit with one of them.

I had given up the riddle, and we were leaving the lake when, suddenly, by the greatest good luck, the bird came up close to us. There it was in the sunlight, with its dark crown, white neck and breast and mottled back—a diver surely. But which? And then the idea came to me—of course, winter plumage. I knew it was not the great northern diver, for I had memories of watching one on a winter's day at Paignton in Devonshire; but for the others, I had been put into the wrong train of thought by my memories of Gould. His illustrations are of birds in their summer plumage and, although in the case of some species—golden plover and grey phalarope, for example—he illustrates both the winter and the breeding dresses, he has no illustration and little to say about divers in winter. I turned to Witherby's *Practical Handbook,* which seemed to point to the black-throated diver, but I could not find the dark crown which I had seen so plainly —Witherby writes of "brown washed greyish." I did not get the answer till it was given me by Authority at the British Museum, who convinced me that my bird was a black-throated diver, and suggested that the dark crown might be due to the contrast of pale neck in the low sunlight.

And so, we shall hope, now that the wind may ruffle the water in that broad lake once more in winter, other divers may puzzle watchers in years to come.

And Frensham Great Pond? The water took longer to come back to those eighty acres than the smaller lake by Sunningdale. It was in mid-July 1945 that I drove out to see what changes, if any, might have come with days of peace. I had heard that the pond was filling again—or rather was being filled, for all that area of Surrey had passed into Government hands—and I wondered what English skill could have done to bring back the beauty which German purposes had destroyed.

We drove out from Milford on the road to Thursley, and there, between those two villages I realized was one of the great changes—a perpetual loss to the Surrey countryside.

Here, where Witley Common first begins to open out to Ockley Common, Elstead and Thursley, bricks and mortar stand stiff on either side of the road. In the war of 1914 that natural stretch of heather and gorse had here and there been flattened with concrete and cement, but in twenty years had somehow recovered much of its wildness. To-day it is common land no more. Pines still fringe part of the road, but beyond is Aldershot in miniature, parade ground and camp for all time.

Thursley still keeps its cricket green bordered with bell heather, and on that July day a family of missel thrushes dotted the mown turf, grey in the sun—grey as the distance towards which we were driving. That was the sudden realization which came to me, standing for a moment to look out from that open space with its memories of schoolboy cricket matches in days past—the sudden knowledge that the distant rim of Surrey common, which once could remind me of Scotland's moors, was ashen grey. I had not stood on that little green since before the war. We were coming to a greater change still.

So we went on to the edge of what once had been a pond. We stood there on a strip of grey-white sand. Far out, beyond the notice which used to warn bathers of the danger of deep water, lay sandy flats of stones, reeds, rushes, willow-herb mauve-pink against a bank of willows. In the middle distance stretched rippling water between streaks of rushes. And the birches, that forest at which I had stared in October two years ago? They had vanished. Instead, lines of rushes and streaks of water. We travelled round—threequarters of a mile from where we stood—to the far side of the pond, and there caught sight of two men in thigh-high rubber boots cutting the reeds with fag-hooks. We walked out on the dry floor of the pond to ask what had happened. A genial country-man told us. The birches had been cut by hand. A hundred pioneers had done it, under Government orders, for the Government now owned the pond and all the neighbourhood round. Had they tried bulldozers? Yes, but only one, and he had gone down with his nose into bog. And now they were cutting the reeds. The pond was filling, by the little stream running in at the side from the south—I had noticed that the bed of this stream, a tiny tributary of the Wey, had been cleared and deepened—and it was expected that it would take in all six months to fill to the old level.

What of the birds? we asked. Oh, the birds were all right. They had never left the place, though some of them had changed over to a small pond on the other side of the road past the hotel. There had been duck—"hundreds of duck"—there were coots, moorhens, dabchicks—yes, even the grebes. Just then I heard and caught sight of a moorhen, fifty yards out, paddling among the rushes. Yes, it had a nest there. Three of the chicks had hatched, and there were other eggs in the nest.

We asked about the other pond known as Little Frensham Pond, though the maps show it a straggling sheet of water stretching two-thirds of a mile in two directions. The Little Pond, we knew, like its neighbour, had been drained lest it should serve as a guide to enemy airmen under sun and moon. But the Little Pond, we were told, had been left to itself. Like its neighbour, it had changed from water to wood, and the birches growing on its floor had not been touched. Were they likely to be cut? No one knew.

I thought of the Little Pond as I saw it first years ago, a lake among heather and pines. I had missed my way then among the woodland rides, and had suddenly found myself on the bank of the pond, looking down on a sheet of water-lilies; I remembered the wonder of it, the July wind faintly touching those innumerable chalices, the broad surface of white and gold and green. And to-day? We set out to see. Lane End, the Ordnance map marks the sandy road leading from the highway, and we made our way down to it to find it truly named. It ended on the border of a desert. I had seen something of what we were likely to find, as we travelled by the road east of the Great Pond, but I had not realized what lay beyond. South, east, west, wherever the eye travelled, stretched the same white sahara. There were ridges, slopes, mounds, but they were all part of the same vast, dead space, the same grey-white slough of sand. You could not drive a car over it; there was only one way to come in sight of the Little Pond, to walk up and down over the ridges of sand ploughed there to the horizon. We climbed a ridge that

31

pushed out into the desert, and looked where the pond should be. There it lay, a grey-green thicket in the distance.

I remembered what had been there years ago, miles of heather, bell heather and ling, purple and crimson down to the banks of the lake glittering in the sun; I remembered the pines and the waterlilies. It was the war, the tanks that had done this, that had left somehow a threatening, living presence behind with what had been done in the sand. And I wondered, could life ever return to that wilderness? Rain and sun, could they ever restore what the years of war had taken? In Scotland keepers burn heather, and it lives young and green the next summer. But to plough heather deep out by the roots—that would be death? I looked out again over the desert. And then down at my feet. There, an inch high in the sand, grew a seedling of gorse, and there, ten feet away, another seedling. In ten years' time, perhaps, in five, three years' time? Would Surrey come again into her own?

The dining-room at the Hautboy Hotel, Ockham
The Parish Church, Farnham

CHAPTER IV

ANCIENT CAMPS

THERE are many new things waiting to be known about Surrey. That is an alluring fact which is realized by no one more fully than the reader of the records of the Surrey Archæological Society, anxious to learn the history of the towns he passes through, the countryside he sees day after day, above all, perhaps, of the so-called prehistoric remains in the county of his choice. And in some respect he is not much nearer the knowledge he hopes for than were the members of the Society when it was first formed. On 12 May 1854, when the inaugural meeting was held at Southwark, how many members present, I wonder, would have realized that in another fifty years' time their great-grandchildren would be almost as ignorant as they were about Surrey's ancient camps? They themselves knew almost nothing, and it was not until well into the present century that we were able to know, or guess, a little more.

We may begin with the list of ancient British camps set out by H. E. Malden in his *History of Surrey*. His first four are those of St. George's Hill, half-way between Weybridge and Cobham; Anstiebury, one mile north-east of Leith Hill; Holmbury Hill, a little over two miles west of Leith Hill; and Hascombe Hill, three miles west of Cranleigh. Other remains which he lists as probably British are those "on Worms Heath, a mile and a half from Warlingham, and a round camp at Camp Hill, a mile from Godstone, on the East Grinstead road." Others which have been effaced, or are now difficult to distinguish, were a camp at Oatlands, Weybridge, which was levelled by the seventh Earl of Lincoln in the reign of George II; Cæsar's Camp, once called The Rounds, on Wimbledon Common; entrenchments in War Copse, near Caterham north of the Pilgrims' Way; yet another Cæsar's Camp, near Aldershot; and irregular banks and ditches on Crooksbury Hill and other slopes which lent themselves to rough means of defence.

Those are the camps, or remains or vestiges of camps,

D

33

which formed the list made by H. E. Malden in 1905. One more camp has been added to our knowledge since. This is Dry Hill Camp, near Lingfield on the borders of Kent and Sussex, which in 1932 was examined and described—discovered would be the better word—by S. E. Winbolt. His description is to be found in Vol. XLI of the records of the Archæological Society, and is the third of the kind for which readers are indebted to him, the first and second being accounts of his excavations at Holmbury and Hascombe. These papers followed the measurements taken and recorded by Dr Eric Gardner in an admirable article on St. George's Hill, published by the Society in 1911, so that of the five large British camps only one, Anstiebury, to-day waits the spade of the explorer.

To take, then, these four explored camps in order. St. George's Hill differs from Holmbury, Hascombe and Dry Hill in that, being in the neighbourhood of Weybridge and made the more accessible to its inhabitants by the generosity of the Egerton family, owners of the hill, the shape of the camp must have been somewhat altered by the feet of thousands of local wanderers, added to the work of foresters planting pines and quarrymen digging for gravel. Add to this alteration the effect of hundreds of years' denudation by rain and wind, and you get a camp obviously reduced in shape and size. But when in course of time St. George's Hill came under a scheme of building development, the camp lay open to the measuring eyes of that untiring searcher into hidden history, Dr Eric Gardner, and he, in the *Collections* of the Surrey Archæological Society, has opened new doors into the past in a fascinating essay.

Of the main ridge, which lies some 220 feet above the Thames, the southern end is prolonged into four spurs, once called—I wonder if the names are still in Surrey speech—Horseshoe Clump, Spence's Thrift, Raven's Clump and Summer's Clump. Within these four spurs lies a rough rectangle, quarter of a mile long and roughly 200 yards broad surrounded by ramparts and ditches, of which the rampart to the north-west was measured by Dr Gardner to be no less than 23 feet in height, and that, we may remember, was a measurement taken after many centuries of denudation by weather. On the north-east side there is a sort of extra enclosure, apparently added at a later date to the camp, and designed to protect its water supply. Even in wet weather to-day you can trace the course of the stream which once formed that water supply; it runs half a mile down the hillside to a pond called Dead Man's Pool. (And I wonder when it got that name.) The camp must have been a complete and formidable fortification.

And how much of the neighbouring country did this British Stronghold, as Dr Gardner names it, command? We may look at the map to-day, and sum up the situation with Dr Gardner. "To the north-west, it commanded the whole of the Thames Valley to Windsor; to the south-west, the Wey Valley to Guildford; to the south-east, the Mole Valley to Leatherhead; but to the north—nothing."

But there was no need for the Stronghold to command the country to the north—from this Stronghold. Its British occupants commanded the country to the north—that is, to the Thames—from another stronghold with which they were doubtless connected. This was a camp situated in the neighbourhood of what is to-day the Oatlands Park Hotel. If we could look at its contours to-day, we should be able to judge in what way the Oatlands camp may have been planned as a sister and assistant of the Stronghold, giving it, maybe, the command of the main crossing of the Thames to the north, for it lies in a direct line from the Stronghold to a ford with a recognized place in history, the Cowey Stakes below Halliford.

But there is little use in puzzling over the possible uses of the camp that is now the grounds of Oatlands Park Hotel, for the owner of the ground in the reign of George II, the seventh Earl of Lincoln, in the process of laying out his estate—incidentally, it was he who dug and filled the lake below the hotel and called it Broadwater—laid the whole camp flat.

It is a curious fact that although the Stronghold is one of the largest and clearly most important prehistoric camps in Surrey, no weapons or implements have ever been found on St. George's Hill. But they have been found in the neighbourhood of the different fords of the rivers surrounding the

Stronghold, the Wey, Mole and Thames, and in reading Dr Gardner's pages in the Surrey Archæological Society's *Collections* it has amused me to imagine that possibly one or two of the Bronze Age urns, which he chronicles as having been dug up in the neighbourhood of Oatlands, were discovered in laying the foundations of the house in which a red squirrel ate nuts at my writing-table.

From 1911 we go on to the next year of exploration— 1930. In that year a locally raised excavation fund enabled Mr S. E. Winbolt to superintend digging on Holmbury Hill. He and his helpers took four weeks over their task, three of digging and one of filling in. Holmbury Camp is in a rough square, with west, north and east sides each of about 220 yards; it lies on the top of a hill sloping up from the foot of the Chalk Downs. Its height is, in the south-west corner, 857 feet above sea level, in the north-east 767 feet. It was a camp which, in spite of the nature of the soil—sand of the Hythe beds of the Lower Greensand—was supplied with water, held no doubt by strata of clay. Even to-day, about 75 yards outside the camp on the north, there is a little pond on a bed of clay, and according to a skilled water-finder there are strong springs running some fifteen feet below the surface. The main entrance to the camp is at the north-west corner, and there is a secondary entrance or postern at the opposite south-east corner.

Digging resulted in the finding of a number of broken quern stones, perhaps representing twenty in all; charcoal and burnt sandstone, the remains of fires; bones of sheep, ox and wild boar; various sherds of pottery, a number of flints and a quantity of sling pebbles. These last, Mr Winbolt states, almost certainly came from Netley, or Ranmore, some six or seven miles away to the north on the Chalk Downs. For the quern stones there must have been iron pivots, but—a puzzling point—"not the smallest scrap of iron of any kind of implement was found." This, Mr Winbolt tells us, has been his experience in working other Early Iron Age camps on sand. Is there some property in wet sand, one wonders, which destroys iron by rust?

Mr Winbolt ends his paper with a delightfully imagined sketch of the life which once pulsed on this sandy height:

"Musing many evenings on this hilltop I pieced the past together thus. The last incoming wave of Brythonic Celts, crossing from N. Gaul, in the second century B.C. penetrated Britain chiefly by the North Downs route which connected Folkestone with Farnham, Winchester and Salisbury Plain. The sand hills close south attracted many groups to settle in such fine sites as those of Oldbury, in Kent, and Holmbury. They brought their Gallic civilization with them : their querns alone imply the growing of corn, and skill in stone work and the forging of iron. Possibly three groups belonging to the same tribe occupied three neighbouring fortified villages, and co-operated in the construction of all three. Some five hundred people (probably fewer) occupied Holmbury, of whom perhaps one hundred and fifty were grown men. On the top and on the northern slopes they pastured their herds and flocks, and grew corn; in the Weald below they hunted the wild boar and other game. They made and drank mead, were fair potters, wove skilfully clothes of bright colours, and cleaned animal skins for their winter clothing. They tattooed their bodies, and, led by the priestly caste of the Druids, practised cruelties in the religious rites connected with their gods of thunder, war, women's crafts and manly beauty—Taranis, Belutacador, Belisoma and Belin. With these were ranged also Nudd, and Lud, and Mabon, and the three Mother Goddesses. There were no pine trees then on the hills; this innovation of about a century and a half ago must be rigidly expunged from the picture. When the Romans came they made little resistance, for they had for many years partially adopted the material side of their culture, and they lived on Holmbury, as elsewhere, practically unmolested till the fifth century A.D. The Saxon invaders came, and the Celtic folk of Holmbury finally trekked away westward and northward by Farnham and Guildford.

"Will this fancy serve?" ends Mr Winbolt. But of such bright imaginings, surely, is history built.

Holmbury Hill was explored in 1930. In 1931 Mr Winbolt went on to Hascombe Hill, where through the generosity of Lord Onslow in financing the work, and by consent of Mr Joseph Godman, owner of the property, he was again

able to carry out excavations. He found the general plan of
the camp to be an enclosure rectangular towards the north-
east, and bounded by a series of curves towards the south-
west. Looking at the plan as sketched in the *Collections*, I
should describe the north-east half as square, and the south-
west half as lemon-shaped : the apex of one right-angle of the
square points north, and of the other east, while the lemon
points south-west. From the eastern right-angle to the further
point south-west the distance is 840 feet, and the broadest
part from north-west to south-east is 500 feet. The whole
area is roughly five and three-quarter acres, as compared with
the eight acres of Holmbury.

Until Mr Winbolt surveyed the camp no one, it seems,
had taken any measurements or had examined it in detail.
The work of exploration was made difficult by natural
features and by overgrowth of brambles and bracken. The
side of the hill on which it stands runs up steeply from behind
the White Horse Inn, and it means a stiff climb of fifteen
minutes to reach it. Bracken seven feet high in the summer,
as I found years ago when I was at work on the *Highways
and Byways*, and climbed Hascombe Hill to find the camp,
makes the recognition of any shape in wooded ground a
matter of great difficulty, and when to bracken is added a
growth of bramble, ordered movement for a single individual
becomes out of the question. For myself, when I tried to
make out the shape of the camp, I own I gave the thing up;
all the more gratitude, then, is due from Surrey walkers and
readers to Mr Winbolt and those who worked with him for
four weeks at a most laborious task.

In the main, his discoveries and the conclusions he draws
from them much resemble those of his work at Holmbury.
The earthworks, he writes, are typically pre-Roman of the
late Early Iron Age. The periphery of the five and three-
quarter acres contained by them is about 780 yards, and we
imagine the vallum and fosse, wall and ditch, surmounted by
a wooden stockade. There is an entrance in the north-east
side of the camp, twelve feet wide and sixty feet long. In the
course of his digging Mr Winbolt found, as at Holmbury, a
fairly large quantity of worked and broken flints; some eighty
to one hundred flint pebbles, average about two ounces, which

were used for three purposes, the larger to be thrown by hand, the smaller as stones for slings, and others used as pot-boilers, some of them fractured by heat; quern stones, used as at Holmbury for grinding corn; and about one hundred and fifty fragments of pottery, all of them of the same type and date, from 150 B.C., hand-made, mostly black inside and red or black outside—the average thickness of a pot would be five-sixteenths of an inch. No food bones were found, and although it seems possible, indeed probable, that at Burningfold and elsewhere in the neighbourhood iron was smelted, and although querns, as at Holmbury, must have been worked with iron pivots, Mr Winbolt could find no vestige of any iron implement.

If so few traces of continued use by inhabitants are to be found, what was the purpose of the camp? As a place of refuge for those living in neighbouring villages, seems to be the answer. Where, then, were the villages for whose convenience the camp was constructed? Once more we are confronted with an answer which is all the more baffling because of simple and natural causes. The villages were situated "possibly along the sand ridge both east and west, now so densely wooded as to make their discovery very difficult." Hascombe was peopled by the same tribes as those of Holmbury. Probably these men of the sandhills were of the same race as the Celts of the Sussex Downs. "They were Brythonic Celts who had been established in south-east Britain from as far back as 500 or 600 B.C., who lived as tribal groups in hilltop citadels." Those of Hascombe Camp probably left their high village soon after the middle of the first century B.C.

"Did they make a new home in the nearby Weald at some such place as Dunsfold, or Cranleigh or Bramley? Or did they make away westward by way of Guildford and Farnham? At any rate we have no proof that the site was again occupied at the end of the Roman period from fear of Saxon invaders, or held by Saxons against Danes."

There is still more, then, to learn about our forerunners in this part of Surrey. "Anstiebury should be investigated," wrote Mr Winbolt in 1931. He himself was to add to our knowledge in exploring a camp up to that time, as we have seen, hardly recognized. Of his work at this camp, Dry Hill,

Lingfield, he writes in the *Collections*, Vol. XLI : "It must always remain a matter for wonder that with the name in common speech and the old-English lettering on the Ordnance map it should have waited until late in the present century for admission by writers into the category of prehistoric earthworks in Surrey."

Dry Hill Camp is the largest earthwork that has been explored in Surrey. It covers twenty-four acres with a circumference of nearly a mile. Its ramparts lie round a sandy hill-top of a height of 565 feet, on the borders of the county adjoining Kent and Sussex, three miles from Lingfield to the south-east. It commands a magnificent view over the Weald. For three weeks Mr Winbolt and his assistants attacked the camp, which they found to be defended for about three-quarters of its circumference by triple valla and two fosses. The camp is roughly pear-shaped, with the stalk to the north-east, and these valla stretched from the north-east along the north, north-west, west and south rims of the camp; on the east and south-east the valla are two with one fosse, while at the extreme south-east the designers depended for their defence simply on the sharpness of the natural slope. In their three weeks' digging the explorers' "finds" were few. Among them were collections of waterworn pebbles, for slinging and hand-throwing; some lumps of iron slag, which suggested that iron-smelting had been carried on; many remains of ancient fire-making, and a few signs of flint-working, but not a single sherd of pottery.

But one remarkable piece of work they did uncover. There are three entrances to the camp, from the north-west, the south-west and the south. About half-way between the south and south-west entrances, in the inner fosse between two valla, they came, at one foot down, upon a hard platform of well-laid cobble stones and iron slag, forty-three feet long and mostly three feet six inches wide, neatly defined on either side; it was about one foot ten inches deep. On the top of the platform at the north-west end they found two much-corroded horseshoes, and near them a corroded door-hinge; and on cutting a section of the platform towards the north-west end they came upon half of a red-and-yellow brick, four inches wide and two and a quarter inches thick. This was decided

to be of Tudor date. As for the horseshoes, an expert, Dr
H. R. Murray, reported that one was of a type worn by
draught horses at the end of the sixteenth and beginning of
the seventeenth centuries, and that the other was of a kind
used over a wide period of time. The type of slag in the platform was that connected with Tudor or Stuart blast furnaces;
so that putting together all the evidence, it was decided that
the platform might be dated about 1600. Here, then, was a
real riddle. By whom, and for what purpose, was a platform
constructed with such care? "It lies inexplicably in the fosse,
and is here described in detail," writes Mr Winbolt in the
Collections, "in the hope that some one may discover its
raison d'être." That hope has not yet been fulfilled.

On one curious point Mr Winbolt does not comment—the
name. Why should it have been called Dry Hill? At the
north of the camp, between the inner and middle vallum,
there is a pond, which Mr Winbolt describes as "always
containing water." We come back to the greatest riddle of
all. "The puzzle here as elsewhere is why a fort made with
so vast an expenditure of labour was so little inhabited.
There was no real difficulty about water supply. The tribal
'camp of refuge' theory seems best to fit the case. It is probable that the area, once cleared of birches, heather, bracken
and gorse, was peacefully pastured, and never witnessed a
battle."

And still, the one remaining of the five great British
camps, Anstiebury Camp, awaits the explorer. As to the other
"remains of works" listed by H. E. Malden, the supposed
British camp on Worms Heath was examined on behalf of
the Archæological Society in 1908, at a place "where a circular shaft in the chalk outcrop on the side of a gravel pit
appeared to be of such symmetrical formation as to suggest
the possibility of its being due to human agency. After
descending to some depth, though the remarkable symmetry
was well maintained, the absence of any pick-marks in the sides
and of any trace of human implements convinced the experts
present that the shaft was the result solely of natural causes,
and the work being unlikely to result in anything of special
archæological interest was abandoned." Last, then, we come
to Camp Hill, which is marked in old-English lettering on

the Ordnance map half-way between Godstone and Tand-
ridge. I can find no reference to the camp in the Society's
proceedings, so that with Anstiebury it must be left to explorers of the future.

And what of the rest of the camps in the Malden list?
There is little to be said. Surrey in the nineteenth century was
not everywhere fortunate in its land-owners, from the point
of view of the antiquary. Of wanton and deliberate acts of
destruction of ancient earthworks the capital example is the
levelling of Cæsar's Camp at Wimbledon in 1875 by its then
owner, a certain Sawbridge Erle Drax, who flattened or filled
in whatever remained of the stronghold. I can find no detailed description of the camp as he found it, nor any exact
measurements of its area before spade and pick obliterated
traces of its two-thousand-year-old ramparts and ditch. Brayley's *History of Surrey* describes what dwellers in Wimbledon saw in the 'forties :

"On the high ground at the south-west side of Wimbledon
Common, and about a mile and a half from the upper part of
Kingston Hill, is an ancient *Entrenchment* of a circular form,
which the country people call the *Rounds*, an appellation by
which it has been known for a long series of years; although
of late it has been introduced into some of our modern maps
by the name of *Cæsar's Camp*. In Camden's time it was
called Bensbury, which that writer supposed to be derived
from *Cnebba's-bury*; Cnebba and Oslac, two of the principal
generals of Ethelbert, King of Kent, having been slain in the
battle fought at *Wibandune* (or Wimbledon), between that
sovereign and Ceaulin, King of the West Saxons. Its area
comprises about seven acres of ground; and is to a considerable extent overgrown by prickly furze. It is crossed by a
cart-road leading towards Combe-lane and Kingston; and on
one side appears to have been defended by outworks. It is not
exactly circular, but inclines to an oval form. The surrounding ditch, which is from eight to ten to fifteen feet deep, is
partially overshadowed by scrubby oaks."

Some twenty years later William Bartlett, in his *History
and Antiquities of Wimbledon*, wrote of the stronghold that
it was difficult to decide as to its origin, "as the plough has
passed over it. But," he adds, "those who visit the spot will

observe that it has a double *vallum*, but not an outer *foss*. The outer *vallum* is considerably below the level of the inner, thereby affording an opportunity for a second line of defenders to hurl their javelins or arrows over the heads of the first line." Well, by 1875, the *vallum*, the ditch fifteen feet deep, the prickly furze and scrubby oaks had been levelled flat, and in 1924 we find Dr Eric Gardner writing summing up the treatment of our prehistoric monuments :

"'Cæsar's Camp' at Wimbledon has been maliciously destroyed; the great camp at Oatlands disappeared under the spades of Lord Lincoln's gardeners in 1756; the mighty works on Hungry Hill, Aldershot, have been used as a gravel-pit; and now it is impossible to form even an idea of the plan of its original defences. 'Cæsar's Camp' on a bold promontory across the Long Valley has been sadly mutilated by the County Boundary Bank and the trenches of various military operations; the interesting entrance to Holmbury has gone to make room for a trackway crossing the camp; the works at Limpsfield and Woldingham are fragmentary; and the lost camp at Wallington was discovered only by chance building operations which disclosed its filled-in ditch."

It is a long list of opportunities gone, perhaps for ever. But may there not be opportunities still to come? I turn back to the last item in the Malden list. "Other earthworks of more doubtful form and origin." Which, and where, are these? I do not know which are those that were in Mr Malden's mind when he wrote his history, but may it not happen that even to-day there are "other earthworks" which have hitherto gone unnoticed? I happen to live on the slope of a hill in Surrey, Hydons Ball, which is the subject of an old rhyme, handed down through who shall say how many ages :

> On Hydon's top there is a cup,
> And in the cup there is a drop,
> Take up the cup and drink the drop
> And set the cup on Hydon's top.

Now who is to doubt that this hill, deep in the Surrey countryside, was linked in the mind of past generations with some kind of rite, or belief, or custom? There will come a day, I hope, when echoes of war will have ceased and some one will make it his happy task to explore this and other hills of the South Country, to see if he cannot bring to light some hitherto neglected vallum or fosse which may have been used before the days of Cæsar by British tribes as a camp of refuge akin to the camps of Holmbury and Hascombe and Dry Hill. If that day should ever come, I shall hope to show the explorer lengths of banks and ditches set about Hydons Ball—banks hundreds of yards long, ditches too deep and wide to belong to the work of any farmer. Few who know Hydons as a name, I think, have ever walked the length of those banks and ditches, or have asked themselves why they should run here or have been sunk there; and no one, I am sure, has ever measured them.

Chapter V

INDUSTRIES

IRON—GLASS—GUNPOWDER—CLOTH—LEATHER—POTTERY
ANCIENT; MODERN

IRON

WHEN it fell to my lot to dig first into the sandy soil on the flank of Hydons Ball, and later, when local needs for water led to the placing of the big reservoir on "Hydon's Top," I realized for the first time what were the beginnings of the iron industry of the Weald. Ironstone lay in open air where before were bilberry and ling. Here and there the soil had been ploughed, as I knew from the old map showing the four old roads, and some of the ground once under plough had been planted with larch, hazel and chestnut; and wherever the soil had been once moved in this way, if it was again dug, the ironstone turned up by the spade was in small, or at all events not large, fragments. But where there was obviously virgin soil, as in ground which grew heather and bilberries, you might come across really large pieces of stone, weighing many pounds. One such fragment, which is before me as I write, measures ten by seven by four inches, and weighs twenty pounds. I could find many bigger. It was stone of this kind which was the material of the old industry of the Sussex Weald and, here and there, of Surrey.

Of Sussex to a greater extent than of Surrey. In Sussex and in Kent, as Mr Mark Antony Lower has shown in an exhaustive article in the *Sussex Archæological Collections,* iron was worked before the days of the Romans, and in due course became an industry controlled by Romans. There are no traces of Surrey ironworks of this date, and for two reasons; one, that iron in quantity existed only in southern and particularly in south-eastern Surrey; the other, that iron could not be economically worked except where there could be carriage by water. Traces of early iron works are to be

45

found in local names, in parts of Surrey near the Sussex
border, and, of course, in many parts of Sussex itself. Instances are Furnace Pond near Worth in Sussex, and on the
Surrey border a few miles away, Forge Pond in Lingfield.
At Alfold, in the Fold Country lying along the Sussex border,
there is a Furnace Bridge. Two miles east of Leigh you may
still find on the Ordnance map Irons Bottom. And of
Hammer Ponds, in local names and language all over these
parts of Sussex and Surrey, there are any number. Streams
were dammed to create at the lower end the necessary water-
power, which worked two pairs of bellows to make a blast
for the furnace and to run a wheel which raised and let fall
a hammer for the smelted iron. John Ray, in an appendix to
his *Collection of English Words not generally Used*, gives a
detailed account of the method of the industry. Lower quotes
from this in the *Sussex Archæological Collections*, and Mr
Montague Giuseppi, in the *Victoria History*, sums up the
main points :

"The mine, as the ore is called, was dug for at a depth of
from four to forty feet or more. Before it could be put into
the furnace the several sorts of it had to be mixed together
to enable it to melt to better advantage, and then alternate
layers of this and charcoal were piled together and the whole
burnt. The effect of this was to 'mollify' the ore and so to
allow of its being broken into small pieces. These pieces were
then put into the furnace, which had been previously charged
with charcoal, and after about twelve hours' melting were
drawn off in the form of sows or pigs. The bottom and sides
of the hearth were made of sandstone, the rest of the furnace
being lined to the top with brick.

"The average amount of iron made in a 'founday,' or
period of six days, was eight tons, the amount increasing as
the hearth grew wider with the continual blowing. If the
hearth was made of good stone it would last forty foundays
or weeks, and during this whole time the fire was never
suffered to go out. The forge or hammer had at least two
fires, one called the finery and the second the chafery.

"At the finery the sows, as they were sent out from the
furnace, were converted into blooms or four square masses
of about two feet in length, and next into 'anconies,' which

46

were bars of about three feet in length with the ends left square and rough. This was done by continual beats of the hammer gradually increasing in force. At the chafery the rough ends of the ancony were drawn out and rounded off and the bar thus brought to its perfected state. One man and a boy at the finery were expected to turn out two tons of iron in a week, whilst in the chafery two men should in the same time make five or six tons. As to the amount of fuel that was consumed in these ironworks, we are told that twenty-four loads of charcoal were necessary to make eight tons of sows at the furnace; three loads of the biggest 'coals' went to one ton of iron at the finery, and one load of smaller 'coals' would draw out a ton at the chafery."

It is all far off and long ago, yet here at my hand is this great lump of ironstone. Here it is, side by side with a list of some of the tools and implements leased in 1666 by Anthony Smith of Rake in the parish of Witley to William Yalden of Blackdown in Sussex. The lease grants to William Yalden

"All that upper forge and upper finery and the lower hammer chafery and iron works called or knowne by the name of Horsebane Hammer alias Cold Harbour Hammer, or by any other name or names, scituate, lyinge and beinge in Witley Heath and Thursley Heath."

And here among the goods, chattels and implements are :

"Imprimis one hammer and anvill with a helve and armes fittly placed, twoe fore spiritt plates, one fore plate, one bottome plate, one twoewer plate, one loope plate, one plate before the finery hole, one fulling plate, twoe hare plates, twoe side plates adjoininge to that worke, two paire of greate tonges, one paire of small tongues, one quashe, twoe fargons, twoe greate clames, one shovell, one chast sledge, a beame way anckrues, a new lock and key uppon the finery doore, and a good lock and key to the dwellinge house."

Anthony Smith, of course, was only one of a number of Surrey ironmasters. In February 1574 a certain Christopher Barker set out for the information of the Privy Council a list of all the iron-mills and furnaces then existing in the counties of Sussex, Surrey and Kent, with the names of their owners. Among the Surrey owners listed in this State Paper are :

"The Lady Bray, one forge in Cranleigh, in the hands of

Gardener. Mr Elderton, one forge in Shiere. Mr Christopher Darrell, one forge and one furnace at Ewood. Mr John Gage, one forge and one furnace, about Copthorne and Lingfield. Bartholomew Jeffreys, one forge and one furnace in Burstow. Lord Montague, one forge and one furnace in Haslemere and thereabouts. Thomas Gratwyck, one forge in Dunsfold."

Summing-up the evidence from State Papers and other documents, Mr Malden divides the iron-producing districts of Surrey into three. Westernmost lies the district which is part of the Sussex iron-centre of Fernhurst and North Chapel; it reaches into the parishes of Frensham, Thursley, Haslemere, Witley, Chiddingfold, Hambledon, Alfold, and Cranleigh. Towards mid-Surrey, to the field district of Sussex iron, belong Charlwood, Newdigate and Leigh; and in the south-eastern corner of the county, belonging to the Worth district of Sussex, stand the parishes of Burstow, Horne, Lingfield and Godstone. Here the iron must have been got from the Hastings Beds, on the outskirts of Ashdown Forest, and the Hastings Beds Mr Malden considers to be the richest in ore of all soils in the Weald.

When you come to try to fix a date at which iron works in Surrey had come to an end, you are in a difficulty. Evidence is negative; you are left with positive evidence that iron was being worked in times far off. Aubrey made the perambulation, which afterwards took the form of a book, between 1673 and 1692, and he writes of two forges existing in Witley Park. But Aubrey, as we know, wrote largely from hearsay, and hearsay is not good evidence for dates. In Ogilby's *Book of Roads*, 1720, iron-mills are marked near the road on Wisley Common, but new editions of maps copy old editions. According to Mr Lower, cannon were being cast at Worth over the Sussex border, within seventy years from 1848; and Allen, in his *History of Sussex and Surrey*, says that Fernhurst in West Sussex was the last place where iron was made in that part of the country, and that none had been made there for forty years. He wrote in 1829. "Seventy" and "forty" are vague periods of time, but if we conclude that the period 1778–1789 was the date when iron ceased to be worked in Surrey, that coincides with the known date when

March sunshine, Coldharbour
The Tower, Leith Hill

the Carron Works were casting guns for the navy in Scotland. The "carronade," a special type of gun invented by General Robert Melville, was cast at these works in 1779.

We may look to-day at an interesting specimen of old Surrey work in iron. In Crowhurst Church, within the altar rails, is a cast-iron slab over a tomb. On one half of it are embossed the kneeling figures of two boys opposite two girls, with a winding sheet between, and below the kneeling figures two coats of arms. On the other half is this inscription, in raised Roman capitals :

HER : LIETH : ANE : FORST
R : DAVGHTER : AND :
HEYR : TO : THOMAS
GAYNSFORD : ESQVIER :
DECEASED : XVIII : OF :
JANVARI : 1591 : LEAVING
BEHIND : HER : II : SONES
AND : V : DAVGHTERS

In this inscription all the letters S are the wrong way round and the F's are upside down. According to Mr George Russel French, describing the monuments in Crowhurst Church, the part of the slab bearing the inscription is to be found locally in the form of fire-backs.

GLASS

Industries belong more often to nations than to counties, but here and there local and natural conditions have led to the establishing of manufactures of national importance. This has been the case with the making of glass in Surrey. It was an industry, so far as English workers are concerned, late in introduction. With the Roman invasion followed Roman craftsmen, who set up glass works in one or two places, notably at Warrington in Lancashire. But with the end of Roman rule came the end, too, of glass-making in this country, and what glass was used apparently came from France and Germany. But it is on record that in 675 Benedict Biscop, abbot of Wearmouth, managed to get some glass-workers

E

over from France, and it is just possible that they may have handed on the rudiments of their craft to Englishmen. If so, it can only have happened locally, and the industry died out.

In the thirteenth century begin the records of glass-making in Surrey. By a deed of which the date is not later than 1230, and may be twenty years earlier, Simon de Stocha, known to have been living in 1226, granted twenty acres of land in Chiddingfold to Lawrence Vitrarius—that is Lawrence the glassmaker. In another deed, dated about 1280, occurs the mention, as a boundary, of "le Ovenhusfeld," the oven or furnace house field; and in a third deed, of the year 1300 or thereabouts, is the name given of William, son of William le Verir of Chudyngfaud.

In 1351 the Chiddingfold works rose into fame. Glass was wanted for the chapel of St. Stephen, Westminster, and the commissioners sent into the country to get it failed, until John Alemayne of Chiddingfold came forward to supply, on 30 October, three "hundreds" and three *pondera* of white glass. A *pondus* weighed five pounds, and twenty-four *pondera* went to a "hundred"; the price of a *pondus* was 6d., so that the whole quantity cost £1 17s 6d. Carriage from Chiddingfold to Westminster cost 6s, plus the expenses of a mounted superintendent, 1s a day for the seven days he took going down to Chiddingfold and back to Westminster. On 7 November following, Alemayne supplied thirty-six more *pondera*, and again on 12 November sixty *pondera*, all at the same rate of payment, and all purchased at Chiddingfold.

Four years later Chiddingfold came into royal notice. Edward III was then building St. George's Chapel at Windsor, and glass was needed for the windows. Chiddingfold supplied four "hundreds" at 13s 4d each—an increase in price of 1s 4d per "hundred" on the glass supplied to Westminster. A curious method of preparing the glass for the painting, which was done at Westminster and Windsor, is shown in the items of the accounts. It was first washed with ale, which was supposed to harden as well as clean it—*tam pro lavacione tabularum vitri quam pro congelacione vitri— viijd.*

Chiddingfold at this time was one of a group of factories in a district which extended into Sussex, embracing on the other side of the county border Kirdford, Wisborough Green, Loxwood and Petworth. These, with Ewhurst and Alfold in Surrey, formed a group which gained its prosperity from the abundance of the natural supply of timber from the dense forest country of the Weald, a cheap and ready source of fuel. With the growth of work and trade we find three families in succession heading the industry; first, the Shorters —the name is variously spelt Shertere and Schurterre, then towards the end of the fifteenth century the Ropleys, and after the Ropleys, until the beginning of the seventeenth century, the chief family of all the Surrey glassmakers, that of Peyto. With the Peytos the industry reached the height of its fame, as headed and adorned by the work of true artists, rather than artisans. In Charnock's *Breviary*, published in 1557, appear the following lines :

> As for glassmakers, they be scant in this land,
> Yet one there is as I doe understand :
> And in Sussex is now his habitacion,
> At Chiddinsfold he works of his occupacion :
> To go to him it is necessary and meete,
> Or send a servant that is discrete :
> And desire him in most humble wise
> To blowe thee a glasse after thy devise :
> It were worth many an Arme or a Legg
> He could shape it like to an egge
> To open and to close as close as a haire,
> If thou has such a one thou needest not feare :
> Yet if thou hadst a number in to store
> It is the better for store is no sore.

The glass, you may decide, must have been better than the doggerel. But that Surrey glass had gained a name beyond the borders of England there exists to-day as witness a map in the greatest glassmaking country of the day, Italy. I shall always remember the pleasure of seeking out and finding, painted on the walls of the Guardaroba in the Palazzo Vecchio, at Florence, a map of England dated 1556, on which the only places marked in Surrey are Guildford, the capital, and Chiddingfold.

But it was the fate of the great glass-making firm of Peyto to see the Surrey industry fade and die. In the reign of Elizabeth, with the need of oak for the ships of Her Majesty's navy, came the realization that the timber of the Weald, instead of carrying the Queen's sailors in water, was disappearing in fire, piled into glassmakers' furnaces. The need for preventing this vast waste came home at last to the minds of Ministers, and in 1615 a proclamation, absolutely prohibiting the use of timber for fuel, brought to an end the industry of the Weald. Glass in future was to be made by a new process. Oak was to give place to coal. The centre of the industry was still to belong to Surrey, but it was to Surrey in London, at Lambeth.

Glassmaking lived again three hundred years later. In *Old Chiddingfold*, a Village Pageant Play, Mr Graham Robertson, in the summer of 1921, brought to the eyes of Surrey of to-day a picture of the life and thought of the old craftsmen, working for Richard Peyto the master glassman, on the day when James's proclamation sounded the knell of their trade. In the fourth Episode, Richard Peyto, already near his end, his hopes centred on the colours of the great Minster window which is to crown his life's work, enters on the arm of Martin, the foreman. He has not heard the news :

MARTIN : Sir, you grow weary. Now at least give word
       That we damp down the fires. Doth not this red
       Content you, Master?

PEYTO :   We have failed again.
       This is but tawny, not the incarnade gules
       That burns about God's fiery ministers.
       Till I may wrest the crimson of my dreams
       From rose and ruby, wine and westering sun
       Feed ye my fires; watch like an Alchemist
       The shifting hues within the crucible
       Until the Red Rose blossom.

MARTIN : (*gently*)   And if it fly us
       As it hath ever flown Philosophers?

PEYTO :   Then I will die i' the seeking. Feed the fires.
(*turning*) : Well, Gregory—well, Miles—what
work to-morrow?
The amethyst goblet for the Mayor of Guildford?
The flagons for the Judge?

MILES :   (*awkwardly*) :   To-morrow, sir?

GREGORY :   (*hesitating*) : To-morrow? Martin knows, sir;
question him.
And—take your rest, sir; leave the work to us.
*The men go out. Peyto is left with his niece,
Margaret, and Martin. From their manner he
realizes that something is wrong. Martin
prompts Margaret :*

MARGARET :   (*slowly*)   On the church door
There hangs a Royal Mandate—"by the
King
A Proclamation touching glasses."

PEYTO :   Well?
(*kindly*) : Why, Martin—Margery? Work for
the Court
You fain would spare me? Rest you both
content.
(*His hand on Martin's shoulder*) : This shall
be yours. My little more of toil
Is for the King of Kings. What further?

MARTIN :   Sir,
None may make glass with timber nor with
wood,
But feed the furnace with sea coal or pit——

PEYTO :   (*wildly*) : We have none—or may come by
none! My fires——

MARTIN :   Are quenched to-morrow.
(*Peyto sinks upon his shoulder. They half lead,
half carry him to the couch*).
*The end is near. The old man lies quietly, as
if asleep. Then his eyes open. He begins in
low tones, which become clear and ringing :*

53

PEYTO : Dark—dark the vaulted aisles and cold;
No lattice flames with rose or gold;
Down the great nave a kneeling host
Awaits my fiery Pentecost.
Tarry but yet! I—I will dare
To draw a splendour down the air,
To kindle in the minster dim
The glory of the Seraphim;
Till ye shall see the Angelic Choir
On wings of light and feet of fire
Sweep earthward at the sacring bell;
Till ye shall hear white Gabriel
Cry "Ave," and the meek reply
"Ecce ancilla Domini."

*As he speaks enter to solemn music certain Visionary
Presences in robes that glow with the hues of stained glass.
They bear white lilies and move rhythmically to a stately
measure. Suddenly in their pacings they pause and melt into
an arc-shaped cluster of jewelled brightness; flame-like shapes
in crimson unfurl great golden wings, and the whole group
bends and converges towards a centre, where a blue-veiled
Figure bows before a kneeling Archangel. The music deepens
and swells into triumphal chords. The old glass-maker starts
up on his couch.*

PEYTO : My work—my Great Work—finished!
(*He staggers to his feet as Martin and the
doctor hurry in*)

Domine!

Nunc dimittis—in pace——
(*He falls back into the arms of the two men*)

So the scene ends—one of the most beautiful that has
graced the Surrey countryside. The Pageant Play was acted
in the open air at Chiddingfold, where I saw it more than
once, and where, on one occasion, as vividly as the play
itself, I remember among the audience the gracious presence
of Ellen Terry herself, a friend of the producer. To his
achievements in poetry and play-writing the author of the
Pageant afterwards added to its record the gift of two paint-

ings, which for inspiration of line and colour are unlike any I have seen. My wife bought one of them, and by good fortune in a raffle I became the possessor of the other. It translates to paper the scene of the death of the old glassmaker, and in the faces of the descending angels and the lighting of its rose and gold it fulfils his dream. The two paintings are before me as I write : memorials of genius.

With the transference of the industry of glassmaking to London—even though Lambeth is on the Surrey side of the Thames—I close its Surrey story.

GUNPOWDER

Chilworth to-day is a long village street. It was a very different sight thirty years ago. Except for a farmhouse with its barns and sheds, and a small wayside inn, there was not a building to be seen on the left of the road for a mile from the level-crossing by Tangley Mere till you came to Postford mill and pond on the way to Albury. Instead, you looked out over the green grass and rushes of water meadows. Beyond the meadows there were trees, alders mostly, and among the trees buildings, but the buildings were not houses; they were windowless and without chimneys. If you were walking, and happened to have an Ordnance map in your pocket, you would find that the strip of trees and half-hidden buildings lying between th Tillingbourne and one of its tributaries was marked Powder Mill.

That was all it was, early in 1914. But from August of that year, until the late autumn of 1918, it was more than a powder mill; it was the Chilworth Powder Factory, one of the busiest places in Surrey. From August 1914, its buildings grew in number and size until the water meadows on the banks of the Tillingbourne were patched and peopled with storehouses, testing-houses, mixing-sheds, magazines, and all the machinery and impetus of a supremely important piece of the business of a great war. Day and night the work went on, and day and night the factory was ringed by a guard of soldiers, a never-ceasing round of sentries and patrols, three and a half miles of them on the rim of water, corrugated iron and barbed wire. It was my lot to be sent to Chilworth, as an officer of the guard furnished by the Queen's West Surrey Regiment, in the autumn of 1914, and at Chilworth I spent two and a half years of the most monotonous work that has ever come my way.

Part of the duty of an officer was to go the rounds, once by day and once by night, of the ring of sentries and patrols. There were eleven sentries, with their boxes placed at chosen points in the circumference of the factory. Going the rounds by night was an easy enough task on a moonlight night, but on a cloudy or rainy night, without moon or stars, you had to know your path through the fields and woods pretty accurately, for though you carried a torch it was only to be used on emergency. In those thirty months I got to know every yard of the three and a half miles of the round by heart, and I believe I could walk every yard by night, as I write thirty-two years later, without a mistake.

To every section of the round belong separate memories. It began, soon after leaving the guard hut, with a six-hundred-yards' patrol to the first sentry-box, running partly through the carriage drive of a fine old house and garden, Chilworth Manor, a drive that ran between big yews and white poplars—I remember a night in which a huge branch crashed in wind just off the road. Next came a stile into a little field in which a donkey once brayed to a patrol; it became, and remained, the Donkey Field. And then, a wet field of which I remember best its crop, turnips, and the sheep feeding on them in the dark. Unless you are a countryman, you do not readily tell a sheep's cough from a man's, and it was possible for a patrol to challenge a sheep; but what I remember best is the smell of the sheep in the mud and the rain; I hated that acrid smell then, but I long now to smell it again. Along the wet path at the bottom of that field visiting rounds went, and came up out of the field to an open space unsheltered by trees; it was a very cold place for a sentry, and came quickly to be known as Windy Gap; but I remember it mainly for another reason, that there were gamekeepers and other countrymen from time to time on sentry-go there, and that near the box now and then a rat trap might be found, and a rat. The trap was an ingenious contrivance, which many years afterwards I saw described in a country paper as a new invention. But it was not new to Windy Gap. Thus was monotony relieved in that cold place.

It was one of these gamekeepers, on sentry-go at another box on the round, who challenged me on a quiet winter night, and as I came forward to him, stood suddenly tense. A sound came from the sky. He stood there, and even as I too listened with him, he spoke—not to me. He spoke to himself twice, softly. "Duck . . . duck . . ." He was no longer a sentry, and I was nowhere in the world in which he lived. It was this same sentry who on another night told me of a day's leave he had spent with his brother; woodpigeons had been destroying the crops.

"My brother, he's out every day after them; they average twenty a day. . . . Puts two or three of them up in an ash— a tall ash, same as that—climbs up. Stuffed ones, we use; eighteenpence they charge us for stuffing one, and that'll last you the best part of a season. . . . Well, you know those wires same as they put on tops of pipes, to keep birds out; well, you gets one of those, and cuts it in half—see? and fastens the bird up on that, and get another piece and stick it up into the throat—so—and then you bends the wire on to the bough and it'll stay there till you take it down. . . . Some-times we bakes 'em. You know; when we picks up one's been dead two or three days, takes him home, put him in and shuts him up in the oven all night; well, that hardens the flesh, makes it all hard, and that'll last you two or three days; after that his tail feathers come out, then his breast feathers; then you got to get another one."

I have written of this gamekeeper-sentry in a book, *Shoot-ing Days*, which dates back to the years of the First German War, but I write of him again here because he belongs in my mind always, he and his fluent, easy talk of country things, to life in Surrey out-of-doors. I think of him, some-how, whenever I think of posts and patrols in the woodland that surrounded part of the factory; he had served his time as a regular soldier, as had others of the factory guard, in the Queen's, and there was no more trustworthy member of the guard, on or off parade, but he was a creature of the woods and wild places, as you knew quickly if you talked to him, there in the loneliness of his post on a dark night.

Of that part of the factory round, which ran through woods on the side of a hill, I have other memories. One is of a night when standing by a flight of rough steps we had made through hazels, I realized that rats were cracking nuts in the boughs above my head; it was a queerly loud sound there in the dark. Another memory is of a night of perfect stillness on which I stood listening to a sound which was new to me, but which I eventually made out to be a pair of brown owls talking to each other, much as swallows or starlings do at nesting time. Another sound I heard one night near the same place was more of a puzzle, which I could not solve till the next morning, when I found that the steep hillside above where I had been standing was a home of badgers. And there, under that hill, tunnelled by badgers, with the lining of the sett tumbled out among rocks and roots, I could listen on a night after rain to the quietest sound of all, the ripple of the little Tillingbourne travelling to the Wey.

One of the sentries—I will call him Private Sexton—preferred any other patrol on the factory round to that path under the hill. To get to the next sentry the patrol had to cross a tiny wooden bridge over the Tillingbourne, and it was misery to him to cross running water. Why, he could not explain, but he feared the bridge and the dark water moving below it. "I'm just a natural coward, that's what I know I am," he told me. But was he? There came a morning after mounting guard at six o'clock, one of the guard, Private Rapley—he was a man of heavy build, and he had run a quarter of a mile at a slow speed so as not to be late—marched a dozen yards down the road and pitched forward on his face dead. Private Sexton and his chum, Private Banks, had picked him up. A week later they were on guard again together, posted to the Donkey Field, and Private Sexton, leaving Private Banks on sentry-go, set off in the ordinary way on patrol to the guard hut. When he returned he seemed cold and silent, and an hour or two later, when it was again his turn to set out on patrol, he hesitated. Private Banks told me later of what he heard then :

"I was almost going to ask you something. But I don't think I shall, after all. . . . Look here, will you believe me?"

"Don't I always believe you?"

"Well . . . Look here. When I got over the stile there"—
he pointed to the corner of the field by the road—"he came
out from behind that tree and walked down alongside of me.
. . . Alf Rapley. It was him right enough. All the way. By me
side. No, he said nothing. When I got to the guard hut, I
goes in, quick. I was as long as I could be in there, because I
knew. . . . He was waiting outside. Waiting for me. But he
didn't come no further than the stile. He stopped there."

He sloped arms to move off. Private Banks surveyed
him.

"Here, you're not fit to . . . Look here, I'll take the
patrol. You stop here."

But he set off down the path to the stile. Weeks before,
when they were on duty together, they had arranged a signal,
a sort of coster whistle, with an answer, so that they could
communicate if necessary. When he judged that Private
Sexton had reached the stile, and would be setting down the
road, Private Banks whistled. But he got no answer.

That is among memories of dark nights. But there were
rounds by day, in sunshine, in wind, in rain, through months
of spring and summer, when the world of easy, happy wild
life in fields and woods showed itself to all who would see it,
careless of gunpowder and men. There were partridges in
furrows and springing corn, a jealous suitor chasing his rival
and back to his waiting hen. There was the Tillingbourne
stream, with the sense of newness and change that is the
spirit of moving water; I remember the moment when I first
caught sight of a mayfly in June, and the vision of those light
falling wings took me back twenty years to a backwater of
the Oxford Thames below Long Bridges, to Iffley meadows
and fritillaries in springing grass. Once, on another day in
summer, I was on my way by a path skirting woodland, and
was suddenly aware of movement coming nearer through the
hedge. There, slipping through bents and bramble, was a
mother stoat leading her family, teaching them, you might
guess, the meaning of sights and scents as they followed her
lead; the little procession went by in what felt like silent
trust.

And once I saw a sight that seemed to belong only to such
a place as the spot we guarded, a place where no man came

from January to December, a place of danger where men were warned of peril and wild creatures knew no fear. At the far end of the factory, under the steep face of the hillside where badgers sharpened their claws on tree trunks half buried in tumbled soil, was an old gateway long disused; you could look over the top into dog's mercury and barbed wire. I stood looking at the face of the hill, trying if I could, to follow a badger's track through into the open, when suddenly I saw, moving quietly through the dog's mercury, a polecat. There was no doubt about it. Polecat-ferrets I know and have often handled, but this was a different animal. It might have been the original of Archibald Thorburn's illustration to Millais's *Mammals of Great Britain*, so like was it in pose and colour to that drawing: I remember to-day the glint of sunshine on the long hairs of that black-and-copper coat. And into the recesses of that green hillside the polecat vanished.

But of all the wild life I watched on my rounds at that Chilworth factory I think most often, and with gratitude for the hours given me there, of the snipe. Between the Tillingbourne and the road lies a stretch of marshy, rush-covered ground which then was, and I hope may be again, the haunt of snipe in winter and spring. I had often before heard and watched snipe drumming over meadows by the Wey, but never until those years at Chilworth had heard the sound of drumming in the night time, or had had the opportunity of watching a pair of snipe for hours at a time during their nesting. I see by my diary that the earliest date on which I heard a snipe drum was on 10 March 1917, at 4 p.m., and that I heard another, or possibly the same bird, drumming at 2 a.m. the next day. Until then I had always associated that fascinating sound with days of April.

Two more birds seldom seen in our Surrey countryside I link in memory with the daily round of the Chilworth guard. On 3 February 1917 I find in my diary an entry of mixed happenings—an "explosion of waste" and "ten tufted duck, one pochard, one female smew on Postford Pond. 13° frost." Postford Pond lies on the extreme east of the factory ground, and in the winter tufted duck and pochard were a common sight, but a smew is not a bird of inland waters, and I shall always think myself lucky to have seen one on a Surrey pond.

Bucknill, I am sure, never saw one in his time, or he would have said so in his *Birds of Surrey*. All he mentions are birds seen by other people, and usually shot, two of them "at some mills near Albury," which I think must be the mills by Postford Pond. And Bucknill, too, was less lucky than I was in regard to the other rare visitor which I saw close to the factory, a black redstart, which on 8 March 1917 suddenly flew up from a field path in front of me as I was setting out to walk to Guildford. It settled close by, and I came back to read in *Birds of Surrey* of the six solitary records which were all that Bucknill had been able to discover, three of which, a wonder to relate, were merely seen near Guildford, and not shot.

As for the "explosion of waste," that too was a record of a curious kind. I not only heard, but saw it at a distance; workmen in the factory had carried out what was described as waste from one of the mixing-houses—so I was told—and the waste somehow blew up. I did not take much notice of it at the time, nor I believe did anyone connected with the factory, but we heard a day or two afterwards from an officer in charge of a store of cordite miles away in Sussex that the explosion had been heard there, and had been supposed to be something very big indeed—one of those strange freaks of blast, as regards acoustics, of which we had so many examples in the war of 1939.

But now for the history of gunpowder-making in Surrey. It was an industry which came first to be established in the reign of Elizabeth, when powder-makers were appointed to their posts by the government, and, as it happened, these appointments were held from the beginning by Surrey men. In Elizabeth's day, when relations with foreign governments were apt to be difficult, it became of the first importance that the supply of gunpowder should be assured in manufactories at home. And the first difficulty in assuring this supply was the production of the main ingredient of gunpowder, saltpetre, or nitrate of potash, which is not a natural product of Europe. Saltpetre, therefore, had perforce to be produced artificially, and it is a strange coincidence, almost prophetic of the conditions of modern warfare and the supply of oil, that the art of making saltpetre was first taught in England by a German captain, one Gerrard Honrick, who, on 13 March 1560, for the sum of £300 agreed to instruct Englishmen in the art, or, as it is phrased in the Elizabethan State Paper giving the text of the agreement, "in the trew and perfect arte of the making of salt-peter to growe in cellars, barnes, or in lyme or stone quarrees." This art, shortly stated, consisted in the mixing together of earth, "the blacker the better," and animal excrement with lime and ashes. And one of the chief sources of the animal matter required was the soil of pigeon-houses. So important was this business of obtaining the ingredient of saltpetre considered that actually in a proclamation by Charles I in 1625 it was ordained that owners of pigeon-houses, stables and so on might not pave them with stone or brick or floor them with boarding, or lay them with anything but good, sound earth.

But this was when the making of gunpowder had become an industry vital to the forces of the Crown. Before Elizabeth's time, we had been obtaining gunpowder in quantity from abroad, and the earliest date of the establishment of a factory in Surrey seems to be 1554, when Henry Reve erected a mill at Rotherhithe. In 1588, the year of the Armada— compare England's preparedness, or the reverse, for war in the year 1939—we were making so little powder in England that there had never been more than twenty or thirty lasts (a last was about a ton) delivered into the Queen's stores. If the Armada had been commanded by a Howard or a Drake! We had no powder to blow fleets out of the water.

As things happened, it was in 1588 that we first hear of a great Surrey family engaged in the gunpowder trade. In January George Evelyn, grandfather of John Evelyn the diarist, and his son were licensed by royal Letters Patent to dig and get saltpetre within the realms of England and Ireland, except in London and within the radius of two miles from its walls, and to convert the same into gunpowder. As to where they had all their mills there seems to be some uncertainty, but their first mills were undoubtedly on the little stream known as the Hogsmill River, which rises in Ewell and flows into the Thames at Kingston. There they worked until 1613, when George Evelyn's son transferred his mills to Godstone. From time to time contracts were renewed, and in a contract dated 1 July 1624 we read that the yearly quantity to be delivered to the Crown was raised to two hundred and forty lasts, or twenty lasts a month, and the price was to be 8½d per pound. But whatever the contracts' terms, and they were renewed more than once, the subsequent procedure seems to have been the same. Evelyn delivered his lasts punctually, and as punctually the king was in his debt. Eventually, in 1636, the Evelyn contracts with the Government ceased. It may have been a relief to be no longer the creditor of the Treasury.

So we reach a definite stage in the history of the gunpowder industry in Surrey. Henceforward the headquarters of the industry were transferred to Chilworth. When the mills at Chilworth were first built is not known, though probably they were set going by the East India Company to supply their own needs. At all events, when the appointment of powder-maker to the king was taken away from, or given up by, George Evelyn's son John, it was given to the tenants of the Chilworth mills, leased to them by the owner, Sir Edward Randyll, Samuel Cordwell and George Collins, who on 1 November 1636 became the only authorized gunpowder-makers in the kingdom.

Their monopoly did not last long. By August 1641 Charles I had set his hand to a Bill "for putting down the restraint of making gunpowder." This became an Act "for the free bringing in of gunpowder and saltpetre from foreign parts and for the free making of gunpowder in this realm." Possibly Charles had in view the obtaining of gunpowder from any and every source; at all events Cordwell continued the supply from Chilworth, and gunpowder reached the King's Commissioners from Hamburg and other sources, good, bad and indifferent. But on the outbreak of the Civil War, Cordwell, finding the surroundings of the capital in possession of the Parliament, transferred the Chilworth supply to new masters, and during the Dutch War, 1652–4, one hundred and fifty barrels were supplied weekly to the Admiralty and one thousand eight hundred barrels were sent to Portsmouth. And, in fact, even with the powder-making industry free to all, it is clear that during the Commonwealth the Surrey makers had a very large share of Government contracts; exactly how much it would need an accountant to determine—anyhow, the business was large.

So we come to the Restoration; and not only of the monarchy, but the restoration by the monarchy of the old office of sole gunpowder-maker to the king. Colonel Daniel O'Neale was the maker chosen, and he delegated part of his authority to the head of the Randyll family, who still owned the mills at Chilworth. It was thirteen years later that Aubrey began his perambulation of Surrey, in which he gives an account of the powder mills as he then saw them. He writes of the number of mills which he saw "in this little romancy vale" as eighteen, of which he says five were blown up in little more than half a year's time.

"'Tis a little commonwealth of powder-makers who are as black as negroes. . . . Here is a nursery of earth for the making of saltpetre; there is also here a boiling-house where the saltpetre is made and shoots; a corning-house and separating and finishing-houses, all very well worth seeing of the ingenious. I had almost forgot the brimstone mill and the engine to search it."

At Albury, too, Aubrey writes of powder mills, and says that the charcoal for the powder was made from the alders which grew there, though he was told by Mr Evelyn that the strongest powder was made of dogwood coals. To-day, either at Chilworth or Albury, we are back among the same scenes of trees and water. Still the little Tillingbourne wanders quietly through the meadows; still the catkins of alders hang crimson in spring, brown in winter, above its stream.

But of the actual business side of the Chilworth mills the main story of later days is that of Sir Polycarpus Wharton, who, on 1 January 1677, took a lease of the powder works for twenty-one years. On that date the mills were in so ruinous a condition that he found himself compelled to spend £1,500 to make them serviceable. Of this sum, in spite of undertakings of repayment, he never received a penny, and all contracts into which he entered were ignored or dishonoured—a miserable tale of characteristically Stuart callousness, which culminated in Sir Polycarpus being imprisoned for debt. And it was debt, though of a different kind, which ended the Randyll ownership of the Chilworth

64

Waverley Abbey, near Farnham

mills. Morgan Randyll, elected as one of the Members of Parliament for Guildford during the years 1680 to 1715, found himself so heavily burdened that in 1720 he sold his estate to a Mr Houlditch, woollen draper and a director of the South Sea Company. When that bubble burst, Houlditch's estate was seized and sold, the purchaser being Sarah Duchess of Marlborough, who devised it to her grandson. one of the Spencers, whose successor, the second Earl Spencer, in turn sold it in 1796 to Edmund Hill, owner of other powder mills near Hounslow.

Here comes a quaint story. Of the Chilworth mills as they existed in 1700, one of them, known as the Lower Works, in 1704 was converted into a paper mill. In 1817 the owner of this paper mill, a Mr Rowland, brought a prosecution against the owner of the Chilworth powder mills "for erecting and maintaining certain powder mills called a corning-house, a dusting-house, a gloom-stove, etc., in the parish of St. Martha at Chilworth." The case was tried before Mr Justice Dallas and a special jury at Kingston, and the full report of the case was afterwards printed in a book, *Chilworth Powder Mills: Trial on an Indictment charging them as a nuisance: by which they were proved to be not only no nuisance but as safe as any, if not the safest, powder mills in the kingdom.* The jury heard only one witness, Major By, R.E., the superintendent of all the King's powder works, and immediately found the defendants not guilty, the judge pronouncing the prosecution to be the most malicious he ever remembered being brought into a court of justice.

And so, through the nineteenth century, powder-makers carried on at Chilworth, with powder gradually giving way to new forms of explosive. In 1905, as we learn from the exhaustive account of the industry given by Mr Montague Giuseppi in the *Victoria History*, one of the directors of the Chilworth Gunpowder Company, Mr Edward Kraftmeier, introduced a new, slower-burning powder to the notice of the Government. It became in time known as brown or prismatic powder, and through Mr Edward Kraftmeier the Government were enabled, with the help of the German inventors, Mr J. N. Heideman and Mr M. Duttenhofer, to get this new powder made at Waltham Abbey and at Chilworth.

An inn yard, Farnham

Next came a further development, the invention of cordite or smokeless powder, which led to a very large extension of the buildings of the company, till the works extended for nearly two miles along the valley of the Tillingbourne. Here the company was engaged in the manufacture of cordite, and another new powder, ballistite, when in 1914 there broke upon England and Chilworth the First German War.

And in that year, as I have said, I was sent as an officer of the guard to Chilworth. There from one year's end to the other the guard ringed the factory with sentries and patrols, and for most of the time the war seemed a thing very far off. But one afternoon I remember when for a few strange minutes it was going on there at Chilworth, by my side. I had climbed up the hill above the factory on which stands the little chapel of St. Martha, a building which you may see far off in that part of Surrey, and which, lest it should somehow furnish a guide to enemy aircraft, was at one time covered in, its roof and its churchyard walls, with boughs and bushes, an elementary form of camouflage. I climbed the hill and stood with my back to the south door of the church. And there, in my ear as I stood, was the war in France. Close to my ear were the sounds of battle, field guns, heavy guns, the shaking boom, the rattle of musketry, as if we were fighting Germans in the next parish. All came to me in repercussion of sound from the oak door behind me. I stepped a yard to the side and I was in the silence of Surrey; a step to my right, and I was in France. I could be in and out of the sounds of battle as I chose, there above the Chilworth factory on a Surrey hill.

CLOTH

Two woolsacks hang one on either side of the Guildford borough arms. They are a memorial. There was a time when the manufacture of woollen cloth was the staple industry of Guildford, Godalming and the villages near. Exactly when the industry came into being no one knows—perhaps it was as early as the thirteenth century—but there are two natural causes for its growth. One was the neighbourhood of the downs where there was good pasturage for sheep; the other,

66

the abundance in the county of fuller's earth—Nutfield, near Redhill, is the main source, which from the earliest times was used for cleaning wool.

From the first the manufacture and trade in woollen cloth was hemmed in by law. In 1391 a statute of Richard II ordained that

"because that of old times divers cloths were made in the town of Guildford and other places within the counties of Surrey, Sussex and Southampton called Cloths of Guildford, which were of good making and of good value, and did bear a good name;

"and because certain fullers and others were found to be wrongfully dealing in cloth before it was fit for market, and were stretching the cloth before sale;

"it is agreed and assented that from henceforth no fuller or other person, whatsoever he be, shall buy within the said towns and counties any cloth before the same cloth be fulled and fully performed in his nature."

Nearly two hundred years later we find other legal restrictions. In 1557–8 it was laid down that no one should make cloth except in a market town where it had been made for ten years past. This was possibly to make it easier for the ulnagers and sealers, the officers whose business it was to see that the cloth was of proper quality. Several cases of prosecution under this Act are on record. In 1561 Richard and Simon Hardinge were charged with having made woollen cloths at Frensham, and Thomas Rosyer was charged with the same offence at Witley. Then in Hilary term 1562–3 six clothiers, all of well-known families of Surrey clothmakers, the Hookes and the Chittys, were charged with having in the past ten years carried on the industry of kersey-making at Thursley, Pitfold and Frensham, and over the county border at Aldershot and elsewhere. They asked to be fined, apparently to save further trouble.

There was another offence which in these Elizabethan days came now and then into court—stretching the cloths with unlawful instruments. In 1565 twelve Godalming manufacturers, among them members of families of repute—Chitty, Hooke, Mellersh, Wood, Chaundler—were accused of having used tentors or wrenches, ropes and rings to strain and stretch their cloths. In 1569 five Farnham clothiers were charged with the same offence. After that for a time there was a lull in the prosecutions, perhaps because they had had their effect, or possibly because the gentle trade of the informer was found not sufficiently paying. But under the Stuarts the informers seem to have sprung into life again. In 1607 Thomas West of Guildford was charged with having had in his keeping and use a certain instrument, namely a tentor, with a lower bar and other engines, wherewith one hundred cloths of white wool called kerseys, rough and unwrought and made for sale at Guildford, were stretched and strained in breadth and length. And in the Michaelmas and Hilary terms of 1610–11 no fewer than twelve others from the same town had to answer charges laid against them by informers of having used "a certain engine called a rope" and other unlawful instruments for stretching cloth.

Thus in Elizabethan days three Surrey towns, Guildford, Godalming and Farnham, had become the chief centres of the industry of cloth-making; and, in spite of prosecutions, the business had spread into neighbouring villages, Wonersh, Chiddingfold, Shalford, Shere. Many Surrey families prospered and became landowners through success in the cloth trade; they were mostly connected with Godalming, but the most famous family of Surrey clothiers belonged to Guildford, that of Abbott, of whom the three sons of Maurice Abbott, Robert, George and Maurice, became respectively Bishop of Salisbury, Archbishop of Canterbury and Lord Mayor of London. Even so, Sir Maurice Abbott was not the first lord mayor connected with the trade of clothier. In 1565 the office was held by a Godalming man, a member of the Drapers' Company, Richard Champion.

But the golden days of the Surrey cloth-makers were to pass. On 26 November 1630 a number of inhabitants of Godalming and the neighbourhood, among them members of the families of West, Perior, Woods, Hackman, Webham, Chitty and Monger, presented a petition to the Privy Council. They represented themselves as clothiers who for many years had maintained as many as 1,400 poor people in the spinning of wool, weaving, working, making, dyeing, fulling and dressing of cloths called Hampshire kerseys. They had sold these kerseys to one Samuel Vassall, a London merchant who traded beyond seas, but Vassall had fallen on evil times and they could find no other merchant to take their goods, so that the poor people they had maintained were in danger of starvation. They prayed the Lords of the Council to make an Order for the selling of the cloths. The Lords in response, not very helpfully, ordered the magistrates of the county living near Godalming to make collections for the unemployed.

Surrey was not the only county in which the cloth trade at this time had gone back. It was the same in Hampshire. State Papers show that in 1630–1 there was a complaint from clothiers of Basingstoke that whereas they had previously made thirty broadcloths and a hundred kerseys every week in the town, they were now making only seven broadcloths and twenty kerseys, and could not sell even those. Trade was as bad in Devon, Kent, Suffolk and Essex. Clearly some major influence was at work, and the cause was doubtless one and the same. The Merchant Adventurers and the London Drapers' Company were at work getting the trade in cloth, wholesale and retail, into their own hands. They were too strong for the provinces.

Aubrey, writing at the close of the seventeenth century, gives a picture of the decay of the Surrey trade. Godalming alone was still eminent in the clothing business, "the most of any place in this country; here they make mixed kerseys and blue kerseys for the Canaries, which for their colour are not equalled by any in England." Of Wonersh he writes that it "has been a village of great note for the clothing manufacture, but has been in its waning condition above threescore years; it chiefly consisted in making blue cloth for the Canary Islands." Here, as at Godalming, the trade seems to have brought about its own end: "the decay and indeed ruin of their trade was their avaricious method of stretching their cloth from eighteen yards to twenty-two or twenty-three, which being discovered abroad, they returned their commodity on their hands and it would sell at no market." And the same fraud, he writes, "caused the decay of the blues" at Guildford.

Only at Godalming did the cloth trade linger on. But

modern conditions of manufacture, possible in town surroundings, were too much for the industry further out. Brayley
and Britton, in an appendix to volume V of their *History of
Surrey,* survey the county scene. They "mark the changes in
remote corners where the minor arteries of trade beat with
feeble intermittent pulsations." The south-west of Surrey
faints and fails. "A few kerseys, woollens, and stockings are
still made at Godalming; but the advantages of steam-power
wherever coal is cheap leave but little chance to other
places." It is the same story with cloth as with pottery and
glass; all goes to London.

LEATHER

In one of the oldest trades in the world, Godalming and
south-west Surrey held a place of honour second to Bermondsey and Southwark, chief seats of the industry in England.
Tanning and other methods of treating the hides of animals,
whether to convert them into leather, fur or parchment, must
obviously have been occupations of countrymen from the
earliest times, and it is just the universal character of the
employment which makes its development in detail difficult
to follow. But early in English history Surrey names are
found in court cases and other records connected with the
trade.

From the first, English law set out to ensure that Englishmen should be supplied with the necessaries of life in good
condition. In 1351 under Edward III the Statute of
Labourers laid down that no shoemaker might be a tanner,
or a tanner a shoemaker. In the reign of Henry VII other
Acts sharply define the work of tanners, curriers and cordwainers—those who tan leather, dress and colour it, and
make it into shoes. Then follow statutes of Edward VI which
deal with forbidden processes of hastening the necessarily
slow production of good leather, and so we come to legislation under Elizabeth and James I, the appointment of official searchers and sealers, and further insistence on regula-
tion of sales outside appointed markets.

All this led, of course, to cases in the courts from which
we can judge the extent of the manufacture of leather in the

county of Surrey. In 1437 we find Richard Couper, a tanner of Oxted, with other defendants in a Chancery suit, described as men of substance "yn there countreys and richesse." In 1483 John Hamonde and Robert Oketon, tanners in the hundred of Godalming, are fined for making excessive gains out of their leather, and John Glover and Thomas Glover, whiteners (*dealbatores*) of tanned leather, are found to be working outside a market town. Another tanner, William Ropley, of Chiddingfold, member of a well-known glass-making family, is accused of the same offence as John Hamonde, making excessive gains. These are just names which chance to occur in law suits, and which point to the importance of the leather trade in the south of the county.

All through the cases that come into court we see the emphasis laid on the need for proper control of the leather industry in all its branches. Fashion, in the reign of Edward IV, could be as ridiculous as it is to-day. Thus in 1464–5 it was enacted that no shoemaker in London or in a circuit of three miles should make shoes with pikes, that is, peaked toes, more than two inches long. In Henry VIII's reign the law went a good deal further. In 1532–3 it was laid down that no tanned leather should be sold in or within three miles of London except in Leadenhall market or in city fairs, and all tanned leather for sale within this three-mile compass had first to be searched and viewed by the wardens of the Cordwainers', Curriers', Girdlers' and Saddlers' Companies.

This Act brought a number of tanners into trouble. Within a year four tanners were summoned for putting to sale in the borough of Southwark a large quantity of hides and calves' skins which had not first been brought to Leadenhall. Case after case of various kinds, in which leather was seized in the Southwark market, came into court, one of the chief practices which were impugned being illegal methods of trying to hasten the process of tanning, and so injuring the leather. Here is the opening of the preamble of the Act of Edward VI for the true tanning of leather :

"Whereas in times past the hides or leather were wont to lie in the tan vats by the space of one year or five quarters of the year, before it was taken out of the same vats or put to sale, now for the speedy utterance and tanning hereof they have invented diverse and sundry deceitful and crafty means to have the same leather tanned, some time in three weeks and some time in one month or six weeks at the most."

Among these deceitful and crafty means were "over liming in their lime pits" and "putting seething hot liquor with their oozes into their tan vats, which they most commonly do practise in the night time," while among the oozes used were mixtures with "ashen bark, tapworth, meal, ashes or culver dung." It is interesting to notice the importance attached to pigeon (culver) dung in early days; it was one of the chief sources of saltpetre in the making of gunpowder. (Tapworth—query, taplash, an old name for the dregs of beer and other liquor.) All these mixtures were forbidden in the process of tanning, and no leather was passed as sufficiently tanned which had not lain in the oozes for at least nine months.

We get plenty of instances of Surrey men summoned for offences under these and other Acts. In 1552 a large quantity of leather was seized in Southwark as having been improperly tanned, and among the twelve accused tanners were two Surrey men, John Cholmely of Blechingley and Thomas Pynnyn of Bermondsey Street. In 1563–4 Robert Clarke, a currier, was charged with having curried four hundred hides outside a market town, in his own dwelling-house in the parish of St. Nicholas, Guildford. In 1568 Anthony Bygnall, a tanner of Shere, was suspected of having sold at St. Catherine's Hill leather which had not been properly examined and sealed, and in 1573 John Bygnall of Wonersh was charged with other Surrey tanners with having used unlawful mixtures in the parish of St. Anthony Undershaft. One of these tanners was the same John Cholmely who had been summoned in 1552; it was his third appearance, for in 1566 he had been charged with exposing for sale two hundred and fifty hides at Leadenhall before they had been examined and sealed. As with other cases, the charges were based on evidence supplied by that product of the times, the common informer.

Other centres of the leather trade in Surrey in the sixteenth century were Reigate, Horley and Godstone. In 1563 Robert Wood of Reigate was accused of carrying on the art of tanning though not having been properly apprenticed, and he again appeared in court in 1566 for selling unregistered leather. Two tanners of Horley, Henry and Nicholas Bray, in 1561 were charged with selling leather there, not in open market, and they were among the tanners who had to answer the charge of using illegal mixtures in 1573. Godstone in 1568 seems to have been a recognized centre of trade in leather not only for Surrey but for tanners in Sussex and London; there were tanners of the same period in Leatherhead, Lingfield, Stoke d'Abernon and Bookham, while at Croydon, in 1564, out of what was evidently a settlement of shoemakers, eight were summoned for having, while carrying on the business of making shoes, engaged in the work of curriers in their own houses.

These various records of cases brought into court, of no great account separately, are of interest in the aggregate as showing the extent of the leather trade in Surrey during the sixteenth century, and also as a measure of the deep interest felt by the community as a whole in the carrying on of the trade honestly, so that buyers could be sure of getting proper value for their money. There were still too many engaged in the trade who were not above taking what advantage they could of local conditions. In his *Description of England* published in 1577, William Harrison, at one time rector of Wimbush in Essex, and afterwards Canon of Windsor, writes, from his knowledge of conditions of country life in his day, of the use of various ingredients instead of oak bark for tanning :

"Only this I wish that our sole and upper leathering may have their due time, and not be hasted by extraordinary slights, as with ash bark, etc. Whereby as I grant that it seemeth outwardly to be very thick and well done : so, if you respect the sadness thereof, it doth prove in the end to be very hollow, and not able to hold out water." (Sadness, i.e. solidity.)

At Godalming, tanning is still carried on. War altered many conditions, but with peace the old prosperity doubtless will return.

POTTERY (ANCIENT)

As with glass, the industry of earthenware in modern times centres in Lambeth. But—as also with glass—pottery in Surrey was being made in country districts at a date early in the Middle Ages. Best of all examples of this early art are the encaustic tiles which were used to cover the floors, and as some think, possibly the walls of monastic buildings, and of all varieties of these tiles those found at Chertsey Abbey are the finest. The question then arises, where were these tiles made? and on this point authorities differ. One theory is that they were made in the precincts of the monasteries, possibly by Italian workmen; this is the opinion of Professor Church, given in his book, *English Earthenware*. Another opinion, detailed in the *Connoisseur* (i. 247) by Mr A. L. Solon, is that the tiles are of exclusively native origin, his reason for this belief being that no example of a tiled pavement has been discovered in mediæval buildings earlier in date than those exhumed from the abbeys of Malvern and Chertsey. He goes so far as to suggest that since the French pavements of the earliest period have been mostly found in provinces under English domination the art of making the tiles may even have been imported from England.

However that may be, the tiles are believed to date from about 1250 to the beginning of the fourteenth century. But of definite evidence of the early existence of an earthenware industry in Surrey the only example, detailed in the *Victoria County History*, is the collection of fragments found on Limpsfield Common in 1863. Here there was actually discovered a potter's kiln, of rough stones laid without mortar, in shape like an oven, about three feet in diameter. And the kiln, or at all events the existence of pottery works in the neighbourhood, can be dated. In the *Victoria County History* Mr Montague Giuseppi, quoting the *Proceedings of the Society of Antiquaries*, tells us that in an extent of the manor of Limpsfield made for the abbot of Battle in 1314, the name of Geoffrey the potter appears as one of the tenants; while in a list of natives of Prinkham in Lingfield, which was held

of Limpsfield, there is the name of Roger the potter. As for
the kind of earthenware made at these works, Mr Giuseppi
describes the pottery as mostly of a grey and coarse material,
and the fragments as consisting "principally of the handles
and rims of vessels of a very large size." Perhaps, he thinks,
the clay on the common was used for making these vessels,
but what led to the site being selected for pottery works was
the abundance of wood in the neighbourhood.

This Limpsfield pottery is the only earthenware described
in the *Victoria History* as definitely old and of Surrey origin.
And having given Mr Giuseppi's description of it, I come
now to the account of another discovery which I believe will
prove of considerably greater importance : indeed, I would
venture to say that had Mr Giuseppi known of it he would
have devoted the larger share of his article to it, given one
condition—that excavation by skilled workers had put him in
full possession of the facts.

Here is the story. In 1909, when it was my good fortune
to come to live in south-west Surrey, and so to come into
close contact with much of the countryside, we built our
house on the flank of Hydons Ball, not far from a smaller
hill in the neighbourhood known locally as the Tolt; and a
year or two later it was our further good fortune to come
into possession of the Tolt itself. It was then that the owner,
the late Mr John Eastwood, told us that there had been dug
up on the Tolt—whether in the course of ferreting or in
some other way I forget—fragments of pottery and scraps
of fused glass, but that no thorough investigation of the
ground in the neighbourhood had been made. We decided to
experiment further with the digging, and I and one of my
daughters spent some of our leisure time in cutting trenches
in various directions and, wherever we found fragments of
pottery, in getting down to the subsoil so as to see whether
the ground had been disturbed at any time, or whether we
had reached the solid, and could be sure that we should find
no further pieces by digging further.

We unearthed a very large number of pieces of pottery of
various shapes, sizes and colours, parts of jugs and of vessels
of a large size, some scraps of fused glass, and, in greater
quantities than anything else, roof tiling. But our digging was

interrupted. There came the building of a sanatorium on ground adjoining the Tolt, which meant that digging could no longer be carried on without onlookers. Then came work which meant that my whole week was spent in London; and then came the Second German War. But I had sent some of the fragments which we had dug up to one of the first authorities on such subjects in England, Mr S. E. Winbolt, and he wrote in reply giving the opinion that the fused glass suggested Roman rather than Surrey-Sussex origin, though the bits of window glass might be dated about 1200. "What perhaps interests us most," he said, "is the tiny piece of stone on which the glaze has fallen; this looks like glassmaking on the spot. The presence of sand and of bracken, for potash, together with the good position, on or near the top of a hill, for draught, would make a suitable place for glassmaking. I wish I could be sure of the date of the pottery; because if I am right about 1180–1200, this glass (if English) is some of the very earliest known."

A little later he came and inspected my drawerful of fragments, and had no hesitation in pronouncing them to be not Roman. We talked in a general way about the possibility of excavation, but such undertakings require money and organization of skilled work, and I gathered that he himself had as much on hand as he could deal with. And then, to the sorrow of all who knew him and his work for archæology in Surrey, in March 1944 he died, and for the time being all prospects of planned excavation vanished.

And that is how matters remain to-day. Two recollections are still in my mind as I think over the possibilities of the future. One is the statement made to my wife, soon after we came to live at Hambledon, by an old man of ninety who had ploughed the Tolt (it was then known as Upper High Field) before it was planted with the Scots pines which grow on its top to-day. His plough "rattled as it went over the ground." The other is of a day when in digging a trench at one place I found that the ground had been disturbed and contained fragments of pottery to a depth of four feet and possibly more. I had no opportunity, as things happened, of excavating further.

What may the future hold? Discovery of pottery-making

on a larger scale and with a richer and more varied output than anything hitherto found in Surrey? Who knows?

POTTERY (MODERN)

To London belongs to-day the trade of the pottery of the common day, but to Surrey the work of the potter artist. In Compton lived that great artist George Frederick Watts, as his paintings live to-day in the separate gallery there and in the art collections of the world; but the work of the master mind remains not only in galleries. In countless gardens through England you may look at the handiwork of the Potters' Arts Guild, a society of designers founded by Mrs Watts at Limnerlease, with the object of developing artist-craftsmen who—in her own words—"would, in the end, be capable of using to the best purpose the very noble material provided by British clays."

Twice in the present century war has interrupted and checked the work of the Guild, but the influence of a master mind has held on still, and will hold on. The Guild designs and manufactures, in red and grey terra cotta, things of use and beauty for the garden, from sundials to garden seats, flower vases, bird baths, bowls. Vases may be tall, to stand on terraces or to set about the angles of a formal border, sundials can be patterned with wings, wreathed with cobras or flowers. Elves sit about the edges of lily ponds, Bacchus drinks of grapes, Pan plays his pipe, Harebell, delicate as her name, holds her chin in her hands; but whether you choose bowl or statuette, Tudor or Greek pot, fruit finial or Italian box, you will find grace, simplicity, distinction. If I am to choose of many garden decorations one that in thought and design seems to me to mark best what has been in the mind and still holds the memory of Mrs Watts, it shall be the bird bath, three feet high for an outstanding feature of garden hospitality, broad in its splash of water and named Martineau after a lady who greatly loved birds, even as did St. Francis, whose prayer speaks in carved lettering from its stem—"Praised be Thou, my Lord, of Sister Water, for manifold is her use and humble is she and precious and pure."

But artistry in pottery is not confined to Compton. From the Losely MSS. Mr Montague Giuseppi quotes a letter written by Sir Julius Cæsar to Sir William More, dated 19 August 1594, asking that the bearer might be given, out of Farnham Park, "certaine white cley for the making of grene pottes usually drunke in by the gentlemen of the Temple." And to-day "Farnham ware" is in request as much as ever. But the green pots, and many other products of the local clay, are no longer made at Farnham; they come from the neighbouring village of Wrecclesham. It was in 1875 that the firm of Harris and Sons was started by Absalom Harris, and at Wrecclesham the firm has established its fame. As I remember it first, at the beginning of the century, its chief product was glazed pottery of a delightful dark green shade, which I have always thought of in the same category, for depth of colour and clearness of glazing, with pottery which I once bought at Jerusalem. And I learn from the *Victoria County History* that at first the firm only made garden pots and vases, bread crockery, chimney-pots and so on, and that the only glazes in use were yellow, red, and chocolate. Then about 1886 they were asked to copy some green-glazed garden vases which had been bought in France but would not stand an English winter; they succeeded in the task, and followed up the one success with others.

In the autumn of 1945, at Wrecclesham, I was fortunate enough to find the Messrs Harris brothers, successors to the founder of the firm, superintending the work, which had been hampered in various restrictions by the war. I was shown a vase of grey clay which they had reconstructed from some fragments of Roman pottery dug up in Alice Holt Forest, a mile or two from Wrecclesham over the Hampshire border, an extraordinarily skilful piece of work. And I spent a pleasant hour watching the different processes of pottery-making to-day, in the use of the grey clay dug from a neighbouring field. I watched the clay being mixed to the right consistency, then being shaped from the wet lump, an inert clod taking on meaning and use; and I found myself thinking in lines from Isaiah and Jeremiah as the wheel spun under the potter's hand, turning and finishing vessel and vase, and—to please a child who was with me—a jug with

78

the face, beak and eyes of an owl. I left the works with memories of an industry in myriad forms of ware and piece, of pot, pan, basin, saucer, mug, of quaintly tiled chimneys, of great bowls of red geraniums out-of-doors, and a lawn and flowers beyond in sunshine of October.

CHAPTER VI

ROADS

STANE STREET TO BYPASSES

Two old roads cross Surrey, one running east and west, the other north and south. The younger road is Roman, the other stretches beyond Stonehenge. East and west runs the ridge of the North Downs, carrying the traffic of to-day, as it carried the Ancient Briton or the Phœnicians trading with him, from Salisbury Plain by the Hog's Back to Guildford, and from Guildford east into Kent:

> There runs a road by Merrow Down,
> A grassy track to-day it is,
> An hour out of Guildford town
> Above the River Wey it is.

That poem in its timeless beauty is of the very self of the old road, its sunshine, its sounds, the horse-bells, the cuckoo —you may hear the cuckoo calling there in those lines in the silence of deep July.

And the younger road, the Roman, is still plain to see, though not for a long distance within the county boundaries. Stane Street or Stone Street—half English, half Latin in its name—starts from Chichester to cross the South Downs in the direction of Pulborough. From Pulborough it runs straight as a die past Billingshurst and Slinfold to within a mile of the Surrey boundary, where we lose it, to pick up the line of the old metal a couple of miles outside Ockley. Past Ockley it again vanishes, and though the Ordnance maps print Stane Street in faint capitals north of Holmwood, and "Roman Road" east of Leatherhead, and though you may pick up the straight line again, pointing past Ewell and

Morden in modern macadam to Tooting, Lambeth and Billingsgate beyond the Thames, they are London suburbs that front the traffic of omnibus and car. Yet even at Ockley, where the green lies by the side of the old road and all is the quiet of England, there can be a vision of Roman armour in the grey distance of that driven line, and in the air an echo of Kipling's song of the Great Wall:

> Mithras, God of the Morning, our trumpets waken the
>   Wall!
> "Rome is above the Nations, but Thou art over all!"
> Now as the names are answered, and the guards are
>   marched away,
> Mithras, also a soldier, give us strength for the day!

To-day's counterpart of the Roman road is the bypass. Just as the Roman road cut straight and hard as the Roman mind through wood and hill, so the modern bypass, avoiding towns, shops, corners and every kind of stoppage or hindrance of fast movement, carries the twentieth-century driver from one point to another with one object only always ahead of his bonnet—to get there. I think often of E. V. Lucas, at work on the *Highways and Byways of Sussex*:

> *To get there first!*—'tis time to ring
>   The knell of such an aim;
> *To be the swiftest!*—riches bring
>   So easily that fame.
> *To shine, a highway meteor,*
>   *Devourer of the map!*
> A vulgar bliss to choose before
>   Repose in Nature's lap!

He wrote that, in his "Song Against Speed," in 1903, and in *E. V. Lucas: a Portrait* I find his daughter writing of him thirty-five years later that "he hated so many of the things which the new order has brought. He hated noise and speed; wireless and words like 'hiker'; bad manners and casualness; most newspapers; the Great West Road; and he liked his car to be driven almost at the pace of a brougham."

If he disliked the Great West Road I wonder what he

G   81

A corner in Albury below Newlands Corner

would have said of the Godalming bypass on a Sunday evening to-day, with a hundred cars crawling lamp to lamp into Guildford. For that procession, more and more crowded at week-ends during the summer months, sums up the answer of the bypass to to-day's votary of the Song of Speed. Most of those aiming at getting there first arrive at the same time.

Yet bypasses can show different pictures. They can be rightly or wrongly planned. And they can make very pleasant travelling, but they differ in outlook. They can take you through open country with views to right and left of field and hill, or you may find yourself looking at nothing but villas. Of the bypasses which I have come to know in Surrey, I like best the road that runs from Milford crossroads, avoiding Godalming, to Guildford. All the way you are in the country. More, for you see different sides of Surrey—sand and chalk, willow and elm, water and distant hills. And of the months in which to see the bypass happiest in the sun I should choose June.

I travelled by the Godalming bypass soon after it was opened, and realized at once how new and separate was the sight it gave me of the Surrey countryside. I saw Surrey as only a bird might have seen it, flying over fields where there was no path. Here the road went high over a valley and I looked straight down on the Wey; here I was passing cornfields and fields of grass of which only the farmer knew the hedges; and there, suddenly, I was travelling north of the Hog's Back. That was in the early days, when the bypass was still almost a lonely road, then—how quick and how complete the change!—the car-driving public became aware of the new road out of London into the world beyond, and every Saturday and Sunday the bypass held its processions, racing through the open, closing in bonnet on mudguard, drivers muttering at the hundreds of other drivers bunched in front. The war stopped that carefree traffic and the bypass became part of a machine.

Days of peace came, and once more I set out by Milford on a morning in June. I had not driven that way for five years and it was a happy thing to see the changes of colour and of growth. Along the sides of the road those who planned the new highway had thought out schemes of shade and

flower, and the saplings dotted right and left had become
trees. Prunus and acacia stood in grass next to bushes of pink
roses, and beyond the avenue they made and the moon-
daisies growing under them stretched pasture and corn. One
sight I did not remember as a scene of the roadside before
the war, though it has always been common on waste land in
Surrey, and that was a caravan of gipsies, their gay clothes
spread to dry on a paling, children wandering and horses
feeding, six of them, in the rough wayside grass. Where did
they get their water, I wondered, in those dry fields? But
gipsies always set riddles. Within a few yards of their caravan, a sight familiar to soldiers of Parliament or Napoleon,
I looked up at a thing new even to war of to-day. Above and
across the easy level of the road stretched a strand of steel
wire, invisible to a landing aeroplane till it should break it
in death. I realized how few were the days since peace had
come to that countryside.

Other sights of that morning's drive I remembered of old,
and shall always think of as the memory and meaning of
peace by an English road. One is the row of elms on the left
of the road as it swings right towards Compton, surely as
noble a company of trees as ever stood above a curving highway into blue sky. And then further on, towards the great
chalk ridge that was part of the old road east and west in
the days of Stonehenge, two signposts of this twentieth century, two crosses, one on each side of the road, standing
witness to the readiness of Englishmen to take a story on
trust without proof of its truth. As you come near to the
Ridge you will see the two crosses marking the route which
the Ordnance maps, too, will tell you ran there, the track
of thousands through the ages, the Pilgrims' Way from
Southampton to Canterbury. But I write of that strange story
in another chapter.

And then, as you pass those signposts, begins another part
of the bypass, as separate and as distinct as any two miles
of travel in England. Suddenly you are aware of a change
of outlook, colour, distance beyond, plants at your side. The
road runs no longer among fields, under trees, in a country
opening out before you. Instead, to your left rises higher
and higher a wall of chalk. You look left and right, and on

your right, too, a bank of chalk grows into a wall; in a moment you are running in a passage between sheer cliffs. I remember well the sense of surprise, almost of dismay, when years ago, at the first opening of the bypass, I came suddenly into that white passage between cliffs. I did not realize on that level road exactly where we were; the white walls on either side are a blind entrance to what lies in front, and in a car you do not have time to look about or behind. But in a moment the knowledge came to me, who had never thought out where the bypass would run, that the white walls on either side were part of the very structure of the Surrey countryside, that the engineer who planned the road on which we were running had cut into, through, under and out the other side of the great chalk Ridge that separates northern Surrey from the south, part of the Old Road of time beyond counting that crosses England east and west, the Hog's Back.

I have sometimes wondered what will happen with those chalk walls. They began crumbling soon after the cutting was made, and a fence had to be put at the foot to stop lumps of chalk from scattering out over the road. In years to come, you would guess, the rains will bring down a big slide now and then, and the silent Ridge will tell the hurt of primeval Surrey that way. The cars will not care. Meanwhile, flowers dress the wound. Mullein sends up tall yellow spikes, drinking what they may from chalky crevices ,and valerian spreads its red panicles on ledges high and low. Are the seeds windblown? There must be plants in gardens near, but when I first saw those cheerful guests of hungry places I thought of the curtains flanking the Guildford tunnel two miles away.

From under the bridge that to-day carries the Old Road over to Guildford the new road breaks out to north and east. I know no other such sudden lighting of a landscape in the county. The bypass slides sideways through the cutting, so that you do not see what stretches beyond till you are free of the chalk walls, and then in a moment you are looking to a horizon spreading to four counties—Hampshire, Berkshire, Buckingham, Surrey, twenty miles, perhaps, of serenest England. But a finer sight waits on a hill below you to the right. The curving road sinks from the Ridge, and as the

Guildford houses grow into view in the foreground there is another higher vision, the noble outline of the chancel of the cathedral. There it stands, a promise to be fulfilled in years of peace. And there is peace already, on such a June morning as that on which I looked again at the cathedral after five years of war, with sunshine on the roses of Guildford's gardens, and screening the great business buildings that stand between cathedral and town front a curtain of willows, and then a long line of Lombardy poplars—how they had grown since I saw them last!—bending green in a wind from the west.

Between Guildford and Cobham, its next main neighbour on the road to London, time and the war have brought changes to what used to be untouched country. Ripley itself, once the recognized halting place for bicyclists on the road south from London, is little altered: still the Anchor and still the Talbot Inn welcome passing guests. But the Hut Pond fringed by the Scots pines of Ockham Common, during the war of 1939, suffered as did other pleasant waters of Surrey. Of Frensham Great Pond and Little Pond, and of Virginia Water, I write elsewhere; they were drained. The Hut Pond was not drained but bushed. When I saw it first after five years, it was sprinkled with island obstructions, big bundles of dead boughs sunk tethered to its floor, and my mind went back through summers and autumns gone to boat-loads of holiday-makers idling happily in sunshine, and to one October evening long ago when with a companion I watched bunches of teal circling and dipping in the twilight over its water. But if the island bushes were new, so also were other islands, close inshore. Opposite the Hut, the edge of the pond—surely an unexpected picture for boating Londoners—is starred with white water-lilies.

I remember the Hut Pond when the Scots pines on its banks were young. To-day they are fewer than they were; I hope some will be allowed to grow old and nobly red in summer sunsets. But there is yet more for the years to redeem from the grasp of war. Once it was happiness on an August day, driving on from the Hut Pond towards Cobham, to look out on the left below the hill of Foxwarren Park over acres of heather, pink and purple among the pines.

85

Then came the roar of tanks, and to-day their tenacious tread still shows on empty sand. In Scotland you can burn heather down to black dust, and next summer the young green springs again from the root, but the grinding weight of chains year in year out is a new test of plant life, and time must be the gardener.

Beyond Cobham Fairmile still suits its name; Esher needs time for new fronts on her thoroughfare, and Sandown's future is as gay as ever. But the Kingston bypass? That still begins by shouting advertisements, and till public opinion silences those affronts, the bypass will keep the name it earned so quickly, as a road planned without thought except for speed. Yet even on the bypass you may still here and there look out over cornfields, and pray that villas, if more are to come, may deepen behind those already there, instead of lining other miles. Villas can be happy things to see in the right place, and even on the bypass roses add their own beauty, but to drive out of town the best way is surely to be able to see wide and far over harvest fields to the hills. And in the war the bypass lost some of the foregrounds it used to have that were not bricks and mortar; Carter's grounds for flower seeds, for example, which used to tell us there were better things to sow than for the kitchen. Or tennis and cricket; they will come back brighter than ever, and we shall see a polo ground again, I hope, instead of potatoes.

But I shall always remember the Kingston bypass as I saw it that morning for a thing unexpected, a new experience of the life of birds; a new problem set me of migrants. Swifts are creatures of mystery. They are latecomers in spring and the first to leave us in summer. They are birds for ever on the wing; *apus*, footless, is their fitting name, for their tiny feet are useless for perching. And a mystery that I have never seen explained is their choice of area. No swifts nest near my house, yet on a summer day the sky is seldom without those sickle-like wings and that swooping, twisting flight above the chimneys; and then there comes a day when over miles of Surrey country there is not a swift to be seen. What the pulse may be that takes them hither and thither through leagues of air over the country that is their summer home I do not guess. But to return to my Kingston problem.

We were running into Kingston Vale, Richmond Park on our left, and as we crossed the Beverley Brook I looked right, and there over Wimbledon Common was a flight, a concourse, a cloud of swifts of such numbers as I had never dreamed. If ever I could write vaguely and with truth of hundreds and hundreds, it was then; I thought as I looked of a swarm of bees. If it had been May I should have guessed they were arriving from Africa; if it were August they might have been going back. But in mid-June? That riddle of swifts remains for me without an answer.

EAST AND WEST

To drive from the Sussex border north-east and east, by Chiddingfold and Hambledon, say, through Bramley towards Dorking and Reigate, is to discover little change in outline or detail over a long period of years—until you come to Chilworth. I have walked or driven over those roads year after year since I began the *Highways and Byways* in 1907, and over them lies the same unaltering peace. But at Chilworth not only the look of the village but the whole atmosphere of the place has changed. When I first saw it, journeying to St. Martin's all those years ago, as I thought by the Pilgrims' Way, it was a collection of sheds and storehouses hidden by alders, so that unless you knew what was the industry of the place you would pass it by without a second glance. When I came to know it in the years 1914–18, as an officer in charge of the guard over the factory, it was a group of buildings solely devoted to the making of gunpowder. Between the buildings and the narrow road leading over the level railway crossing to Albury there was a cricket ground, and through the fields nearby and under the alder trees all round the buildings meandered the little Tillingbourne, down from Postford Pond past the powder mills to the Wey.

And it was there, by the water meadows of the Tillingbourne, that accidentally on my rounds as an officer of the guard, and purposely in hours of leisured watching, I learnt more of the habits of nesting snipe than I have ever had the chance of learning before or since. It was a place of queerly mixed activities, of gunpowder-making first and foremost, of farming, for the in the meadows cattle were grazed for market—I think of those wet fields always with red Devons lazily wandering—and of, for me, the study of wild birds, their flight and times of coming and going in autumn and spring. Above all, the study of snipe, for it was here that with fieldglasses I used to measure the swoop down and the climbing up of the bird "drumming"; it was here that I saw snipe perch on gateposts and the dead branch of an oak, and heard the mated birds answer each other in the rushes and from the air; but I came back always to that sound of sounds of April—the bird sending over the marsh the drumming note which is the riddle still unsolved. Is it from the vibrating feathers of the spread tail, or from the quivering chords of the throat? Once I thought I knew, and said so in more books than one; now—for there are trusted naturalists who have heard the sound from a snipe on the ground—I know that I do not know.

But Chilworth itself has changed. With the end of the war of 1914–18 came the end of the powder factory. Storehouses, mixing-houses, magazines vanished. The cricket ground, which stood bare to the road, became valuable as a frontage for building, and all along, parallel to what was once the wicket, stands a row of cottages. Where once the passer-by might have stood to stare at sentry and patrol, he looks at gardens of marigolds and asters. If you happen to catch sight of an oddly segmented building under the hill above the Tillingbourne you may like to know that what has been used as a cottage was once a mixing-house for explosives. But the magazines, the machinery, the chimneys have vanished; the alders and the willows over the Tillingbourne remain.

Beyond Chilworth on the road to Dorking, Albury stands or sleeps in the sun, and you may still admire a village with chimneys surely built by an artist. Still the Tillingbourne ripples side by side with the road, and still high above road and river the little church of St. Martha outlines its spire to the sky. I shall always have in my mind, when I think of St. Martha's, a sight I saw once in a Christmas week between the wars. The Rector of Albury, the Rev Philip Gray, had somehow contrived that the churchyard with its chapel should be floodlit with electric light, and there it stood on the

hill above the highway, darkness below and glory in the
height above, a vision nearer heaven, as I thought then and
think of it to-day, than all else of earth or sky.

Between Albury and Shere, off a turning from the road
running to Merrow Down, lies the Silent Pool. I wish I
could see it as I remember it in years gone by, clear water
fringed by box trees, a pool dark and shining as the box
itself. It was water in which trout swam lazily up to the side
of a wooden hut, to be fed with whatever food visitors threw
them, sandwiches and all else beside. But when I last saw it
there had come a change. Half the water of the pool had
disappeared, scum lay on what was left, and there were no
trout. I knew that in 1934, when heat and drought had dried
the springs of the chalk downland, the pool had shrunk below
any level known for years past, but the summer of 1945 had
been a season of heavy rains, and some other cause must
have led to the emptying. "Military requirements"—I heard
the obvious explanation, but one expects that easy reasoning
in times of war. Whatever the cause, all who knew the pool
in the years gone by will hope that peace may return to its
brim.

So by the old road you may travel to-day through Albury,
Shere, Gomshall, Abinger Hammer, Wotton and Westcott
to Dorking, and find the scene unchanged. East of Dorking
there are new roads, new, that is, to one who walked under
the Downs as I did before the first war and has driven since.
To-day the road to Reigate runs along easy, sweeping curves
where the walker of past ages trudged by right-angles miles
out of the way, as we who measure distance by time would
calculate things. To see exactly what distance you are saved
by the new routes, it is easier to compare new maps with old
than to look forward and backward and round the corner on
the road itself.

A mile out of Dorking to the east the old road used to
turn sharp left, a quarter of a mile due north, and then by a
right-angle sharp right again. To-day the two right-angles
are bypassed with a road running on by a gradual curve close
to the railway, and a mile further on travelling parallel to
the railway instead of into Betchworth. So it comes into
Buckland from the west instead of the south-west, and takes

the traveller all the way by a broader, safer highway than by what was once a country lane. Will the road become wider still? Perhaps, and still there may be walkers who will prefer the lanes that run to the roses of Betchworth gardens.

But to return to the road west of Dorking. When I last journeyed that way one of my objects was the little church at Abinger, which I first saw in days when it was kept locked, and when to get the key and return it meant an extra two miles or more of walking up and down hill. In later years it came under a kindlier spirit, who invited passers-by with the hospitable notice, "Strangers Welcome. From Open Road to Open Church." And then came visitation of a different kind. In the fifth year of the war of 1939 one of those idly destructive German bombs fell on the little church and shattered it. There, when I saw it, stood fragments of the massive Norman walls, the windows just telling their date by the shape and no more, the churchyard with gravestones leaning this way and that, masonry last touched by Norman hands hurled hither and thither, and everywhere rubble, desolation, image of the Hun. Yet the tree of the English churchyard, the yew, remained unscathed, and there at its side, iron-fenced and grass-grown, stood relics of centuries, the village stocks. I left that ruin, and looked back again; there by the wrecked nave in the churchyard soil shone a single spray of ceanothus—blue sky opening from cloud.

I came back from Dorking south by Holmwood, to glance once more at the straight-driven miles of the Roman road through Ockley and its village green, level and broad enough for more than village cricket; past Ewhurst to Cranleigh, with its space of noble turf and memories of tennis tournaments following cricket matches, and home by Painshill and Parkhatch, where the quiet brown deer feeding seemed already to efface the trail of other occupiers, noisier tenants of wartime. There was left that afternoon a sense of change to days of peace.

BYWAYS

I come back from main roads and bypasses to lesser lanes; from the highways connecting town and town to the byways between village and village. With me they are a magnet. For

they are of the countryside itself; they belong to the air and
life of wood and field, and the thought and work of farm
and cottage; they are of the heart of Surrey. The great roads
that run through county after county belong to the cities
from which they come and go; they are for travellers, for
business, high days, holidays; but the lanes belong to the
quiet feet of everyday. I knew what the difference was on a
day when I first came to south-west Surrey; it was an afternoon in June, I had left Weybridge in the morning—Weybridge, where for a year and more the new motor-track had
brought noise and dust to what had been peaceful riverside
—and we walked for the first time down a lane that runs
under beeches between banks of sandstone. It is one among
a few that I have come to know better than any others—to
know and to think of in the same way.

For I like to go back through the years. With all of us there
are places where we can look at the scene and realize that
we see the same sight that our grandfathers saw, and their
fathers before them. That is true, in its main big features, of
all English landscape. Mountain and valley, hill and dale
are the same as fur-clad Briton saw them. In dusk, in twilight,
we see the horizon Cæsar knew. But the happy thing is to be
able to look at the small things near you, the little features
of the road at your elbow, and to know that those too are
unchanged. And that is the happiness to which I come whenever I find myself in that lane, where we walked when I first
came to live in south-west Surrey, all those years ago. It is
one of three or four which lie close to one another nearby,
all of the same kind, and each asking an answer to the same
question. Each runs down the side of a steep hill, with very
high banks out of which jut and curl the roots of beech trees
grasping the sand. How did those narrow, sunken byways
first come there? Thirty feet high on either side the banks
rise, and I stand and stare at them, wondering who cut into
the flank of the hill so deep to make a road, and when and
how they did it. All that can have been changed through the
years has been the road surface. To-day we walk or drive on
asphalt where our forefathers trod or rode over broken
stone and mud.

But the little narrow lanes between farm fields or through

woodlands are the fascinating places. War has changed many miles of Surrey, but by Hambledon and Hascombe I can still find byways unaltered through the years, and imagine myself in company with Cobbett on one of his *Rural Rides*, or I think of Miss Mitford violeting with Lizzie and the white greyhound, or of Kingsley striding along and counting the trout he is going to catch next week under the crest of Siabod. Here to-day are the trees, the turf they saw. Oak and beech spread new in sunlight, hart's tongue fern clusters green in shade. It was all the same a hundred years back.

SMUGGLERS' PATH

Or should it be the plural—paths? When I first came to live at Hambledon I heard of one path only, which was the trackway running from a lane bordering Hundred Acre over Hydons Ball. I remember it as it was first shown to me, a sunken way through holly and juniper, heather and whortle-berries—"hurts" in the speech of the countryside. You could trace it right over the hill, or rather over the flank of it, for the path avoids the top, a length of a mile or more from the lane south of the Ball to other lanes on the north side towards Godalming.

But, of course, I soon discovered other tracks running in the same direction, north from the sea of the Channel. There must have been old pack-horse ways without number in the country north of the forest land of the Weald, and you can trace two or three of them over the Ball to-day. But what has always interested me is not the existence of the paths running north, but the tracks at right-angles to them. These, as I reason, are as direct evidence as you could wish of the use of the track by smugglers. They would know that the excise men, the police of the day, were on the lookout for them when there was "a run," and by suddenly changing from one north-going path to another by one of these cross tracks could bypass the men waiting to intercept them.

To-day, of course, the various tracks are less easy to follow than they were when I first used to find my way— more than thirty years ago—over and about the Ball. Rain has washed in the sides and filled the middle of the old paths.

And if in the thirty years they have changed so that I can see the difference, what must be the change in the hundred and fifty years since the smugglers ran their silk and brandy past the men watching for them? But there is still a fascination in treading again the old trackways through the holly and juniper, over the heather and the "hurts," and in picturing the scene as others saw it all those years ago, in moonlight and cloud when "the gentlemen" went by.

Chapter VII

THE PILGRIMS' WAY

It is a salutary task to have to rewrite a chapter already written. It was thirty-eight years ago—in 1907, but how short a while it seems!—that I was asked by Messrs Macmillan to add *Surrey* to their series of *Highways and Byways,* and for the opening chapter I chose the subject of the Pilgrims' Way. And I read all I could about it. At the back of all the books, of course, there were the beginnings of English history, and in particular what could be known of the oldest English roads. Then came questions as to who used these ancient highways, and why and when men travelled by them; and of those highways there was one long route which must always be in the mind of dwellers in the south of England, the great Road by which men would go east and west; the Road that ran through Salisbury Plain by Stonehenge to the North Downs and by them to Canterbury and the eastern ports.

As to the existence of this great Road, that we can take for granted. But was it used by pilgrims to Canterbury? That is a question which is well enunciated in the opening sentence of an article printed in the *Surrey Archæological Collections* (XLI, pp. 1–33), entitled "The Pilgrims' Way from Shere to Titsey as traced by Public Records and Remains," by Edwin Hart, F.S.A. "The Old Way, along the North Downs, usually called the 'Pilgrims' Way'," writes Mr Hart, "has been the subject of many interesting books, yet not much has been done towards collecting and explaining the evidence available both as to its age, meaning and continuity, and also as to its actual course in detail." Mr Hart then devotes his thirty pages to an examination of the course of the Road, but it cannot be said that in so doing he does the same in detail for the Pilgrims' Way, for the simple reason that he does not show that it was used by pilgrims. He seems to be satisfied that it should be "usually called" the Pilgrims' Way.

And so, I must confess, I myself was satisfied, when I set

94

out to write a chapter on the subject for *Highways and Byways* in Surrey. It did not occur to me to doubt the credentials, as regards mere fact, of so many who had already written of the Pilgrims' Way. There was H. E. Malden, the honoured antiquary and editor of the *Victoria History of the County of Surrey*; there was Edward Brayley, author of the *Topographical History of Surrey*; there were Manning and Bray, whose *History of Surrey* is a classic; the *Surrey Archæological Collections, passim*; there was Mr Hilaire Belloc's monograph, *The Old Road*; and beyond all, as an authority not to be questioned, there were the Ordnance maps, with the track of the Pilgrims' Way marked in old-English lettering. Who should dispute these bibles? No one had done so, I believe, when I began to read the text-books; how should I have done so? How would anyone do so to-day? Well, let us see.

In the forty-fourth volume of the *Surrey Archæological Collections*, published in 1936, appeared an article of thirty-six pages by Dr Wilfrid Hooper, entitled "The Pilgrims' Way and its supposed Pilgrim Use." Almost simultaneously in Vol. XXI of *History*, the quarterly journal of the Historical Association, for June 1936–March 1937, there was printed an article, "The Pilgrims' Way," from the pen of the late C. G. Crump, Assistant Keeper in the Public Records Office. Both these papers are trenchant criticisms of the theory that the old Way east and west through southern England was used by pilgrims to Canterbury. Together they form an extraordinary indictment. I will take Mr Crump's article first.

Mr Crump begins by stating that he has always believed the idea of the Pilgrims' Way to be "a fond thing grounded upon no certain warranty of criticism," and even to be intrinsically absurd. But he finds that in the course of years "the army of true believers had grown very large and very fierce." He takes the authorities arrayed against him, "a formidable band," in order.

First, Andrews and Drury, who in 1769 published a map of the county of Kent, on a scale of 2in to the mile. Next, the makers of the maps in Hasted's *History of Kent*, published in folio in 1778–89. Next, Manning and Bray, whose

History of Surrey was published in 1804–14, and Brayley, with his *Topographical History of Surrey*, published in 1850.[1] Last, he lists "the note on the Pilgrims' Way or Path towards the Shrine of St. Thomas of Canterbury" which is printed on pp. 215–19 of the Rev Arthur Penrhyn Stanley's (better known as Dean Stanley) *Memorials of Canterbury*, published in 1855, and which he describes as the best monograph that has appeared on the subject, but only as a fair statement of a weak case.

To take these, then, in chronological order. The first mention of the road is on the map of Andrews and Drury (1769). Go to Otford Station, north of Sevenoaks in Kent, and follow the road which crosses the railway eastwards. The road becomes a field path after about five miles, "and that five miles is the only Pilgrim Road that was known to exist in Kent in 1769."

Next comes Hasted's map-maker of Kent in 1778–9. He takes us further east. To find the stretch which he marks on the map, go to Whorn's Place adjoining Cuxton on the north-west bank of the Medway as it runs to Strood and Rochester. The road which leaves the valley to pass along the slope of the down is marked on Hasted's map as the Pilgrims' Road.

Now for Surrey. Manning and Bray, in their *History of Surrey* (1804–14) write of two lengths of road as parts of the Pilgrims' Road. One is between Reigate and Merstham :

"A lane in the parish of Merstham retains the name of Pilgrims' Lane. It runs in the direction of the chalk-hills, and was the course taken by pilgrims from the west who resorted (as indeed from all parts) to Canterbury."

The other is between Titsey and Tatsfield. In Vol. II, p. 408, it is described as the "Pilgrim Road (so called from the passage of pilgrims to the shrine of St. Thomas à Becket at Canterbury) which is now perfect, not nine feet wide, and still used as a road."

Brayley, in his *Topographical Survey*, adds one more portion, at Albury, in a short paragraph : "The ancient path called the Pilgrims' Way, which led from the city of Win-

---

[1] This is the date given by Mr Crump. My own copy of Brayley is in five volumes, of which the first is dated on the illuminated title-page 1841. The remaining volumes are undated.

Pilgrims' Way, looking east from St. Martha's Chancel of Compton Church

chester to Canterbury, crosses this parish, and is said to have
been much used in former times."

So that up to 1850 all we have, as testimony to the existence of a Pilgrims' Road east and west through the south
of England, are three short pieces of road in Surrey and one
fairly long stretch in Kent. Witnesses to these stretches of
road date from 1769 to 1850. Thomas à Becket was mur-
dered in 1174.

But let us look a little more closely at Brayley's statement
about the path at Albury. Two points of interest are to be
noted : (i) that he is the first writer to use the term "way"
for what others have called a "road"; (ii) that William Bray,
co-editor with Manning of the *History of Surrey*, who died
in 1832, aged ninety-six, does not mention this path at
Albury. Could the name Pilgrims' Way have existed in his
time?

So we come to Dean Stanley's *Historical Memorials of
Canterbury*, with the note in the appendix entitled "The
Pilgrims' Way or path towards the Shrine of St. Thomas of
Canterbury." This note was contributed by Mr Albert Way,
whom Dr Wilfrid Hooper describes as well known in his
time as an antiquary of repute, and in it Mr Way purports to
bring together "the evidence of local tradition." What he
does, in effect, is to construct a possible itinerary from Farnham to Canterbury, and to suggest that it was by this route
that pilgrims travelled. He begins with Henry II's journey
from Southampton, and adopts Dean Stanley's suggestion
that the king chose "the Way" for his journey to Canterbury
in 1174, "a hypothesis," as Dr Hooper points out, "which
has since been widely accepted and serves as a basis for the
assumption that Henry's example set the fashion which
quickly established the Way as the popular route." But what
evidence is there? It is quite possible that the king travelled
from Southampton to Farnham and thence by the Hog's
Back to London. But onwards from there? The king left
Southampton on 8 July and reached Canterbury on 12 July,
and the Pipe Roll contains an entry of the charge incurred
for hiring horses for the use of the sailors following the king
to London. It is difficult to see how the theory started that
from Guildford, where the king had a castle, he should have

H   97

preferred any other road to Canterbury than through London. Why should he be supposed to travel to London via Canterbury rather than to Canterbury via London?

Hitherto—up to 1855, when Dean Stanley's *Memorials of Canterbury* was published with Mr Way's note to the appendix—we have dealt mainly with conjecture, as to the possibility of the use of a Way into Canterbury following the old road running east and west. We now proceed to something more tangible, not as proving that such a Way existed and was used by pilgrims, but in the adopting of conjecture in the form of print by no less an authority than the Ordnance Survey. During the years 1861 and 1871 the Ordnance Survey was at work on the large-scale maps of Surrey and Kent, and the officer in charge of the survey in south-west Surrey was Captain (afterwards Major-General) Edward Renouard James, R.E., described by Dr Hooper as a writer "who, to his technical qualifications, added a taste for archæology and a whole-hearted enthusiasm for the pilgrim theory."

Captain James set out his theory of the route taken by supposed pilgrims in a pamphlet entitled *Notes on the Pilgrims' Way in West Surrey* published by Stanford in 1871. This was republished some thirty years later under the title *Three Surrey Churches,* and this is what Dr Hooper has to say about General James's statement of the case. "It opens," he writes, "with the damaging confession that the subject of the Pilgrims' Way had been little studied in West Surrey and that 'very many persons in that neighbourhood' were in ignorance of the very name. He propounds the theory, which has since been applied to ancient tracks in other counties, of a winter way and summer way, which he illustrates by taking the Hog's Back as the upper way, carrying the winter stream of pilgrims, and the parallel track along the valley to the south as the lower way favoured by the summer stream. He places great stress on the local fairs and the dates on which they were held, professing to see in these strong corroborative evidence of pilgrim patronage. He refers particularly to the annual fairs of Wanborough, Puttenham, St. Catherine's, Shalford, and Guildford."

Dr Hooper then deals with these fairs one by one:

"Wanborough fair may be at once dismissed since it was

not instituted until the eve of the dissolution. Puttenham
fair, which had died out before 1871, fell on the 27th of June,
the third day after the feast of St. John Baptist. Guildford
fair took place at Whitsuntide, to which date it was shifted
from Trinity shortly after its institution, on account of the
number of neighbouring fairs held at the same season. Shalford fair was held on 14th to 16th August, that of St.
Catherine's on 21st September."

But were all these travellers, some of them, presumably,
from the Continent, following the same route as that of
Henry II, through Southampton, Winchester and Farnham,
planning the same journey with the same idea of attendance
at fairs?

"To fit in these dates [Dr Hooper continues] with the
movements of pilgrims to and from Canterbury requires no
little ingenuity, but Captain James assumes without condes-
cending to proof that they were persons of unlimited leisure
who spent months on the journey. The feast of Becket's
translation, which attracted the chief concourse of the year,
fell on 7th July, so that the pilgrims attending it were free
to return from Canterbury a month or more before Shalford
fair, and over two months before St. Catherine's. Yet his
readers are seriously asked to believe that the ordinary pilgrim took upwards of a month to perform a journey of 80
miles, a progress of less than 3 miles a day. If this can be
credited then clearly the dates of the fairs were of little importance and the evidence based on them is worthless, for
whatever the dates fixed there would have been on this
hypothesis pilgrims constantly on the road coming or returning in connection with the summer or winter festival."

We have seen that the earliest mention of the Pilgrims'
Road on maps belongs to Kent, in 1769, and that there is no
mention of such a road in Surrey until Manning and Bray's
History was published in 1804. Let us look for evidence
next in writers. Camden's *Britannia* was published in 1586.
As Dr Hooper observes, "Camden and his school had a
ready ear for the legendary and frequently retailed local
traditions though at times with evident incredulity. If any
had been current concerning the Way when they wrote they
would surely have picked them up in one or other of the

parishes along its course." Camden has not a word of any such tradition. Aubrey, again, who died in 1697 and left behind him his *Natural History and Antiquities of Surrey,* loved nothing better than current gossip. He is silent as to the Way. But there is another writer whose silence is even more remarkable, and that is Cobbett. In his *Rural Rides* he was continually travelling by roads in Hampshire, Surrey and Kent, and in his *History of the Protestant Reformation* he has much to say about pilgrimages. Could he have omitted mention of pilgrimages by the Way to Canterbury if he had ever heard of it? And there was no keener student of every aspect of English roads. This, for instance, is what he writes of riding to Canterbury through Surrey:

"I have often mentioned, in describing the parts of the country over which I have travelled, the *chalk-ridge* and also the *sand-ridge,* which I had traced, running parallel with each other from about Farnham, in Surrey, to Sevenoaks, in Kent. The reader must remember how particular I have been to observe that, in going up from Chilworth and Albury, through Dorking, Reigate, Godstone, and so on, the two chains, or ridges, approach so near to each other that in many places you actually have a chalk-bank to your right and a sand-bank to your left, at not more than forty yards from each other."

No word here about a winter and summer Way for pilgrims! Cobbett wrote about his rural ride by Canterbury in 1823. He would have been a valuable witness if Captain James, writing in 1871, could have quoted him. Yet with all this lack of evidence, from witnesses whose testimony would have been invaluable to his theory, Captain James, in charge of the Ordnance Survey large-scale maps of Surrey, did not hesitate to print the words "Pilgrims' Way" on the maps, following a line of his own supposition, and so through this invention led to the unquestioning adoption of the whole Pilgrims' Way theory by the writers of the two chief books on the subject, Mrs Henry Ady (Julia Cartwright) and Mr Hilaire Belloc.

Mrs Henry Ady's book, entitled *The Pilgrims' Way from Winchester to Canterbury,* was published in 1892. The authorities on which she depends for her case are Captain

James's *Notes on the Pilgrims' Way in West Surrey* and Dean Stanley's *Memorials of Canterbury*. And this is what Mr C. G. Crump has to say about it, as a book containing "many statements of medieval facts which, could they but be verified, would prove the presence of pilgrims on the road." Mr Crump continues, quoting from Mrs Ady:

"The Pilgrims' Way 'goes through Shalford Park up Ciderhouse Lane where the ancient Pesthouse or refuge for sick pilgrims or travellers, now called Ciderhouse Cottage, is still standing.' No authority is mentioned for this story. On the next page we find that the Prior of Newark 'owned most of the hillside, and the names of Farthing Copse and Half-penny Lane, through which the pilgrims passed on their way to St. Martha's Chapel, remind us of the tolls which he levied from all who travelled along the road.' Again there is no authority given, and yet a toll on a public road exacted by a religious house must have left some trace of its existence. Or turn to Otford, and we find that 'the first resting-place the pilgrims would find on this part of their route would be the archbishop's manor-house at Otford.' Were pilgrims entertained there? It is not a case of a few pilgrims now and then but of numbers of pilgrims. If so, there must be some authority for this statement; yet none is mentioned. It must not be thought that these are picked cases; they occur throughout the book."

Can you come to any other conclusion than that Mrs Ady in writing her book had always at the back of her head, besides Captain James's *Notes on the Pilgrims' Way*, the old-English lettering on the Ordnance maps placed there by Captain James?

And now for Mr Hilaire Belloc's book *The Old Road*. This was published by Constable in 1904. It is a beautifully printed volume of 172 pages, with illustrations by William Hyde and six large sheets of maps reproduced from those of the Ordnance Survey, on which a single red line is printed showing the Pilgrims' Way running from Winchester to Canterbury—a single red line all the way.

That red line sums up the purpose, the underlying impetus, and the explanation of the making of the book. It is born of the idea that on a certain date in the twelfth century the Old

Road, the highway running east and west through southern England, became the Way from Winchester to Canterbury. That date was the murder of Thomas à Becket in 1174. From it, onwards:

"All the West suddenly began to stream to Canterbury, and à Becket's tomb became, after Rome, the chief shrine of Christendom.

"Ireland of the saints, South Wales still tribal, still in a way unfixed, leading its population to far adventures and to the attraction of distant places, all the south-western peninsula of England, Brittany for ever mystic, the mountain masses of the Asturias which had themselves preserved an original sanctity, the western ports from Vigo to recently conquered Lisbon—the only ports by which the Christian enthusiasm of the Spaniards conquering Islam could take to the newly opened sea and to the north—all these sent their hordes to converge on Winchester, and thence to find their way to Canterbury."

Now that is a fine example of Mr Belloc's prose. But— did these things happen? All the West began to stream to Canterbury, perhaps. Pilgrims, yes; but to Canterbury via Winchester, Farnham, St. Martha's Chapel and the rest? Mr Crump sums up these questions:

"What evidence is there that anyone ever travelled from Southampton to Canterbury by this route? Mr Albert Way can suggest one traveller. 'It has been supposed, with much probability,' he says, 'that Henry II when he landed at Southampton, 8 July 1174, and made his pilgrimage to à Becket's tomb, may have approached Canterbury by this route.' I do not know who made this guess, but I suspect that it was the Rev A. P. Stanley. Mrs Ady adopts this conjecture and states it as a fact. 'This was the route taken by Henry II . . . in the month of July 1174.''

So once more he repeats the vital question, the question on which depends the truth or falsity of the supposition that there ever was such a thing as the Pilgrims' Way:

"Is there any evidence that anyone ever travelled by that route from Winchester to Canterbury?

"The best answer I can find is that given by the English Place Name Society in their volume of *Surrey Place Names*

(p. 8) : 'Pilgrims' Way. Although there is no medieval evidence for this name, there is no doubt that the road follows the line of an ancient trackway, and further there is no doubt that it was from an early date used by pilgrims to the shrine of St. Thomas of Canterbury (cf. the history of the chapel of St. Martha, infra 244).' To tell the story of the chapel of St. Martha needs more knowledge and more skill in dissecting myths than I possess. All I can do is to urge as humbly as I can that it seems to me that an error has ventured to insinuate itself into this article, and that the sentence 'and further there is no doubt' should in future read 'but there is not a shred of evidence.'"

If there is a severer indictment of any theory of place names, or of any story invented round them, I do not know it. But even so, having a great respect for the work which has gone to the making of such a book as *The Place Names of Surrey,* I turned to p. 244 for "the history of the chapel of St. Martha." This is what I found :

"The ancient church of St. Martha here was early granted to Newark Priory, dedicated to St. Thomas the Martyr. This may have led to confusion in some of the later forms, helped by the resemblance of *Martha* and *Martyr*. Perhaps the hill was always known as Martyr Hill, and the church and parish as (St.) Martha's."

That is all.

And now, with those words as my text, that "there is not a shred of evidence" that the road east and west was used by pilgrims to the shrine of St. Thomas, I come to the end of this chapter. And to the end of all belief that there is, or ever has been, a Pilgrims' Way from Winchester to Canterbury; and last, and least important, to an explanation of how I came to write a chapter in the *Highways and Byways of Surrey* supporting that belief. It is a simple explanation. I accepted the Ordnance map. It never occurred to me that out of a mere theory, based on the fact that Henry II journeyed from Winchester to the shrine of St. Thomas à Becket at Canterbury, and on the occurrence of the name Pilgrims' Road for two stretches in Kent in the eighteenth century and three short stretches in east Surrey in the early nineteenth century, a single Government official would have added the words Pilgrims' Way, printed in old-English lettering, to maps accepted in Great Britain as authoritative evidence of historical fact. So, with other Englishmen, I accepted the theory. I did not, however, accept Mr Hilaire Belloc's elaboration of it, as expressed by him in his book *The Old Road*. Perhaps I may quote one passage, in which he writes of the compulsions of the pilgrimage :

"The pilgrim set out from Winchester : 'You must pass by that well,' he heard, 'it is sacred' . . . 'You must, of ritual, climb that isolated hill which you see against the sky. The spirits haunted it and were banished by the faith, and they say that martyrs died there' . . . 'It is at peril of the pilgrimage that you neglect this stone, whose virtue saved our fathers in the great battle' . . . 'The church you will next see upon your way is entered from the southern porch sunward by all truly devout men; such has been the custom here since custom began.

"From step to step the pilgrims were compelled to take the oldest of paths."

That idea, involving the notion that all pilgrims followed the same single road, which Mr Belloc traced in red ink through the length of the Ordnance maps, seemed to me contrary to human nature, and I gave reasons for rejecting it. But I did gladly accept the theory of the Pilgrims' Way, just as I now sadly abandon the whole invented story.

CHAPTER VIII

CHANGES

THE FOLD COUNTRY—LEATHERHEAD MILL POOL—VINE
COTTAGE

THE FOLD COUNTRY

YEARS ago I set out to walk from Baynards Station, on the line between Guildford and Horsham, by Alfold and Dunsfold to Milford. I was then adding chapters to the *Highways and Byways in Surrey*, and it was my first sight of the Fold Country, that corner of the county lying deepest in oak woods and primroses. Of all the walks I took in making the book that was the happiest. It was May the 1st; April had ended in north-east winds and snow, and there on the Surrey roads it was full sunshine. I saw my first swallow, I heard my first nightingale of the year. I knew what Surrey could be at its best.

Years later I passed by some of those roads and lanes again. Not all of them, for some had vanished. It was the last day of May 1945, and in the years between the Fold Country had changed. Two great wars had blasted the face of Europe, and Surrey had suffered as had Italy and France. The Fold Country was an aerodrome. Oak woods had been uprooted, engines of steel had torn out by the roots cottages and fields of corn. If I looked for swallows I caught sight of swooping planes. If I listened for a nightingale, drone of bombers drowned other sounds.

I had known, of course, that this change was coming; I had heard and seen the change. During the years that followed the outbreak of war in 1939, all that corner of Surrey between Blackdown on the Sussex border and Godalming, the nearest of the old Surrey towns, had altered to suit the times. But I had not known all that the alterations meant. In those years cars were forbidden luxuries; you might travel by omnibus, or you might walk, but omnibuses went only by high roads, and walking by lanes meant many miles and little knowledge of what lay at the end of them. What we realized at Hambledon, which is the village of my home, was that our world was one of new sights and noises. By day we watched squadrons of planes, singly and in hundreds, flying out south and east; by night we listened to the sound of planes, our own or our enemy's, high over darkened villages. But towards the end of the war all the planes we saw by day were our own, and we found ourselves watching a sight becoming day by day the same, of fighters and bombers circling and recircling to float down one by one to a distance towards the Weald. That was all we could tell or know of the Fold Country that had been flattened into an aerodrome.

Then, on that 31st of May, I drove out to see what had happened; I drove by roads I had known years before, and I drove towards roads which I thought I should know and could use again. And I was blocked. The old road was forbidden. War had taken from me the Fold Country I had known and loved all through my life in south-west Surrey.

Perhaps it was a wood over which I sorrowed first. There was a wood at the side of the road between Hambledon and Cranleigh which I used to know as a roost for starlings. It was a wood of blackthorn, into which on evenings in winter starlings used to drop at sunset and chatter themselves to sleep. All the branches of its trees and the ground under them were white with the starlings' droppings, and the sound of their wings as they rose and fell and swooped to their roosting-places was like the sound of the sea. I had watched them, I remembered as we came near to the place on that 31st of May, on evenings in January and February 1940, when we were already at war but had not realized what the war was going to mean. As we drove down the road I looked to the left, at the place where the wood should be. It was gone, and in its place was a field of level, springing corn. When were the thorns uprooted, I wondered, and what of the starlings? What were their thoughts when they found their winter home vanished, and where did they go? Those were questions not to be answered. War had taken life from that wood; that was all I could tell.

There was more to come. We drove on, and my guide

took me down a lane I had known years before; it was linked in my mind with memories of steeplechases, the point-to-point meetings which had been held April after April at the end of the hunting season, when followers of the Chidding-fold Hunt had met again to watch their friends in the races. How well I knew those fields, those hedges and ditches, the horizon beyond which horses and riders vanished to reappear for the finish at the straight! I could see it all again, the gaiety, the colour, the noble grace of horse and rider; I could hear the shouts. . . . And suddenly I was in silence and in a cold wind that blew over a plain I had never seen before. There had been oak woods at the sides of the lane by which we had come. The woods had gone. The lane had come to an end. Instead, in front of me stretched a vast flat space, a mile-wide level with a mile-deep highway broadening out to where I stood. Here at my feet were buttercups and moon-daisies; there in the mid-distance were the huge noses of steel machines lifting into the sky, monstrous waiting insects. . . . But there had been buildings, I thought, somewhere to the right of the lane. I looked again. "There is the hunts-man's cottage," my guide told me, pointing, "and there is the groom's cottage. But the stables and the kennels—gone. And here it was a copse, but they pushed it away with bull-dozers. And there was a house there"—he pointed again—"which they moved. It was on a concrete foundation, and the Canadians moved it, just as it stood, foundation and all. There it is, away to your right." I looked, and there was a cottage, tiled, tarred planks, windows, chimneys, set down five or six hundred yards away, and beyond the cottage more aeroplanes, rows of them, iron-grey, lettered, painted. And in front of me, I stared again at it, the long, broad, grey run-way, flat in the sun. I was in a dream.

We turned back down the lane. "We can go to the cross-roads," my guide told me, "but beyond that you'll be stopped." And we went again down a road once familiar. Suddenly it became unfamiliar. We were running along a newly made road, with the soil turned back, yellow, naked, to the side. "It's part of the bypass." Further still, and the new road was edged with charlock. And then, at cross-roads, I found myself looking at an old cottage I had known in the years that were gone, an old Surrey cottage, tiled, brick-and-timber, a little garden in front, and to left and right notices on boards, red paint on white, capital letters. "R.A.F. Dunsfold. All visitors and new arrivals to report to guard-room." We went away. We were on the perimeter of the aerodrome, it seemed. We were faced with other notices, yellow and black. "Camps 106, 107, 103, 104, 105. 18 A.G.R.A. Camps 96, 108, 109, 110, 111, 112, and 113 Bde." A black board; "113, 114, 115 and 178 Bde." My mind went back through the years. A nightingale singing in a Dunsfold hedge . . . There was still elder in flower there in front of me, to remind me of the Fold Country I had known.

"Air Ministry. No Admittance." There in front of me was the bridge over what remained of the Wey Canal. We turned and started for home, and as we turned there came again that vision beyond the hedge. Hangars, low curves of corrugated iron, and, beyond the hangars, fighter planes, grey painted, yellow, black, red in circles, huge letters, wings outspread, and beyond the fighter planes bombers, monstrous noses uptilted to empty air, waiting. . . . There came back to me verses :

As I beheld the living creatures, behold, one wheel upon the earth by the living creatures, with his four faces.

The appearance of the wheels and their work was like unto the colour of a beryl; and they four had one likeness : and their appearance and their work was as it were a wheel in the middle of a wheel.

When they went they went upon their four sides; and they turned not when they went.

As for their rings, they were so high that they were dreadful, and their rings were full of eyes round about them four.

And when the living creatures were lifted up from the earth, the wheels were lifted up. And when they went, I heard the noise of their wings, like the noise of great waters, as the voice of the Almighty, the voice of speech, as the noise of an host : when they stood, they let down their wings.

When I read the first chapter of Ezekiel fifty years ago I used to wonder what it meant.

We came back home by Dunsfold and its green—its green with the old blacksmith's shop, and the Bricklayers' Arms, and a cottage on the green covered with white roses, and another cottage with scarlet geraniums climbing to the windows—all as it used to be, years ago, in the Fold Country.

LEATHERHEAD MILL POOL

When I drove up to London that morning in the June that came with peace, the changes that struck me most were the growth and colour of trees and plants, the flowering prunus and the poplars on the way to Guildford and the gaiety of the villa gardens that did their best to shame the blaring advertisements of the bypass. And I drove back from London hoping that all the other changes I might see would be happy, but I own it was with doubt. For I came back out of town by another road, and of one change I had been warned. It was at Leatherhead. Thirty years and more before, at work on the *Highways and Byways,* I had walked into Leatherhead from the west, and thought that there could be no more happy entrance into a country town than the approach to the fourteen-arch bridge that spans the Mole, spreading as the river did into the breadth of a pool unequalled in the Surrey I knew for the depth and clearness of its water.

This time I came into Leatherhead by the north, wondering on the way what Fanny Burney at Chessington would have thought of the new neighbours at the Zoo. Would she have danced a jig round the mulberry tree on Mr Crisp's lawn, as she did when *Evelina* had taken the town by storm? And did she in those days, I wondered, look with delight into the depths of the mill pool from the bridge? I am sure she did. Well, I hoped to do so again, and when I came out of the town over the bridge I looked for the pool and could not see it. I went on further and turned back. I did not know where I was. There was no pool. I came back to the bridge and saw that the only way I could see the river under its arches was to trespass on the ground of what appeared to be gas works. Then at last I could stare at the fourteen arches

—stare, because they stood high out of water. The river ran under them, shallow as a brook. Cress muffled its flow. Nettles, eight or ten feet high they seemed to me, standing out of the bed of the stream—nettles, of all plants to meet in what was once mid-river—nettles rose opposite, under bricks and concrete. The pool was gone, the pool that I had thought the clearest, deepest springing and loveliest in Surrey.

I thought again of the pool as I used to know it, I remembered as if it were yesterday the length and the breadth of it, two hundred yards and more of stream, eighty yards from bank to bank, and all of it translucent over its chalky floor, a deep blue-green. I thought of the water as I saw it all those years ago, welling up into the current of the river from unseen, unplumbed sources below. I remembered the birds on it, swimming and diving: I had counted in their tens coots, moorhens, dabchicks, and up under the arches of the bridge a bevy of swans. And to-day? There were no coots or dabchicks to be seen; true, you cannot see far, for factory premises block the sides, but there would be no depth of water for dabchicks to dive in. When did the change come, I wondered, and why? What had become of all the water of the long, broad pool? I could only guess. I left the river, left the bridge standing there high above the shallow stream, left the gas works and the concrete, thinking back through the years, and as I looked back from beside a barbed-wire fence coiled among hops and valerian, my last glimpse and memory was of the far-side bank and a clump of forget-me-nots.

VINE COTTAGE

"Our valley, green enough in its disordered way, has been reclaimed from the waste chiefly during the last half-century. Fifty years ago it was for the most part a common traversed by sandtracks where now are the hard roads." Thus George Bourne introduced readers of *The Bettesworth Book* to the neighbourhood of the "shaggy waste-land" which is the background of *Memoirs of a Surrey Labourer, The Wheelwright's Shop,* and those other transcript-portraits of Eng-

lish country life of the beginning of the century, unequalled
of their kind in literature of the day.

Ever since I read *The Bettesworth Book* I had wanted to
see the setting in which it was written, but it was not until
an August day in 1945 that I could fulfil my wish. Vine
Cottage, The Bourne, Farnham, is the address in the reference books, and it is not easy to find. When I looked at the
turning off the road towards which I had been directed I half
wondered whether a car driven down that tiny lane could be
turned and driven up again. I remembered the description of
the place given by George Bourne (his real name was George
Sturt) in his introduction to *The Bettesworth Book*. Bettesworth, he writes, did his share towards taming "a very
savage track of English earth." The garden "owes much to
his labour in helping to form it thirty years ago. On the sheltered south-western slope of a spur of hill jutting into the
valley it was still at that time an almost unmanageable sand
heap, very steep. Aided by Bettesworth, the owner terraced
it up with low walls and grassy banks." And cautiously
descending the approach of the sand heap, we found ourselves on the other side of a wooden garden door, looking
at the terraces and the walls.

There they were, as George Sturt and Bettesworth his old
gardener used to know them, the little terraces mounting up
the sandy hillside, the stone walls one above another, and the
neat, small lawns bordered with marigolds and phlox. There
were the trees above them, as the two gardening together
used to see them, birches, Scots pines, a single larch—I could
imagine Bettesworth's eye running over the ground under it,
dried out by the roots—and an acacia beyond, graceful
against the August blue. There was blue plumbago, too, in a
terrace bed, and I liked to think of the garden as it must
have been in May with lilacs, or with apple-blossom falling
to the lawn. But the apple trees themselves, two of them,
were an unhappy sight, withered and brown—the hot sand of
the hill had been too much for them. And I wondered, indeed, how the owner of the garden had contrived to provide
any sort of mulching or food for the roots of what he had
planted—a beech hedge and a yew hedge, for instance, to
border the lawns terraced out of the solid. All I could see

for watering was a small pump, immediately in front of the cottage door.

Behind the cottage, higher still on that hungry hill, lay other plots of soil, each worked to its separate space; scarlet runner-beans, more apple trees, a crimson rose, a bed of herbs; all, I would guess, as Bettesworth and his master had levelled them, for who else would face such labour? I left the garden, looking back from the wooden door at the arches cut in the yew and beech hedges, the cobbled ironstone path under the cottage windows, and at its side the little pump.

Mill on the Mole, Leatherhead
The New Cathedral, Guildford

CHAPTER IX

FIELDS YESTERDAY AND TO-DAY

I LOOK back through the years. Among the happiest memories are those of farm fields through the seasons, of sights
and sounds; of great horses slowly pulling a plough, the
driver's gripping hands, his corduroys tied to the knee, and
the wet ridge falling from the share; all in the silence of
autumn. Of the sower, scattering his light wealth to right, to
left; of winter wheat springing, of larks lifting from green
drills, their song beginning, rising by that stairless spiral into
blue air, descending with the sudden slant to earth that is the
end. Of the scent of beanfields; the warmth of new-mown hay
in swathes; lucerne crimson in a strip across the hill, and the
breath of mustard flower down a lazy wind. Of days in
August, the blue sweeps of the reaper and binder tossing
sheaf after sheaf from the lessening rectangle of corn. And in
September, best of distant sounds of harvest, vibrant from
half a mile, the hum of the threshing-machine.

These were of days in peace, and of the small farm. Perhaps the farm paid not much to the man who ploughed and
sowed its fields; he had few hands to help him, whether it
was pleaching a hedge of hazel or shocking the corn his
horses drew to the rick. His was the Surrey countryside as
we knew it before the first great war, and in the years that
followed, through the awakening days of the 'twenties and
'thirties, when it was slowly borne in upon us that we needed
more than one man's brain to get the profit that lay buried
in each acre of sand and clay. Then came the second great
war, and we found ourselves looking out on another countryside. It was petrol that brought the change, and the tractors
that petrol drew, but above all it was the superseding of the
small by the Committee, the public body known in
county after county as the Loamshire War Agricultural
Executive Committee, that was and as I see it is the forerunner of the Entity that means State ownership of the land.

But I am not concerned with politics here, nor with the

huge debate and its issues which the change to State ownership will bring. Here I write of things seen and heard as the
change comes about, and first of things heard. It was in a
winter month of the second war that the thought came home
to me more insistently than before with the sounds of ploughing. For it used to be a quiet thing, ploughing; you saw the
pair of horses, the chestnut and the big roan, pace slowly in
the winter sunlight from hedge to hedge. To-day they are
not horses, but machines, one following another, and they
pull, not one share to a plough, but four side by side, so that
a ten-acre field becomes new soil in an afternoon. And the
machine sends out not a mere sound, but a noise.

That is the change, the harsh rasping of gear and cog-
wheels in place of the silent trudging animals; and the new
noise wakes in memory old and loved sounds of the village
and the field, the sound of scythes being sharpened over dewy
grass, the swish of a horse's tail and the stamp of an im-
patient hoof, and beyond those two sounds an echo of old
fashions of England, the musical ring and clang of the village
smithy as we heard it years ago morning after morning, and
pictured the iron white-hot and red-hot from the forge, and
heard and smelt the hoof hissing as the shoe was fitted to its
horn. Shall we hear those sounds again?

The fields themselves change, and the paths about them.
The oldest inhabitant—how often we have heard of reference being made to him when questions have been raised as
to local customs, rights of way, commoners' rights, and other
matters of the unwritten law of the countryside; and how
much valuable material for the proper conduct of country life
could be stored up, if his evidence could be taken down by
competent witnesses properly attested and entered in parish
registers or other records of the kind, to be collected and
added in print to county chronicles—eventually the history
of the nation at home! Year after year of this change in the
look, the use, the occupation of the fields emphasizes an evident need—and will the need ever be realized?

Here, in matters small as well as great, the sudden
destroyer—and revealer—is war. Twice in this generation
has war invaded the inner life of village as well as town,
farm fields side by side with growing suburbs, and among

things of country knowledge that are being wiped out to-day, as they were wiped out twenty-five years ago, are memories of rights of way. Records of a single Surrey parish became known to that parish in the first great war and again in the second, but they were known to that parish alone, and the county never heard of them; how could the country at large ever know? Yet it was country life that was being destroyed. And there must have been during the same quarter of a century of English history thousands of parishes with the same story to tell and the same story untold.

Here, then, in a few words, is the story of one Surrey parish. I write elsewhere of a field within a few hundred yards of my own home, a field known for I do not guess how many years as Hundred Acre. Before the war of 1914 it was rough pasture, and across it, with a stile at each end, ran a footpath, an old right of way which I used to value as a short cut from the heather and sand of Surrey to the clay and primroses of the Weald. Then came the war; it was ploughed and the old path disappeared. It does not matter? Well, people walked by that path before the days of bicycles and cars, and now they go round the field by a lane. Except for old sake's sake, perhaps it does not much matter. But another path nearby is different. It is a long path across two fields, and in the war of 1939 it was ploughed up for the first time. It has been ploughed up each year since. In the old days, when those two fields were rented by a small farmer, it remained what it always had been, the way to the church and the village for those who live in houses to the east of Hambledon; it was and is a right of way to Hambledon from Hascombe and beyond. But with the fields taken over by the Surrey War Agricultural Executive Committee the path has been destroyed every year, and those who use it have had to re-tread it over ridge and plough in winter and ever since. It remains a right of way, but what rights can those who use it exercise? They can write to the Committee?

Fields have changed, and the landscape with them. Colour has gone from the farm. The farmer we knew grew a variety of crops, wheat, barley, oats, mangolds, clover, seeds, kale, and he grew some of them in strips. Committees have no time for strips; they think of acres in hundreds. Four fields together are potatoes, five side by side grow turnips. Sheep arrive in lorries and eat half the roots; the rest are ploughed in. Potatoes are turned up by the spinner and piled in clamps. That is a new spectacle. Clamp after clamp in row after row along the side of thirty acres of field—it is something the village has not seen before.

Strangest to village thought, perhaps, has been the new crop, Jerusalem artichokes. In days gone by, artichokes belonged to the kitchen garden, a row or two planted where they could be conveniently dug and banished, for they are a difficult crop to get rid of. But acres of them, in rows a quarter of a mile long, are a different proposition. When they were first planted, they puzzled the village. How would they be marketed? To what use could you put tons of them? Ground up, for coffee, was one of the current answers. But they set more than one riddle, the year they were first planted. A visitor from London, walking by a field whose crops she had known in other seasons, gazed at tall, unfamiliar stems with yellow blossoms swaying in the sunshine and returned home wondering what the farmer wanted with so vast a quantity of sunflowers.

It was all so new to the village when they saw it first. Miles of potatoes, of roots, of artichokes; miles of those three. And machines; the spinner for the potatoes, moving along row after row, throwing the pale tubers right and left, to be lifted into pails and emptied into sacks and heaped in clamps, hundreds of yards side by side. And the baler; that intricate, lengthy contrivance, binding, pressing, packing the trusses of straw one by one, from the loose stack where the landgirls forked it to one end of the machine, to the other end where more landgirls piled it for the lorry, to be drawn away to the stockyard a mile away. All by machinery. And the new machine, too, for the artichokes, the engine pulsing along the lined ridges, the engine that drove a triangled share under the roots, lifted them, passed them along and over a moving screen of wire and dropped them in a ball of caked earth and couch-grass, to be handled and picked and chucked into baskets and carried to sacks waiting again for another lorry, then to be driven away—for what? Vegetable market, no doubt, somewhere, but you heard again that incredible countryman's whisper that they were somehow going to be used for coffee.

Yet one more of the changes which the days of the second great war brought us, one more thing new to the life of the countryman, is the field road. A field road is not a path. With field paths all of us who live our lives in the country have been familiar since childhood. They are narrow, and are trodden by wayfarers singly; we do not walk two abreast by field paths. And they have a single object—they are short cuts from one point to another, and as short cuts they cross fields by the quicker way from entrance to exit, as often as not diagonally as a line from one corner of a square to the opposite. And they have two separate characteristics; they are open on each side, so that you walk in sun and wind, and they are hardly ever straight. Often they cross a field which once a year is ploughed, and then they are re-made by villagers treading them out again; but the field throws the walker from side to side, once more every autumn as it has thrown him year after year. Some slight slope, invisible to the casual eye, deflects the traveller this way or that, and the field path once more runs athwart the furrows, with the same unbending purpose and the same swerving curves.

But a field road is different. It is a new thing in the life and everyday work of the countryside, the life and the work of the village through the centuries gone. Ten years, five years ago, last year perhaps, it was not there. The tractor has made it, petrol has driven wheels over it, the wheels have dug in their teeth, the weight of the steel heart of the engine has pounded it flat. It goes in new directions, never across a field, but along by the side. Here it cuts through a hedge, there it breaks down a hundred-year-old bank; it lessens by its width the area of the field that can bear roots or corn. And in a thousand other ways it leads once more to the thought of the difference that has come to farm fields, in the taking over by War Agricultural Committees of acres which used to be the care of the farmer working for himself and his family.

Then take the question of hedges. It has been my lot to look out over fields which until the second great war were worked by a single farmer. With the limited labour he employed he yet was able to keep his hedges as they were intended when they first separated Church Field from Ten Acre, Crowledge Field from the Grove (I give the old names) and the rest, and somehow with that labour he ploughed, sowed, rolled, reaped and ploughed again, and kept his hedges properly pleached and trimmed. Then came the war, and with labour and wages difficulties the farmer had to give way to the Committee, who apparently had no difficulty with wages or labour. And labour was employed not only in ploughing, planting, sowing. One day in early spring, walking out over familiar fields, I found every hedge cut to the ground. Hedges had not merely been lopped or trimmed, they had vanished. Gone was hazel, ash, thorn; my line of sloes, from which in autumn we had gathered baskets of that fruit of grape-like bloom, was a row of inch-high stubs. I wrote to the Committee (you do not meet, you cannot talk to Committees); the answer was that these things had happened "in the interests of good husbandry."

Well, good husbandry ought not to be a difficult business with unlimited labour; and with Committees, and perhaps with State ownership in days to come, labour seems to be there for the asking. It was a new sight for the village when potatoes were first gathered from the field by boys, girls and old women, twenty of them at a shilling an hour. But girls and old women can have quiet minds. When they are driven back to their lodging in the Committee's lorry they leave quiet fields behind them. Not so all farm workers hired by the hour. One day in the sixth year of the second war a telephone message called me to a field next our village church. There I was shown a gap in the churchyard oak paling and the charred remains of a five-barred gate. Irish labourers, I was told, lacking an easily built fire of hedgerow sticks to boil their kettle, had taken down part of the paling and with the extra material of a broken-up gate which had been taken off its hinges for the admittance of a tractor, had boiled their kettle and made tea. There before me lay the remains of the gate.

In time an enquiry was held. In time the Irish labourers, I understood, were questioned, but they could not decide how the paling or the gate had caught fire. And in time an excellent new five-barred gate arrived, to be stored by a neighbour's kindness in a barn close by. And I have wondered since whether there might not even be further changes as regards labour in days to come. After all, the State as owner could not be compelled to replace its own five-barred gates.

But if, in future, there were no hedges? Without hedges, I have heard it argued, you would not have shelter for the thousands of sparrows which in autumn destroy wheat along the edges of farm fields. Would you not? I have a higher opinion of the mind of the sparrow than to believe that you could get rid of him so easily. He would soon find some other resting-place than hazel boughs or may trees, or even my hedge of sloe. It would not be sparrows whom you would banish by cutting down the hedges, it would be other birds. It would be thrushes, blackbirds, yellowhammers, the life and song of spring and summer, the welcoming shelter of migrants, warblers, whitethroats, nightingales, the shade and protection of the farmer's best friend of the fields, the nesting partridge. And a question which I have asked and to which I have never had an answer from the hedge-cutters' committee man : what do you gain from the bare hedgerow that you do not lose by the tractor? Sunshine instead of shadow on a growing crop? But the tractor robs you of the space of a highway down the length of the hedge. For every hundred yards of your tractor's road you lose four hundred square yards of crop—a tenth of an acre. It is a sum worth thinking out.

There is another sum, of which the factors are not reckoned in yards or shillings. It is the sum of the difference that is in English hedges, the life, the shade, the flower, the song that belongs to them and, for an example separated by the Channel, the open, unfenced acres of France. It is the difference between two minds—those of Thomas Hardy, perhaps, and the author of *La Terre*. We shall come to State ownership in time, I do not doubt; but we shall come back again to Hardy.

CHAPTER X

IN THE WOODS

BLUEBELL WOOD named itself. It is a narrow triangle with the longest sides each of some two hundred yards, and it borders plantations of chestnut and larch. It is not itself a plantation, it is natural woodland of different trees, oak the best of them, but there are fine hollies, and the undergrowth is hazel. Fifty years or so ago its owner, for whatever reason, planted laurel and rhododendron here and there among the hazel, and to-day there are trusses of mauve in June, and the laurel lifts its bright racemes. But the spirit and the light of the wood lies under its trees, in the spread profusion of blue-bells that sheet its floor. I know no other flower that has the property of bluebells, to flood a wood with lakes of colour, ultramarine deep and scented near at hand, spreading and fading to an even distance of mist, to a greyness that yet is blue.

To enter the wood as I like best to come into it, you climb a bank where there is a gap in the pleached hazel of the fence, and you are at the opening of the path which turns a corner a dozen yards away, beyond which you cannot see. The path runs forward among bluebells, among the long leaves thrust the curled fronds of young bracken, and here and there plants of campion not yet in bud. On a morning of sunshine you look up and find the colour of the floor below you in the sky above, a sky beyond a broken canopy of white, the flower of wild cherry trees. Three tall cherry trees stand at the opening of the wood and arch their branches over the path, and it is from those branches and the boughs of oak beside them that I listen April after April for the voices that belong to the wood in spring. It is from those branches of gean, that tree with the cold, virginal name, that year after year comes the repeated greeting of the chiffchaff; it is from overhead, in that white flower under the sky, that there falls the voice of the willow wren, and that the wood wren sends out its quaintly halved sharp twitter and shivering trill.

I have walked through the wood often in winter, with the

bracken high and dry and amber brown climbing into the hazel, and holly berries gleaming above snow, and redwings quietly chattering in the tops of the oaks. I have followed its path in July, and watched white admiral butterflies float over honeysuckle and settle and drink at blackberry blossom among the hollies. But I remember it best as I first saw it on a day in April when I followed a tiny sidepath clustered at its edge with dog-violets, and saw pearl-bordered fritillaries fanning their wings in sunshine on the turf. The violet-grown track joins the path through the wood, to wind again through bluebells, till at the turn among the trees the path is a voyage over a lake of blue, and the light on it spreads and swims through stems and boughs to dark beyond. Suddenly it opens out to join the broad right of way through the chestnut, and looking down you realize that the path has ended as it began with white, but here the white is under your feet, in a cloud of wood-sorrel.

Leaf in March

The Forrard Oak—that is the right word, *the*, to use, for there is only one. When I write that there is only one I mean that there is no other like it known to books on forestry, nor, I believe, to Kew; it is not the common oak, *Quercus pedunculata,* nor the durmast, *sessiliflora,* nor the Turkey oak, *cerris*; nor does it resemble the American oaks, white or red. So far as I know, it has never had an acorn, and nobody knows how, or when, or whence it came to be where it is.

If anyone should happen to be travelling at the end of March on the Southern Railway from London to Portsmouth and should chance to look out of the window at bare woodland between Witley and Haslemere, he may perhaps catch sight, soon after leaving Witley, of a tree in fresh green leaf. That is the Forrard Oak. It has been known by that name among Surrey folk for I do not know how many years, because of its forward foliage, breaking full into leaf as it does at the end of March, whereas its English relations, common and durmast, and its more distant cousins, Turkey and the rest, wait till late April or May. You can see it in its brave new clothes from the railway carriage, or, as I think better, from the top of a stretch of land presented to the

National Trust some years ago by Mrs Abel Smith and Mr Graham Robertson, which lies just north of Sandhills, best of all tiny Surrey villages in its tiled cottages among apple trees and bluebells. And for that matter I have often wished that the National Trust could buy the Forrard Oak in trust for the nation. A few years ago, thanks to the pleas of local residents and the generosity of buyer and seller, it escaped the axe while all its surroundings perished. Could it not be secured for the future, to break into new leaf year after year, new life among lifeless things? England could not possess a happier tree.

I write of only one Forrard Oak. Will there ever be another? I have seen two saplings, a few months old, miraculously grafted by a forester's skill. It is a question whether they will survive. But the Forrard Oak, columnar, gracious, nobly boughed, survives—as yet.

Fire Flower and Groundsel

Three acres of forty-five-year-old larch wood stood there a year before, and I went on a day in July to see what changes twelve months had brought. In my mind were two visions; the first of the wood as I had known it through so many summers, tall, straight stems alive with green and the rosy flowers of March hardening into cones in June; and the other, fallen trunks lying by the remains of December bonfires and the havoc of furrows deep ploughed in sandy soil by the timber merchants' tractor.

I had not guessed the sight that would meet me. One thing I had expected, the fire-flower, as countrymen in Surrey have come to call the willow herb, *Epilobium angustifolium*, that follows fires on commons and in woodland, and covers ashen floors and blackened tree-stumps with red-purple spires of blossom. (How oddly to-day read the pages of Bentham and Hooker, even the revised edition of 1908 : "Widely spread over Britain, but not common.") And there, over half the space which the woodmen had emptied of timber, the fire-flower stood and glowed sweet and cool, hiding furrow and sawn bole and the dark patches of bonfires washed by rain.

Fire-flower spread over half of the three acres; but the

other half! Till I came near I did not recognize that film
of yellow-green. Then I saw that the whole area was filled—
not spread, not carpeted, but waist-high filled—with groundsel, not the garden weed, but the larger, taller *Senecio sylva-
ticus,* three and four feet above tree-stump and charred frith.
How long had the feathery, wind-borne seed lain dormant in
sunless undergrowth before the timber-contractor's axe had
let in light and warmth to the cold humus of the wood? In
thirty years I had never seen groundsel there; I had never
thought of the plant except as an easily-dealt-with nuisance
of the kitchen garden. I stared at the acres which had been
visions in turn of larch roses, dog violets, campion, blackberries, and wondered how to deal with so omnipresent, so
overwhelming a weed. I thought not of fire-flower, but of
fire.

Birch-sown Acres

There lay before me then, that day, one of the problems
of a countryside at war; just a small problem, what to do
with a weed. But far greater problems remained beyond.
All over England, you realized, it had happened—acres once
woodland lay bare to the sun and the wind and the rain. And
not for the first time, in the same way. It was, it is, part of
the story of war, from the days of the Armada to the Somme,
from the Somme to Dunkirk, from oak to pine and fir; the
need is for timber, and the face of the countryside gives way.
And the need follows for years after the war, with the
changed landscape follow changing plans for the future; the
big question is the same, of replanting.

Here and there, of course, that is a problem of forestry
on a large scale, beyond the means of the plain man. But
with other woods the problem of the future is taken out of
the forester's hands; the trees settle the days to come for
themselves. We cannot everywhere replant larch, and perhaps would not if we could, for larch is only a crop, whether
it is cut thirty or a hundred years old, and when cut sets its
problem over again. Instead, there are woods that replant
themselves. You may go out over acres that were larch or
pine three or even two years ago and find birch seedlings as
thick as grass; there were parent trees, perhaps, within the

range of blowing winds, and they have scattered their million specks of air-borne life out over the desert.

And the future? A friend wrote to me in the later days of the war of 1939; he, too, had looked out over acres that once were timber, and the growth was young and strong. "Birch is the curse of Hampshire." Well, in my part of Surrey I am not afraid of the curse. For these birch-sown acres the future will hold no money. There will be no market; the days are past when birch brooms were sold by the thousand in Southwark, as the *History of Surrey* tells you they were. I like to think of simpler days still:

> O spread ageän your leaves an' flow'rs
> Lwonesome woodlands! zunny woodlands!

There is comfort to be had from trees in Surrey as well as Dorset, and in sunlight and shadow I read again William Barnes.

Woodman's Axe

Memory goes back to a day in the war. I looked at the trees on the hill—the Tolt, of which I have written elsewhere. They were to be felled, hundreds of them. I thought of the change it would make in the landscape; I should miss the young green and the rosy plumes set about the boughs in March, and the yellow needles in the winds of October. And that afternoon, as I watched the two woodcutters at work, I pictured the hill in earlier days before the change came and the larch was planted and furrows lay in ploughland over High Field and Poor Field, as an old map tells me those sandy spaces were once named. Now it was to be bare soil once again. Eighty trees had already come down. "How long does it take you to fell a larch?" I asked one of the woodcutters. He had not thought of his work in that way; his standard was the cubic foot. Three of them had once cut 3,000 cubic feet in a week—five eight-hour days— and that included clearing brambles, cutting pulp wood out of the small stuff and doing all the burning that was needed. But a single tree? The two of them would try. There would be first the shaping of the stem with the axe above the "claws," and then the work of the cross-saw.

He got ready with the axe, and I took out my watch to count the strokes—down, up, right hand, left hand, a hundred and twenty-four in three and a half minutes; then the cross-saw with both of them, and in six minutes from starting with the axe the angle of the tree changed; it crashed. But the branch of a small oak caught its top, and would delay the trimming; he was not satisfied, and went with his axe to another tree. It was the same size, but he was faster, he finished with the axe, one hundred and five strokes in three minutes; two minutes more with the cross-saw and it too crashed; three minutes more, and the trash, the branches, were cut from it and the larch lay naked, once a tree sixty to seventy feet high, now a pole of twenty cubic feet, ready for the lorry. "We shouldn't always work like that," he said. The sweat stood on his brow.

Grace of Cherry

We look down, not up. It is a very wide truth, governing and explaining many things in the countryside. Our natural way is to use our eyes on their own level, or below us, and it is seldom that we throw our heads back and look as high as we can. And that is the general rule of English writing of country sights : that it is concerned with what is round about us rather than above our usual vision. So the poets of the flowers of spring find their first subjects on the ground— "daisies pied and violets blue, and ladysmocks all silver white," and daffodils which we "weep to see haste away so soon." They are all of the meadows, the fields, the lea.

But of the flowers of the trees in spring we shall find less poetry. Perhaps it is easy to understand why the elm should have inspired few writers, for its blossoms, although they cluster into crimson crowns in April, are separately small and lacking in outline; and for that matter, since they belong mainly to the top branches, many of us would never see them close at hand unless the tree were somehow broken, or maybe uprooted by a spring gale. But there is a tree of the woods, and here and there of the hedges, which we can all see and yet of which few poets have written—the wild cherry. Is there any lovelier sight of the opening year? I can find in all the woods nothing more delicate or graceful than its flowers in their bunches of three and four and five, along the branches spreading up and about and down over hedge. It is a slenderer, weaker bloom than that of our orchard cherry, but its weakness is its beauty, and the tree as a whole is a mist, a cloud of light.

And of all flowering trees it deserves least to be picked and brought indoors. If the ends of a bough are clipped, to make a bunch of flowers for a vase, the branch from which those blooms are cut will die. It is as if it ended its life in protest; very well, if you cut me, I shall not bloom in your reach again. But the reason of the branch's death is plain to see; the bough hangs down, the sap runs in April to fill the buds, and if you cut the bough it bleeds to death. And so, perhaps, it hangs out its message : look up for flowers.

After the Gale

In January they were standing. They were part of the old woodland, of the natural jungle of this corner of the world as I first knew it thirty years ago; two noble oaks among holly and bracken, wild cherry and amelanchier and mountain ash. Under them in January bluebells were pushing green blades up through peat and rain-rotten leaves, springing stitchwort and dog-violets and honeysuckle. There they stood as we had known them all our lives through.

And then came February. In the last hours of January a wind had sprung up from the south-west, quickening as darkness fell; then in the first hour of the new month the wind blew to a gale and from a gale to something more. From midnight onwards grew a sound I had heard but once before, a deep continuous roar, a bellow unending, till I think the mere ceaselessness must have numbed all hearing, and I woke in the February dawn to no more than the wind of twelve hours ago.

I had known there must be trees blown down; some had fallen even in the wind before the gale. But I had not expected to see what the morning showed, larches lying flat and huddled, twisted and leaning at angles, larches laid in rows, in swathes as if a scythe had swept them, six, seven here, a dozen there, fifty along the edge of the wood. Yet larches, one knew, could be uprooted by a gust, and this had been a tempest. But I did not think to see two oaks as I found them. It is not merely a strange sight, it is one of haunting unhappiness to see great trees heaved from the earth, their roots that had gripped the ground so strongly stretching up into cold air, with soil and stones still clinging to them. And as I looked the thought came—they are not dead, but dying, not mere matter but sentient; they had felt the wrench that tore them out, they had known what was coming, what had come. And they had left—no, they were leaving us as we stood there. I had not thought till that February morning what it was to lose such friends.

Flower of Wilderness

But in looking at these acres shorn of their trees, and wondering what will take their places of Nature's planting, it can be interesting to watch the changes summer by summer. When I stared first at four-foot groundsel standing over shaven larch stumps, side by side with the fire-flower that had made me guess at burning the new weed to prevent its seed covering other acres. I had not thought—who does think of such things in times of quiet growth of trees in a wood?— of other seeds, stronger perhaps than the invading *senecio*. Next summer brought its answer. Side by side with the fire-flower came a new carpet over the ground, and it was not groundsel, but an acre or so of pink campion. True, there were plants of groundsel here and there opening into yellow, and threatening other drifts of seed, but the campion seemed that third summer to be the stronger fighter, if so gentle a substitute can be said to fight. And there were yet other helpers in the wilderness, herb robert for one, shading its geranium flowers into russet and maroon; and quietest and lowliest of all, the heath galium, or as villagers name it better in English, white ladies' bedstraw. I made up my mind that day, watching the third round, so to speak, of the fight that began the day that the larches fell, to wait for the round —timed for three hundred and sixty-five days—which should decide.

Gipsy Singing

There came a later day. Over a desert of litter, of shaven

trunks and stumps sawn close to the soil, a team of men with a Fordson tractor and all its attendant machinery were piling together the dismembered poles that once lived as trees. I was reminded, looking on, of a passage in George Bourne's *Memoirs of a Surrey Labourer*. Forty years before, in sight of the spot where I stood, Bettesworth had watched the getting-up of three big elm trees into a timber carriage, with running-chains and all, by a carter "with only hisself and the hosses . . ."

" 'Twas over there on the Hog's Back, not far from Tongham Station. We all went out for to see'n do it—'cause 'twas in the dinner-time he come, and we never believed he'd do it singlehanded. The farmer says to'n, 'You'll never get they up by yourself.' 'I dessay I shall,' he says; and so he did, too. Three great elm trees upon that one carriage. . . . Well, he had a four-hoss team, so that'll tell ye what 'twas. They *was* some hosses, too. Ordinary farm hosses wouldn't ha' done it. But he only jest had to speak, and you'd see them watchin' him. . . . When he went forward, after he'd got the trees up, to see what sort of a road he'd got for gettin' out, they stood there with their heads stretched out and their ears for'ard. 'Come on,' he says, and *away* they went, tearin' away. . . . The old farmer says to'n, 'I never believed you'd ha' done it.' 'I thought mos' likely I should,' he says. But he never had much to say."

I thought of that scene, watching the red-painted tractor spirting its blue vapour, puffing, grunting, backwards and forwards among stumps and prostrate poles. I should like to have heard Bettesworth's comment. Seven men were at work, driving, sawing, piling, and the foreman jotting cubic measurements in his book. Forwards and backwards went the tractor, like a trained animal digging its claws into the churned soil, and somehow like animals, collared and chained and told where to go, the sawn logs followed it. Neither men nor tractor rested, save that once one of the men, a dark-eyed gipsy, drew himself up and shouted a snatch of song into the mist. I went back home in the fading afternoon light, and once more from the distance behind me came that sound of a Surrey winter day, the echoing tenor of a gipsy chaining and piling logs.

128

Autumn in a Surrey beech-wood—Leith Hill
Harvest at Gatton

Woodland Torn

It was in July 1944 that there came to our quiet country-side a thing unknown before, even in five years of war. Up to that time we had seen and suffered, as had the rest of the South Country, in wreckage from bombs, craters in farm fields, broken homes; all that had been the common fate of England. But stretches of woodland laid flat in summer—that was new.

I walked over to look at the place. We had heard the engine—the "doodlebug"—on its way, and some of us saw it fall; then came the noise, a sort of loud slap, different from the shaking thuds of other days and nights. But I had not guessed what I should see. I made my way through the woodland, and I came suddenly on an opening where two men were at work sawing up trees. They had felled several, three of them oaks in full greenery, a sight woodmen do not expect, and there were others near, splintered and cracked. Was this the place? I asked. No, but a couple of hundred yards further on; they had been told to begin clearing the damage here. I went on, through undamaged boughs and fern, to come suddenly on a scene, strangest of its kind in all my knowledge. Over a space of an acre or more of hill-side trees lay, smashed, uprooted, naked. Oaks stood bare as in winter. Pines reared stems without a bough. A beech up-raised slender twigs, disbudded to the sky. Hollies, the queerest of green skeletons, leafless, somehow looked in-decent. Stranger even than they was the bracken; it lay flat on the peat save for a few green spikes upstanding like masts, without a frond. And over all that slope of hillside spread a carpet of oak leaves, inches thick, filling the rabbit buries, covering roots and moss and sandy soil, and all the leaves fresh and young. Oak leaves in autumn, yellow, copper, brown, we have known all our lives, but green oak leaves lying piled and scattered, everywhere motionless, brought to an end all of them, dead—I had not thought of that. And that group of trees I had passed on my way blasted, and other trees round untouched, how had that happened? Does anybody understand?

In time, no doubt, we shall learn. Science will discover what is the energy, as regards direction and distance, of this

Richmond Bridge
On the North Downs: chalk pit near Ockley

and that form of modern explosive. I have no scientific knowledge, and could deduce nothing of value from the few facts
which seem to be part of the story of bomb damage in my
neighbourhood. In one case a bomb dropped within a few
yards of a house, blew in the french window of the dining-
room and shattered other windows, but did little other
damage except smashing a fruit tree in the kitchen garden
two hundred yards away; and in another case a bomb which
made an enormous crater in a grass field brought down all
the ceilings in a house near, without hurting its neighbours,
while it blew in the window of a church a mile away and took
a door off its hinges in a house half a mile distant in another
direction. If I can suggest any parallel in the direction taken
by unseen forces it would be in the action of frost traceable
in May, for instance, in strawberry beds, where the berries
can be seen blackened in lines at right-angles to each other.
But I write in both these cases of damage done by blast without, of course, knowledge of all the facts.

But how many new facts we need to know! In this corner
of Surrey, just for one example, things happened as a consequence of a bomb falling on a wooded hillside which no one,
I dare say, would have predicted who saw what had happened on that day of war in July. On a day six weeks later—
just six weeks—I went again to that broken acre and found
a sight beyond all thought. Those trees which I had looked
at as bare skeletons, stripped of every bough, were in new
green leaf. From stem, trunk, broken shaft there was young
growth springing. All the trees were alive, and each tree in
its new life showed its own individual habit afresh, different
from its fellows in colour and strength and form. Here was
a chestnut, quick and sappy, thrusting out soft wood with a
new, easy push into the air. Here were hollies, smooth and
grey of bole and stem, prickly with red-brown spiny foliage
at the end of each stripped bough, and only at the very end.
There, twenty yards away, was a great beech lifting slender
shoots to the sky, each tipped with opening green. Above all
in their individuality, here were oaks, some split and leaning,
some half-uprooted, all strangely shattered. One in particular, stripped of every branch as by some giant chisel, stood
perpendicular as a telegraph pole. It was clothed on all its

upright length and height with tiny clustering twigs two or three inches long; somehow it looked as if the little clusters had been bound on. Oddest of all were other small clusters bursting from wrinkled oak trunks, as if the sap insisted on outlet, close to the ground.

I have never seen anything else like this. It was a sight new to the Surrey countryside. The nearest parallel I could think of was hazel or chestnut, cut in their eight- or nine-year rotation, growing new from old. But this was another, nobler growth. It looked as if in that broken acre there were hurt, wounded things trying to be English trees again.

English Snowdrops

Every January I try to make the journey. It is to a wood nearby where snowdrops grow in wide sheets, as naturally spread as windflowers or primroses, flowers of the wood itself. There is a saying in my part of the country—it may belong to other counties besides Surrey—that where you find snowdrops growing wild you are looking at church property. I do not know why this should be so, unless it is that the yew, our noblest evergreen and a tree belonging everywhere to churchyards, is a symbol of eternity, and that so in the same way the snowdrop, our earliest and purest flower, belongs to thoughts of new life. It carries a message we all understand when we see it growing in a churchyard.

Is there any flower of winter days more essentially English? Yet there are botanists of to-day who are at pains to insist that the snowdrop is not indigenous to this country. I say insist, because theirs is seemingly a self-imposed and unnecessary task. On what grounds do they claim that it is a foreigner? I have never been able to understand. Is it because Bacon in his essay "Of Gardens" does not include the snowdrop among the flowers of January and February? But then among the flowers of April and May he doesn't mention the bluebell. For me, at all events, the very name is enough. The Latins named the crocus, the violet, and even the rose, but they were English from the beginning who talked of buttercups and daisies and snowdrops. And last, who could doubt it as English who had seen it as I see it year by year in my South Country wood, sheeted as the bluebell its neighbour, the one as blue as the English sky, the other as white as country snow?

Vision of Woodcock

To wander through unspoiled woods—that is one of the best things in these days; and it is not as easy as it used to be. In Surrey, which is a county blessed with commons, we have seen what tanks can do to what were once untrodden ways by heather and gorse and sand and stream; which is inevitable damage, no doubt, in such times as we have lived in, but an unhappy business for all that. So that to walk in one of the best of all woods in Surrey, and to find it the same, unchanged in its trees and flowers since I first saw it, half a lifetime gone, and to find it unchanged is fortune for which to bless heaven.

I know no happier stretch of country free to all than this wood. Through part of it runs an old road, and a road, too, unusual in its setting, for it is bordered by avenues of trees; not, I think, meant to line the road itself, though they do that for part of its length, but planted in rows as we to-day plant larch. They are Turkey oaks, which I guess by the size to be a hundred years old or more, and they tower straight and tall on each side of a broad green path that never knew macadam, though once it led to the cathedral town of Sussex. There lies the charm of the place, in those high avenues and in the flowers below them, primroses springing from wet clay, anemones in the wind, and on the brim of a deep ghyll, over a clear stream sparkling ten feet down, woodsorrel, slenderest and most delicate flower of all.

But I look back on one afternoon in that wood which holds a memory separate from the rest. It was a day in April; we had turned in our walk, and I called to my spaniel to follow. We went back by the path we had come, and the spaniel hunted busily nose to ground beside us. And suddenly my companion spoke. "A woodcock!" It rose from under the spaniel's nose and fluttered down a dozen yards away. We both had the same thought. There, open to view, where the mother bird gay in her spring dress had risen among oak leaves and naked saplings, lay the nest with its four eggs, rounded, brown-blotched, lilac-grey—the sudden, unhoped-for vision of a Surrey spring. There we left the chestnut-bright mother to come back to her brooding.

Blackberries of To-day

Three-quarters of an inch long—it is an odd description of a blackberry, and August is early in the year to make it. But three-quarters of an inch is the average length of black-berries in a fine summer, or rather autumn, in part of south-west Surrey to-day, and when I first saw the sight it set me wondering. For blackberries in days gone by, and fruit of a smaller size for that matter, used to belong to September.

It was in August 1943—the date is worth remembering—that I first saw a basket of those big blackberries carried up to the house of a neighbour, and a fortnight or so later I found myself pondering over a possible reason. I was walking by the edge of a piece of rough woodland in which two years before the brambles had been cut down to further the growth of some overhanging laurels, and I found myself looking at blackberries as big as the basketful at which I had stared in August. Such blackberries had never grown there before. Instead, the bushes used to carry fruit in small clusters, which did not ripen till later in the year—in mid-September perhaps. But there they were, on strong young canes (as I found myself thinking of them, in terms of rasp-berry growing), dark, ripe fruit, shining in the sun. Surely the seasons had changed? Or was it the mild winter and the May without frost? And then, as I gazed, I caught sight among blackberry bines of a different leaf, a spray, a branch, a strong plant of a different kind—a loganberry.

That suggests a question. It is only in the last few years that loganberries have found a place in the nurserymen's catalogues, and so have been set in rows, in fruit gardens side by side with gooseberries, currants and the rest. And season after season we have watched new varieties following in their wake—Laxtonberries, Veitchberries, Boysenberries and others. Is it possible that these new fruits, flowering and pollinated in the same countryside next to the blackberries of the wood, have transmitted some of their qualities to their wild neighbours? And would the cutting back of wild brambles have something of the same effect as the removal of old canes from the raspberry beds? Are the new, early-fruiting blackberries, in short, the result of recent additions to cultivated fruit gardens? Here are thoughts for years to come.

Carpet of April

Here, in a world where we grow hazel and chestnut as crops for cutting in rotations of years, carpets in the woods change with the years in turn. But the day returns each year in April, the day when "longen folk to goon on pilgrimage," and every year I too long for my pilgrimage. It is to the same spot each returning spring, and surely none of those who journeyed with the Monk and the Prioress and the Wife of Bath set out with greater hope than I of sights and sounds of other years, of flowers in the old places, of scents I know, of the singing birds and one song, one voice, beyond all other voices.

It is under hazel that the carpets change most. They can be unexpected. Two April days I shall always remember, each with its own carpet, in the same acre which lies by the path of my pilgrimage. In the spring that followed the cutting of the hazel the floor of the wood lay bare to the sun. I came to it on a day twelve months later and it was a sheet of violets. Next year, in the shade of hazel grown tall again, they had vanished. Instead, a few yards away, another sight lit the woods. Through the breadth of a corner of Fourteen Acre—that name of old England!—shone celandines among the green of to-morrow's bluebells. And I was back with the sight of them to a wood beloved of other Aprils gone—a wood to which I once journeyed from Surrey, a wood above the Irish Lee, sunniest place of those past days with celandines, campions, gorse. I can never again make that journey, but that Irish river, with the primroses on its banks, and peacock butterflies above the primroses, and sandmartins like grey moths flitting over its stream, is linked always in my mind with the Surrey spring. But it is the primroses that are the strongest link of all; there is no flower with the gift that belongs to primroses, of taking those who see them once more in April to the earliest days of all.

One other sight belongs to my day of pilgrimage. Here in

this corner of England we are still happy with fresh wells and springs, but they have to be harnessed here and there as houses draw near to their source in the woods, and building them in means digging in the clay of the Weald. One April day I came to where clay had been turned a season or two before, and I looked to see the yellow loam spread far and wide. Instead, the carpet was of yellow colt's-foot—surely a flower of forgiveness for invasion. And as I stood gazing there came on the wind the voice loved beyond others, the first cuckoo of the year.

The Lightning-stroke

"Did you hear that very loud crack in the storm the other night?" a friend asked me, speaking of the thunderstorm of 14–15 July 1945, the longest and most violent in my memories of Surrey. I heard many loud cracks, I told him, as indeed I did, for I lay awake till four in the morning in alternating light and dark, but I had not thought of any one clap as much louder than the other hundred or so. But there was one which was more of a crack than the rest, he told me, and it must have been the one that struck the chestnut. Had I seen it, the chestnut near the gate behind the house? I went to look.

In the coppice of the hill on which the house stands, oak, larch, birch, hazel, are a number of Spanish chestnut trees, some seventy feet high. It was one of these that had been struck. I caught sight of it from a path through the woods close to the garden gate—a sudden vision of grey-brown among strong, yellow-green foliage, in the August sunshine. There it stood, a thing such as I had not seen since many years ago I looked at a solitary ash on a hill in Sussex; and it was different from the ash, for I saw that first on a day in autumn when the leaves had fallen, and this had happened in high summer. From near the top the tree was split, a fissure travelling clean through the trunk down to the ground, two inches wide to half an inch, hardly swerving in the perpendicular from head to foot—I thought as I gazed of the sound and the sight of a woodman's hatchet splitting hazel for hurdles. On each side of the gap long strips of bark had been torn from the stem; I picked up one of them fifteen inches long, pointed at each end and sharp as a knife. But the tree as a whole was the thing that held the eye. There it stood among its fellows, seared, shattered, dead among the living. That tree, not a hundred yards from where I lay listening to the storm, had taken the blow, and I stood looking at the happy trees all round it.

CHAPTER XI

AN OLD FARM ACCOUNT BOOK

I HAVE been privileged to read, copying when I pleased from its pages, an old account book belonging to a farm of which the fields lie next to my house and garden. Great House Farm was its name, and the accounts run over the four years 1850–3. They are written in an old-fashioned. almost scholarly hand, in what used to be called the Italian style, angular and pointed, and here and there the spelling, especially of names, is strictly phonetic—perhaps the labourers could not spell their names to their employer.

Entries occur in the book in sections, separated by blank pages. The main entries are of wages, but for different forms of employment. Wages are paid, not week by week, but at intervals, to names which live in neighbouring Surrey villages to-day—Boxall, Pickett, Over, Denyer, Hammond —and the rates range from 1s 6d to 1s 10d per day. But in other respects prices are difficult to range as high or low. Farm pests for instance suggest odd comparisons. There must have been enormous numbers of sparrows in the farm fields. On 25 July 1851 there is an entry of six hundred sparrows at 8d, 4 shillings, and on the following 7 January eighteen hundred sparrows, 12 shillings. Rats were paid for at a penny a dozen, but there are few entries : "dozen half rats, 1s 6d"; and "rats 5½ dzn. 5s 6d" are two for February 1852. Moles seem to have been comparatively scarce. In July 1852 I find two entries : "J. Pannell, catching 3 dzn. mouls, 6s," and in December "J. Pannell 3 mouls 6d." Eggs, at a penny apiece, are seldom mentioned; on 7 March 1852 we read "2 dzn. 10 eggs 2s 10d." Here and there we find ourselves guessing at conditions of farm labour. It must have been thirsty work dealing with overseas manure in summer; we get entries in June and July of "half a gallon beer sowing guano." Sometimes we wonder how prices were fixed : for instance, "11 June 1851, whashed 194 sheep; 18 June, paid for shairing 194 sheep, £1 19s."

All this was a hundred years ago, in days of window taxes and turnpike gates. But throughout the fascination is in the combination of fine, legible writing with spelling you can hear —"a niew lantern, 3s 10d," "one cashuelty sheep," and "Recd, from Mr Matthews 6 lbs yellow sweed seed."

"Labour 1850 Great House Farm" is the heading of the first right-hand page, but preceding it, on an unruled left-hand page, are the following entries, without a heading:

Dec. 28	Sent to London 60 sheep	
	Sent to Gosden two pigs	
Jany 4	Sent to London 60 sheep	
6	Sent to Gosden 2 pigs 49 stone	
23	Sent to London 40 sheep	
Feby 15	Sent to London 44 sheep	
17	Delivered to Mr Hoad 1 fat Hog at Chidingfold at 3s 2d per stone	
22	Sent to London Six Beast	
29	Sent to London Six Beast	
March 2	Delivered to Mr Goff 2 fat Hogs at Guildford at 3.2	
March 7	Sent to London 4 Beast	
9	Delivered Mr Goff 2 fat Hogs at 3s 2d	

There follows the first page of wages accounts, for example:

		Days	£	s.	d.
Oct. 26th	Richd Mitchill	11		16	6
	Geo Boxall	11		16	6
	Math Young	11		16	6
	Hy Edwards	11		16	6
	Jhn Nolder	11		11	0
	Thos Pickett	11½	1	1	1
	Thos Hammond	11½	1	1	1
	Hy Street		2	0	0

Next follow entries sometimes without names:

			£	s.	d.
Dec.	7	52½ Rods hedging at 4½d		19	7¼
		13 Dozen Stakes 1s 1d: rods 1s		2	1
		2 Hundred Faggots		3	0
Jany 18 1851					
		Trenching 136 rod of ground	4	10	8

			£	s.	d.
Feb.	1	Trenching 1 Acre 19 rod, 8s pr rod	5	19	4
March	15	Wm Buss planting 13 Thousand 100 chesnut 2s	1	6	2½
	29	Richr Furlonger Tying hay 25 loads 8 truss	1	17	10
April	22	Wm Nolder & Jas. Enticknap Tying 17 Load 24 Truss Straw		17	8
	26	Rd Mitchil howing Wheat in the Crouch field 2 acres 2 rod at 4s		8	0½
		Geo. Boxall hoing wheat in the Chrouch field 2¼ acres 26 rd. at 4s		9	7½
May	10	Sarah Hammond 10 days		6	8
		Maria Boxal 10½		5	3
		Mary Earl 10½		7	0
		H. J. Edwards howing wheat in the Smalberries 2½ acres 33½ rod, 3s 6d per acre		9	5½
	24	Wm Denyer Howing 9 acres Barley at 2s 4d per acre	1	1	0
June	5	Paid for Mowing 35½ acres of grass at 2s 3d per acre	3	19	10½
		R. Mitchil Haying at 2s 4½ days		9	0
		3½ days		5	3

Six other labourers working in all twenty-two days at 2s
per day and twenty and a half days at 1s 6d per day earn
£3 14s 9d, and three women, Sarah Hammond nine and a
half days, 6s 4d; Mary Earl twelve days, 8s.; and Maria
Boxal twelve days, 6s., earn £1 0s 4d; making a total for
"haying" of £4 15s 1d.

			£	s.	d.
July	25	Richd Furlonger Thatching hay rick 18 sq at 10d sq.		15	0
		6 Hundred sparrows at 8d		4	0
August	13	Flat howing and setting out 1 acre 3 qrs 27 rd Sweeds in the Grove at 5s per Acre		9	7½
		Howing Sweeds in the Wool field 1, 3, 4 at 4s, first time		7	1½
Sept.	1	H. Squelch Reaping Wheat 5A 2 qr. 31 rd. at 9s	2	11	3
		W. Denyer howing turnips in the feathercombs at 4s 2. 0. 11		8	4

			£	s.	d.
		Thos. Earl, H. Edwards, T. Over, H. Squelch mowing 62 acres barley at 2ˢ 6ᵈ	7	15	0
		J. Goodchild harvest month (and others)	2	0	0
	27	T. Earl, A. Edwards, Thrashing rye 11 qrs at 3ˢ	1	13	0
Nov.	8	H. Edwards, T. Over, thrashing 13 Qrs, wheat 2 bushels at 3ˢ	1	19	9
1852					
Jan.	5	Killing 2 pigs		3	0
		Fagots 500 at 1ˢ 8ᵈ		8	4
	7	R. Furlonger tying 29 loads Hay at 1ˢ 6ᵈ	2	3	6
		18 Hundred sparrows		12	0
Feb.	2	Dozen half Rats		1	6
		W. Denyer, F. Edwards hedging 34 rod at 4		11	4
	14	W. Denyer, F. Edwards 38½ rd. hedging at 6		19	3
		288 fagots at 1ˢ 8ᵈ		4	9½
		Rats 5½ dzn.		5	6
March	1	T. Earl, H. Edwards, thrashing barley 29 qrs. 6 Bush	2	9	7
		Rats 3½ dzn.		3	6
	29	H. Boxall making 8 sheep cages at 7ᵈ each		4	8
July	19	W. Denyer howing 3 acres sweeds in the Smallberrays at 5ˢ		15	0
		J. Earl, W. Nolder, W. Denyer Rineing 3100¼ Bark at 1ˢ 4ᵈ	2	1	8
	26	J. Pannell, catching 3 dzn. mouls		6	0
August	2	J. Nolder, howing in the Crouch field sweeds 1 a 3. 20. at 5ˢ		9	4½
		Howing turnips in the Great Bittams 3 a 0 qr 20 rd. at 3ˢ 6ᵈ		10	11
	30	T. Pickett reaping wheat in the Pound field 1 a 3 qr. 17. at 10ˢ		18	7
Dec.	20	J. Nolder		2	0
		Two dozen rats			
		J. Pannell 3 mouls			6
	31	Elliott 2½ days bricklaying at 2ˢ 10ᵈ		7	3
Recᵈ from March 29th 1852 untill April 11, 1853			548	18	8
		Paid Do	543	11	9¼
		in hand	8	4	11¾

(At the end of each quarter he makes up his accounts, and enters the amount "in hand" or "behind.")

	£	s.	d.
April 25, 1853			
Elliot 1 week bricklaying		17	0
digging 40 rod of ground at 2ᵈ per rod		6	8
J. Furlonger digging 159½ rd. at 2ᵈ per rod	1	6	7
Boocom digging 88 rod at 2ᵈ per rd.		14	8

(He is evidently doubtful how to spell the name which we spell Bookham.)

	£	s.	d.
May 15 Boocome digging 30½ rod of ground at 2ᵈ per rd		5	1
Elliot bricklaying 12 days	1	14	0
27 B. Gill making 294 oak fagots 123 fir at 2ˢ pr do		8	5
2 loads wood at 2ˢ per load		4	0
W. Boocome 6½ days 16ᵈ		8	8
W. Boocome 7 days		11	8
June 4 W. Coal, G. Hedgler, R. Smith, digging 30 loads building stones at 2ˢ 3ᵈ	3	7	6
25 loads small stones at 2ˢ 3ᵈ per load	2	16	3

I think there must have been some argument as to the price paid for digging these "building stones" and "small stones," for under 14 June are entries of payments to the same three men, Coal (Cole?), Hedgler and Smith, eighteen loads building stones at 2s 6d., £2 5s, and four loads small stones at 2s 6d., 10s. These building stones and small stones I have no doubt were dug from the Bargate stone quarry which lies midway, at an angle, between Great House and Feathercombe.

Here follow, from other later pages, various entries in the accounts:

	£	s.	d.
March 24, 1852			
Recᵈ of Mr Hoad for one fat pig 33 stone 2 lbs. at 3ˢ 2ᵈ per stone	5	5	3½

Then on two pages, date of year not entered :

		£	s.	d.
Total received from April 12th until May 10th for Laibour and rates bill		60	6	3
For two cashelty sheep		2	2	2
		62	8	5

			£	s.	d.
July	19	Recᵈ for 1 cashelty sheep		10	3
Nov.	21	For two cashelty sheep	3	5	6

These are only two or three entries which precede other entries. Sixty pages later in the book I find three pages of entries mainly concerned with sheep "cashelties" and otherwise. Again, the pages do not show, except for one entry, the date of the year :

			£	s.	d.
Nov.	16	Sold one cashelty Sheep		7	0
	26	Sold Three sheep skins		6	6
	30	Recᵈ for one cashelty sheep		15	3
Decʳ	8	Recᵈ for one cashelty sheep		7	4½
	21	Recᵈ for one cashelty sheep		10	1½
Janʸ	11	Recᵈ for one cashelty sheep		8	1½
March	1	Recᵈ for one cashelty sheep		15	6½
	11	Recᵈ for one cashelty sheep	1	13	11
	11	Do. one —	1	15	0
May	2	Recᵈ for 2 cashelty sheep	2	2	0
July	19	Recᵈ for 1 cashelty sheep		10	3
Octʳ	11	Recᵈ for 1 cashelty sheep		14	3
	12	Recᵈ from Mr Furlonger for 2 cashelty sheep	1	15	3
Decʳ	6	Recᵈ for two Sheepskins and fat		8	0
	13	Recᵈ for 10 Sheepskins		16	0
Janʸ	21	Recᵈ of Mr Furlonger for 1 cashelty sheep	1	4	0
March	5	Recᵈ of Mr Furlonger for 2 cashelty sheep	1	17	3
	24	Recᵈ of Mr Furlonger for 1 cashelty sheep	1	1	9
	29	for 1 cashelty sheep		14	10½
	30	One cashelty sheep		18	9
April	5	One Do	1	1	0
	8	Recᵈ of Burdock for 2 sheep skins		4	0

May 1852		£	s.	d.
4	Rec^d for 2 horses	3	17	0
28	Rec^d for 1 cashelty sheep	1	4	1
June 11	Rec^d for 1 cashelty sheep	1	10	0
Septr 13	Rec^d for one cashelty sheep 5 stone 5 lbs.		11	5
Decr 9	Rec^d of Mr Chatfield for one horse hyde		5	0
	One bullock skin		4	6

When I read these entries of "cashelty sheep" I was puzzled. What were these "cashelties," and why did they differ so widely in amount? A day or two after reading them I happened to be able to ask the question of a butcher of the name of Furlonger, a descendant of the Furlonger mentioned in this account. He told me that his family had been in the business for two hundred years, and explained the term, which is still used in the trade. A casualty sheep is one that has fallen lame or sick, and has had to be killed, or perhaps has been found dead. A sheep fallen on its back, for instance, may not be able to move, and dies where it lies—one of the tragedies of a shepherd's calling. Sheep killed, or dying, in this way are of differing values; some furnish butcher's meat, others may be only fit for other purposes.

Follow three pages, with entries not fully dated, and sometimes difficult to separate and decipher. They deal with sowing corn, harrowing, rolling, etc. The names of the fields vary in spelling.

Hambledon. Sowing wheat (probably in 1851, but the date of the year is not given.)

Novr 14 & 15   Crouch field, 13 acres, harrowing 4 times. Rolling once, three horses.

Novr 16   10½ acres, 3 times harrowing, 1 rolling, 3 horses.

25   Great Bittams, 15 acres, harrowing 5 times. Rolling once, 3 horses.

Decr 6 & 7   Hill field 3½ acres, 2 bushels per acre, harrowing three times. Drilling rye.

Heath field 6½ acres, 2 bushels per acre, harrowing three times.

11   Sowing Rye 9 acres, harrowing three times.

April 2   Sowing Barley 9½ acres 3½ bushels per acre. Small harrowing three times. Rowling once, one horse.

April 3 Drilling the bottom field, 9 acres, 3 bushels. Drag harrowing twice, small do twice, Rowling once, one horse.

4 Sowing Hambledons, 11 acres, 3½ bushels. Drag harrowing twice, small do three times. Rowling twice. Two horses.

11 & 12 Sowing Sixteen-acres, 3½ bushels. Drag harrowing twice. Small harrowing four times. Rowling twice. Two horses.

19 Sowing 16 acres in the Tolt 3½ bushels. Do Drag harrowing twice, small do 3 items. Rowling once. Two horses.

May 1 Sowing 7½ acres in the Tolt 3½ bushels. Drag harrowing three times. Small harrowing twice. Rowling once, two horses.

Sowing Hambledons. Sowing seeds (entry undecipherable). Rowling in, two horses.

Sowing Heath field seeds, 6½ acres, and howing in.

Sowing Wheat 1851

Upper Pockril* 6½ acres 2½ Bushels pr acre. Rowling once, 4 horses harrowing 3 times.

Lower Pockril 8. 2½ do. Rowling once 4 horses harrowing 3 times.

Pound field, 10½ at 2½ do. Rowling once 4 horses, harrowing 4 times.

Drilling 9½ acres. Rowling twice, 4 horses harrowing 4 times.

Sowing 8 acres in the House field 2½. Rowling once, 5 horses, harrowing 3 times.

Drilling 15¼ acres 2½. Rowling twice 5 horses harrowing 4 times.

Feb⁷ 27 Sowing oats in the Wool field 5 bushels pr. acre. Drag harrowing 1 time. Small harrowing three time. Rowling twice 1 horse.

March 10th 1852 Sowing Barley.

7½ acres in the upper 14 Acres 3½ bushels pr. acre. Drag harrowing two time small do 3 time. Rowling once 2 horses once 1 horse.

11 Sowing the Feathercoombs Barley 10 Acres 3½ pr. acre. Drag harrowing two time small do 3 time. Rowling once 2 horses once 1 horse.

* i.e. Poker Hill. A local map shows two fields, Upper Poker Hill, 6 acres 2 roods 26 poles, and Lower Poker Hill, 8 acres 0 roods 36 poles.

Pyrford Mill on the River Wey, near Ripley

Mar. 18   Sowing the Grove Barley 11 acres 3½ bushel. Drag harrowing 3 times small do two time. Rowling once 3 horses twice 2 horses.

April   5   Sowing 62 acres seeds. Sowed pr. Acre 1½ gallon Bents 1 galn. red clover 1 qrt. white ½ gallon trefoil. Rowling in 1 horse.

Here follow five pages of entries of purchases of seed, oil cake, guano and so on. Guano was apparently the stock dressing of the period. These are some entries:

April 26 1851   Received from Mr Mathews
                8 bushels red clover seed
                2 bushels white do
                4 bushels trefoil
                11 bushels 3 galons Bents

May   9   Received from Jhn Wilkins 38 bags Peru guano 50 cwts 1 qr. 24 lb.

     12   Rec^d from Godalming Wharf 47 bags guano. Weight cwts 60 qrs. 3 lbs. 11.

June   5   Rec^d from Godalming Wharf 84 bags guano.

     25   Rec^d from Mr Mathews 6 lbs. yellow sweed seed. do 20 lbs. red round Turnip seed.

Oct   13   Rec^d from Mr Stafford 1 ton best oil cake £7. 15s.

Dec.   2   Rec^d of Mr Stafford ½ ton oil cake at £8. 5–£4. 2. 6.

April 19 1852   Rec^d from Hambledon Union 16 sacks gypsum at 2^s 9^d.

June   7   Rec^d from Godalming Wharf 80 bags guano 5 tons.

     21   Rec^d of Mr Mathews 10 lbs. red round turnip seed.

     30   Rec^d of Mr Ellis 30 lbs. green round turnip seed.

July   3   Rec^d of Mr Wilkins ¾ ton Peru guano.

Godalming Wharf lies at a bend of the River Wey, at a short distance east of the road running to Farncombe and Guildford. The river has been deepened and dredged to form a right-angle, with the sides of the wharf—originally, no doubt, faced with planking but now solid with concrete—lengthened so as to berth three barges. I stood by the wharf on a day in May 1945 and found pleasure in looking out over a Surrey scene unaltered since John Wilkins, perhaps, took his loads from the barges a hundred years before. Still the

On the Wey Canal, Byfleet

river runs shadowed brown and green under the willows; still the hayfields stretch rich in the sun.

Next come pages showing various payments, for farm necessities, rates, taxes and other expenses:

Hambledon, 1850

			£	s.	d.
Nov^r	5	Paid Mr Jhn White for 11 dozen hurdles & stakes	4	5	0
Jany	10	1851 Paid Wm Smithers for 13 dozen hurdles and stakes	5	10	6
	13	Paid Wm Gill for 4 dozen hurdles	1	12	0
Feby	6	Stack of Fagots	3	0	0
April	23	Paid Isaac Smithers for 12 bsl Potatoes at 1ˢ 8ᵈ	1	0	0
		Paid J. Bennett Window Tax half year	2	7	10½
June	15	Paid Mr Elwin for a Wagon	3	0	0
		Paid Mr Lickfold for a Wagon	10	0	0
	30	Paid Jhn Over for Beer and Plowing	4	18	6½
Jany	21	1852 Paid Isick Smithers for 4 dn. Hurdles at 6	1	4	0
June	18	Paid for Shairing 194 sheep	1	19	0
Oct^r	15	Paid Mr Furlonger for meat for Harvest Supper	1	8	8½
	25	Pd. A. Lintott for Beer	1	0	0
Nov^r	12	Pd. R. Furlonger for 14 hundred sparrows		9	4
Feby	12	1853 half Ton coals from Godalming Station		11	6
Augst	17	Paid Mr Jno Peto for repairing the Farm House	20	2	11

Follow more blank pages, and we come to the last entries in the book. These are mainly of small household and farm necessities, interspersed with payments of turnpike-gate tolls, thus:

			£	s.	d.
	15	A new Lantern		3	10
		A new Sive		3	6
		3 lbs. candles		1	4
Nov^r	14	Hireing horse and cart to take a sheep to the Butchers		2	6
		Turnpike gate			6
	23	7 packets blue vitriol		3	6

			£	s.	d.
Dec^r	16	¼ lb. Saultpeter			3
		1 lb. Brimstone			6
	21	Turnpike gate			9
Feby 24, 1851		2 lbs. Brimstone		1	0
		½ lb. Saltpeter			3
March 10		400 8^d nails		2	8½
		8¼ lb. Hoop iron at 2^d		1	4
		2 lb. shot			7½
		¼ lb. Powder			7
April	19	Turnpike Gate 50 sheep			5
	23	Turnpike Gate 1 horse			6
May	30	1 Drag Rake		9	0
		2 Wood Rakes		1	2
		1 new Scythe fitted complete and rubber		7	6
June	14	½ galn. Beer sowing Guano			6
	16	½ galn. Beer sowing guano			6
July	5	½ galn. Beer sowing guano			6
	7	1 lb. Powder		2	6
		4 lbs. shot		1	0
	15	1 galn Beer for drilling and sowing guano		1	0
Sept^r	22	2 Ball Filis*			10
Oct^r	11	A niew Lantern		3	6
		A niew Pail		2	0
Nov^r	15	Turnpike Gate 2 horses		1	0
	22	Box of gun caps		1	6
		Turnpike gate 1 horse			3
	25	Turnpike gate 4 horses		1	0
	26	Turnpike gate two horses		1	0
Dec^r	6	Turnpike Gate 2 horses			6
	28	Turnpike 60 sheep			7½
Jan^y	4, 1852	Turnpike gate for 60 sheep			7½
	17	Turnpike gate			3
	27	Turnpike gates		2	0
	25	Turnpike gate 40 sheep			5
Feb^y	15	Turnpike gate 44 sheep			5
	22	Turnpike gate 6 Beasts and a Man to drive them		1	0
	29	Turnpike gate 6 Beast and a man to drive them		1	0

* Possibly some kind of yarn (Filace?).

			£	s.	d.
March	7	Turnpike gate 4 Beast and a man to drive them		1	0
	30	2 Balls Filis			10
		2 dzn. 10 eggs		2	10
June	5	Paid Mr Forkner for carting three fat pigs		7	6
	7	2 Balls Filis			10
July	3	2 skid irons		7	0
	17	Canister Powder		2	6
	19	Paid J. Over for 14 gallons Beer 1 S for Haying and Driling		14	0
Sept^r	29	2 Balls filis			10

Last, on the two unruled fly leaves at the end of the book, these entries :

Left-hand page:

June   4   Whashed 194 sheep.

Feb^y   8   Sold Ja^s Miles about 3200 hop poles £22. 8. 0. at 14 shillings pr hundred.

March 4   Sold to Mr Ellis £1. 14. 1700 fagots at 2 shillings pr. Hun^d.

(The 194 sheep which were washed on June 4 are doubtless those which are entered on a previous page as having been sheared on June 18.)

Right-hand page:

Bay Mare	April 25
White Sow	Novr 3rd–Feby 29th
1 Black Sow	Novr 3–Feby 25th
1 Black Sow	Novr 25–March 16
White Sow	Novr 25–March 21
March 17	White Sow
Black Mare	April 19
May 24	two Black Sows
27	one White Sow.

These entries, which no doubt are of stock-breeding, are the last in the book. As to one other set of entries, the notes of payments of turnpike gate-money, I can trace from local inquiry nothing much further. Here and there remains a building, as for instance a tiny wayside house on the road from Witley to Chiddingfold, and here and there a name, such as Gaston Gate, on the road north from Cranleigh. But of local memory or tradition of such payments, made less than a century ago, I can hear nothing. In the Haslemere Museum, however, are two of the original wooden boards showing the official charges. See the chapter "Three Museums."

CHAPTER XII

WOMEN'S INSTITUTES

THIS chapter is not a history of Women's Institutes. But it can be interesting to set by the side of first beginnings the happenings of later days, and here for remembrance' sake is the tale of the birth of the first Women's Institute of all.

It was at Stoney Creek, in the fruit belt of Ontario, Canada. There, in 1897, Mr Erland Lee, member of one of the Farmers' Institutes which have done so much good in Canada and the United States, invited Mrs John Hoodless (whom he had previously heard lecturing on domestic science at Guelph, the capital of Ontario) to address a mixed audience of men and women. The address was such a success that it was decided to organize "a Women's Department of Domestic Economy in affiliation with the Farmers' Institute." This department held its first meeting on 25 February 1897, and as a consequence of the meeting decided to be called "The Women's Institute of Stoney Creek."

That was the beginning of the whole movement. And the official historian comments on the fitness and significance of names and dates. First, it was in the year of Queen Victoria's Diamond Jubilee that this original Women's Institute got going. This is significant because, though institutes "really belong to the twentieth century," they "pride themselves on preserving all that is best in the ideals of Victorian days."

Next, the name—Stoney Creek. "It was because the farmers' wives of Stoney Creek became acutely aware of the *hardness* and *narrowness* of their lives that they determined to band together and sow the unlovely soil with the seeds of fellowship."

And the names of those who helped start the movement. "For their first president," the story goes on, the members "chose Mrs Hoodless, whose name quaintly suggests that she had 'come out of her shell,' and the first lecturer to counsel them in their task of making the wilderness to blossom was Miss Laura Rose."

That was in 1897, and for a summary of the facts I am indebted to Mr J. W. Robertson Scott's *Story of the Women's Institutes*, published in 1925. Mr Robertson Scott, editor of the *Countryman*, has faced and succeeded in many difficult tasks in his time, but I doubt if he ever faced and finished a harder labour than the piecing together, from a thousand sources, the story of the greatest social movement of the English countryside.

To-day (1945) the Women's Institutes throughout the country number 5,887, of which 129 belong to Surrey. No political party could afford to ignore, or indeed would think of ignoring, resolutions passed by the institutes at their annual meeting in the Albert Hall. As good an example as we are likely to see of the influence exerted by such resolutions was the passing in 1933 of the Bill making illegal the taking for sale, or selling, of British singing birds. This Bill was opposed in all its stages by a small section of the House of Commons, headed by Major J. W. Hills, on the strange grounds that it "carried with it class legislation" in that it "affected very largely the class that kept birds." Another member opposed the Bill "because it came from the House of Lords." If anything could have been needed to show the absurdity of such arguments, it was the resolution passed by 8,000 delegates of Women's Institutes at the Albert Hall meeting in 1933, in favour of the Bill. This resolution was put before the meeting by a delegate from the Surrey village of Hambledon, and I do not think it is overstating probabilities to suggest that the unanimous vote of those 8,000 delegates influenced the Prime Minister, Mr Ramsay Macdonald, when he made the Bill a Government measure in the ensuing autumn, so that it then and there became the law of the land.

There will be other resolutions of the same kind, I do not doubt, in the future, and other Prime Ministers will pay them the same attention. For it is as a consequence of long experience of Women's Institutes that it has become realized by politicians and plain men alike that a vote carried by

Women's Institutes, either at the vast concourse of an annual general meeting or at a monthly gathering in a village, represents English common sense, whether you or they are talking of national needs or cooking parsnips.

Here, for example—and I think the intelligent foreigner could learn therefrom something of the history of England—are extracts from two programmes. They are of the monthly meetings of the Women's Institute of a small village in southwest Surrey, Hambledon, and show in turn the title of the lecture, or talk, or debate at each meeting, the subjects chosen for competition, and (I only give a few examples of these) the motto or quotation chosen for the month. One of the programmes is for a date in peacetime, the other for a year during the recent war. Here is the first:

January 11
    To be usefully and hopefully employed is one of the secrets of happiness.—SMILES.
Talk: Dressmaking—renovations and children's clothes.
Competition: Child's frock, hand-sewn, not to cost more than 1s 6d.
February 8
    Nature is the living visible garment of God.—GOETHE.
Talk: The growing of plants from seed, bulbs or cuttings, with demonstrations.
Competition: List of twelve "don'ts" in gardening. Collection of Eggs for a Hospital.
March 8
    Rough ways often lead to great heights and views of beauty.—ASTER.
Lantern Lecture: Art and Folk Customs in the Tyrol.
Competition: Bulbs.
    Friday, 31 March, 10.30 a.m.—Annual Meeting of the Surrey Federation at the Market Hall, Redhill.
April 12
    Have I not told how the Universe has nothing better than the best Womanhood.—WALT WHITMAN.
Debate: The Married Woman and the Spinster.
Competition: Knitted fancy scarf.

May 10

> Costly thy habit as thy purse can buy,
> But not expressed in fancy; rich, not gaudy :
> For the apparel oft proclaims the man.
>
> —SHAKESPEARE—*Hamlet.*

Talk : Agenda of the National Federation Annual Meeting.

Competition : Dress Parade of home-made dresses, material not to cost more than 5s.

June 7.—Annual Meeting of the National Federation at the Empress Hall, Earl's Court.

June 14.—Garden Meeting.

> It is a comely fashion to be glad
> Joy is the grace we say to God.
>
> —JEAN INGELOW.

Dance Demonstration.

Competition : Best list of names of the flowers seen in the garden at the meeting.

July 12.—Garden Meeting.

Talk : Rural Architecture.

Competition : Best plan of a six-roomed cottage.

August 9.—Garden Meeting.

Talk : League of Nations Union Speaker.

Competition : Best home-made handkerchief with an initial.

September 13.—Garden Meeting.

> What do we live for if it is not to make life less difficult for each other?—GEORGE ELIOT.

> Members' Meeting and Hambledon Old Ladies' Tea Party.

Competition : Best bottle of home-made wine.

Special Competition : Potatoes.

October 11

Talk : Technique of Acting.

Competition : Best exhibit of potatoes cooked in a variety of ways.

November 8

Talk : British Empire Cancer Campaign Speaker.

Competition : Menu of the midday meal of a man and his wife, a child of four and a grandmother for a week.

December 13.—Annual Meeting.

Demonstration : Knitting and sewing for exhibition.

Competition : Best-dressed doll, cost not to exceed 6d, not including the doll.

Election of next year's Committee.

Exhibition of members' work done during the year.

Collection of Christmas stockings for Children's Hospitals.

That was a pre-war programme. And here are some of the items in the programme for 1945 :

January 10

Talk : Holland, Land of Dykes and Windmills.

Competition : Telegrams.

February 19.—Cookery Demonstration.

Competition : Dried-milk and Egg Custard.

March 14

Speaker—British Empire Society.

April 11

May 9

Politeness is like an air cushion—there may be nothing in it, but it eases the joints wonderfully.

Talk on Birds.

Competition : Darned woollen socks.

June 13

Demonstration on Glove-making.

Competition : Naming Wild Flowers.

July 11

Talk on Madame Curie.

Competition : Cleaned Leather Shoe.

July 21

Produce Guild Show.

August 8

Talk : Soft Toys.

This was a garden gathering, and I, as in other years, after the women's meeting, was able to join with those who had been present. There are few pleasures greater, for one whose chief happiness is in garden sights and sounds, than to accompany village friends by flower beds and borders. They have their own gardens of flowers, as they have their fruit trees and vegetables, and their quiet comments are those of judges. August is the month of phloxes, heliotrope, geraniums, marigolds, sunflowers, and they see in another gardener's grouping and perspective comparisons with what they grow in their own. Here and there a shrub or a tree will be new to them; I am the lucky possessor of *Eucryphias* of different heights and ages, given to me years ago, and these in August are a perpetual source of pleasure and surprise, with their branches rich under blue and cloud with white, roselike flowers humming with bees. August is a silent month for birds, but you may hope for the woodpigeons' croon, *Tak two coos, tak two,* mingled with village talk and praise.

But the Produce Guild Show of July deserves a word to itself. All Women's Institutes have their Produce Guilds, but I had the good fortune to be present at the first exhibition held in Hambledon, and to see for the first time what a small village community can bring together.

I had no idea how good and how varied the produce could be. Bottled fruit, jam, honey, potatoes, eggs, any and every kind of green vegetable—I looked at stall after stall, and could see very little difference in the quality of exhibits from those of far bigger shows held in other days. Peas, for example; there the pods lay split open—could any peas anywhere be greener, younger, larger, more obviously fit for the table? Or beans, broad or runner; or lettuces—were there ever any crisper or fresher?—or cabbages better worth boiling, or potatoes newer or cleaner, or salads more compact of everything with which salads should invite? Who would not be a vegetarian? Honey was there, in sections and jars, and where should bees have a better chance of storing for themselves and ourselves than in the Surrey countryside? I heard, by the way, the remark that bees got much good from willowherb, the "fire-flower" that to-day clothes so many acres of what was once Surrey woodland; I had never thought of the fire-flower, except for its beauty, bringing any benefit to the countryside. Then there were eggs, with separate awards for white and brown, and one of the three judges who had travelled to our village especially to help us (that is one of the happiest points about Women's Institutes, the way they all help each other) told us how to judge an egg—a thing I had hardly thought of outside an egg-cup.

At this gathering a last surprise awaited me. There had

been an award offered to children for the largest number of dead white butterflies. And there were no competitors. I suppose that most members of the institutes in any part of England know that the caterpillars of certain white butterflies eat cabbages, though probably not all of them could tell you which are the only two whose grubs do harm, or how many other species of white butterflies there are which are completely harmless. At all events, here at this Hambledon Women's Institute exhibition there were no entries for the butterfly-killing prize, and I was glad for the children of our village.

CHAPTER XIII

FALLOW DEER TO FROGS

IT can happen to few of us in Surrey to-day to be able to chronicle anything new in natural history. That is true especially as regards animals. But we may have our own experiences, perhaps differing from or at all events worth comparing with those of others. I have lived most of my life in the south-west corner of Surrey, within a few miles of the borders of Hampshire and Sussex—a district less altered than most of Surrey by building—and here are a few entries from the notebook of memory.

First, of deer. If you look at the maps of those three counties, Surrey, Sussex and Hampshire, you will see that there is a big triangle, with its apex at Guildford and its base running from Petersfield to Horsham, of almost uninterrupted woodland country. Beyond Petersfield east through Romsey lies the New Forest, beyond Horsham St. Leonard's Forest, woodlands throughout. It is all of it country in which, at all events till the last few years, which have altered so much that was old and quiet, deer could live and sleep and breed. Deer live in these woods to-day.

That can be said with certainty at least of fallow deer. All through these woods of south-west Surrey deer are natives. And if we may believe, as I believe, that fallow deer are indigenous to England, we may hold that the deer which sleep in our woods and run through our gardens to-day—I found the slot in my kitchen garden only three days before writing these words—are directly descended from primeval English ancestors. That is to me a happy thought, looking at droppings along larch trees or tracks in snow on a newly sown field of corn. There have been crosses of English blood with foreign, of course, for the story of English kings and queens is full of records of such importations, and there must have been many escapes from time to time from the herds of Surrey parks. But I should guess that always, since England was an island, fallow deer have shed antlers and dropped

157

fawns in Surrey woods, and that even to-day, perhaps, the deer who ran through my garden may have found woodland still untouched and quiet enough for courtship and easy feeding.

That used to be so once, I am sure, but the past few years have brought changes. How great those are it is hard to say; perhaps only a complete survey, or census, of areas once covered with trees could establish the point. I can only speak with personal knowledge of a few acres, and as regards those the change came with the war of 1939. Not many months had passed before communications reached me of which the purport was that it was desired to inspect certain areas of woodland of which I was the owner. Inspection duly followed and a correspondence, the gist of which was that it would be as well to be a willing seller, else purchase might follow without choice in the matter. So the trees disappeared. Some of them I did not regret, for they were big old trees which seemed to be dying one by one, and it was clearly better that they should be felled while the sap was still running and the grain of wood sound, rather than that they should come to an end by wind and beetles. But there were others which were young trees still, and growing.

There was one deciding factor in any case. Larch trees are only a crop after all. It was Gertrude Jekyll who first made me realize that, talking over the felling of certain trees on Hydons Ball, the hill on the flank of which my house stands. Larch trees must be cut some day, soon or late; that is their fate and purpose. So they were cut, young and old, the old trees whose rings I counted to make their age one hundred and eight years, and the young trees which I knew to be forty-four. They were cut, and the woods that they had spread about us vanished. I remembered, as I saw them day by day disappearing, the sorrow with which other writers before me had seen the same thing; I thought of J. A. Gibbs in his Cotswold village watching the timber merchants carrying away the elms which he had hoped would frame a cricket ground, as on Upper Club where he had played at Eton. And of Theodore de Banville :

"*Nous n'irons plus au bois, les lauriers sont coupés*. And the deer among the trees—

Les lauriers sont coupés, et le cerf aux abois
Tressaille au son du cor; nous n'irons plus au bois . . ."

Well, my trees too were cut down. And the deer? I wondered. Would they still run where the larches and birches
had sheltered them? Where would they sleep? I found some
sort of an answer to the questions even while the larches
were being felled, for I could see their slot in the fields and
droppings in what remained of the woods, but it was a
different countryside for miles, and it might be that soon the
sense of the herd would tell them that their home was gone.
How long would it be before that loss, too, would add itself
to the consequences of war?

Memories of earlier days remain with me. First and chief
is the memory of a fawn, of a graceful young thing so close
to me that even then I found myself thinking of Lewis
Carroll and Tenniel's inspired drawing, so near was I to
wonderland. I have written of that morning—to-day it seems
the vision of a dream—in *English Wild Life*. I can hear
again, after all the years, the patter of the fawn's light feet,
I can see the dark eyes of the young creature trotting up to
me as I sat among the chestnut trees. And then the wind
changed, perhaps, or I moved, and the fawn knew its danger
and leapt away from me. I sat waiting, and the mother came
following out of the trees, saw me and bounded after her
young one into the greenwood.

That was the happiness of a dream. There are other sides
to such chances of the woods. Only a few yards from where
I sat that morning in the chestnuts I was walking a year or
two later down a ride, when I came upon a sight I had not
guessed could be possible. On the slope of a bank lay a young
fallow buck, dead—choked by a wire noose. It was a snare
carefully set, with knowledge of the track of deer in that
wood, of the height at which the creature carried his head
and of the way he must fall from the bank to strangle himself. I have never been sadder over a wild creature's end.
And I never knew how the snare was set, or by whom. By
gipsies, we supposed, for in those days there were many of
them in the lanes, and the woods all round had been very
wild places till the builder came into that part of Surrey, but
if it was a gipsy who knotted that noose he never followed

up his night's work. Perhaps he was wanted for something else and had moved on.

Since those earlier days of my life in Surrey I have walked and driven many miles through woods and commons and have seen few deer. Turning the corner in a quiet car, perhaps, I have come across buck and does from time to time, and have had that bright glimpse now and then of graceful creatures raising their heads and leaving the glade as empty and silent as woods can be. And I have thought often over the question that these deer in Surrey set to those who look for them, knowing that they must be within a certain limited space of countryside and yet seeing them so seldom. How and where do they spend their lives? There must be many of these wild creatures within a few miles of me as I write these words, yet if I were to be set the task of looking for them I should not know how or where to begin.

It is a curious contrast, the life of fallow deer in a park and in the woods. I can walk from my garden to-day through woods and lanes to the borders of a park two miles away and look out over the wall at a herd of deer grazing in sunlight, careless on that open turf of the traffic whose sound comes to them from dawn to dusk, and yet I know, as I look at them, that there must be other deer perhaps as near to me as they, hiding in the shelter of the woodland I have passed through. For the deer of the park life by day is in sunshine, unfearing of the men driving close to them by road, while all through the day other deer are hiding in bushes outside the park wall, in fear of men going about their daily work. In the park the deer feed by day on grass set apart for them, and sleep by night; outside the park wall others sleep by day, and by night come out to feed wherever they find food near them, perhaps in crops of farm fields, perhaps in allotments or cottage gardens. We who live near them do not see them, and no doubt if we did they would be shot, for a cottager does not grow food for trespassers, but I have wished often that I could watch deer in Surrey outside a park.

Fallow deer are still with us, but I am not sure about roe. For myself, I have only once seen a roebuck, and that was in the early days of the first German war, when I was driving

The King's Stone, Kingston-on-Thames

down a lane on the business of calling up reservists of the army, and a buck dropped over the ledge on my right, trotted quietly in front of the car for twenty or thirty yards and leapt over the hedge again. And as it happened it was from one of those very reservists that I next heard of roedeer in Surrey. He was an old regular soldier who had been employed in a garden near, and as I was talking to him one night when on duty as one of the guard over the Chilworth powder factory, he told me that roedeer ate his roses and that he used to wait up at night for them with a shotgun. He was afraid that they would finish his roses while he was on sentry duty, but I thought it more likely that actually the war would finish the deer, for food was scarce and shooting was not then a difficulty. But I was wrong, for twenty years later, on 3 April 1935, two of my sons, setting out with spades on a digging quest in the Tolt, a wooded hill near the house—a quest of which I write elsewhere—put up a roedeer from the brambles, and by a quaint coincidence one of them startled a roe in the same place on the same day two years later. More, for on 4 April 1941, the other son walking with my daughter in the woods half a mile away caught sight of a buck and a doe. And so in the second German war the numbers of roe in the neighbourhood may have been not very different from those in the first. If so, and if no more woods need be felled, there is still hope for the most beautiful of wild creatures. They fed on a neighbour's roses when I first heard of them, and I could watch them to-day— perhaps not for very long—if they were hungry among mine.

Of another native of this island, less graceful to look at but with as ancient a right of possession, I find it difficult to write with regard to dates and numbers. I have written in another chapter of my first acquaintance with Surrey badgers, by night on a hill at Chilworth, and since that early introduction I have come to know them as neighbours near at hand—at one time too near for pleasure. For many years after I first came to live at Hambledon all I saw of badgers was an occasional glimpse of a grey creature by the side of the road, caught in the light of a motor-car driven by night : I remember in particular one night, or rather early morning, when driving down home from London I caught sight of a

M 161

badger opposite Busbridge Church in the middle of the road, puzzled evidently by the glare of the headlights; then, as we stopped the car, it shuffled to the side of the bank, slipped through the iron fencing and was gone. Next day I came back that way to measure the space between the rails and found it less than four and a half inches. That was the nearest knowledge I was to have of badgers for several years. I knew of an earth in the bank of a lane, about a mile from the house, where the dug-out soil used to tumble into the narrow roadway, and I had heard, too, of badgers in a neighbour's garden; I remember Sir Herbert Jekyll telling me of the damage they had done to his lawn at Munstead. But of first-hand knowledge of the harm a badger could do in a garden I had none, and little thought what it could be or mean to a gardener.

Then came the spring of 1940. I never knew whether it was a single badger or a pair, nor at first did I realize what was happening, for the damage done was very like what I had seen before on the edge of a golf green, and that, the greenkeeper told me, had been done by rooks. And I remember thinking at the time, looking at the divots of turf lying next holes and scattered soil, that it must be in that way that rooks get the earthy tufts of grass they need for the foundations of their nests. But I was soon to learn that the earth diggers were not rooks. A badger was digging for Joe Bassetts—the Surrey name for the grub of the cockchafer— I was told by a gardener as soon as he set eyes on the scraps of turf, and that it was indeed a badger soon became plain by other traces which he left behind him, and which destroyed for me the name given him by other observers of his habits. It was my old friend J. E. Harting, for fifty years editor of the natural history columns of the *Field*, who first wrote, I believe, of the badger as a cleanly animal which dug holes into which to deposit its droppings, and it was he who gave it the name of the inventor of the earth closet. But the badger who dug for Joe Bassetts in my lawns had no thought for hiding any of his misdeeds. Wherever he dug he also befouled the ground, and left his traces for all to see. As for Joe Bassett—I would give much, by the way, to discover the origin of that nickname, universal in south-west Surrey, and

I believe also in neighbouring parts of Hampshire and Sussex —he seemed to me to dig anywhere and everywhere, on the chance of finding food; or else the scent of the cockchafer grub is so universally pervading that it infects the soil for yards together.

Whatever may be the facts as to Joe Bassett, what was plain enough for months after badgers came to look for him in my garden was the extent of the damage. There were two stretches of turf in which Joe lurked and his hunter looked for him. One was a piece of sloping ground leading down from the house to the rock garden; that was the first place in which badgers dug, and for months together they came every night. The other was on a level rectangle of grass originally intended for tennis, and surely no tennis lawn was ever more thoroughly excavated. It measures sixty yards by thirty, and over every square yard of the surface there were holes and upturned roots. I tried to discover from which direction the diggers came, and where they had come from, but in vain. The whole garden is surrounded by wire netting, but badgers care no more for those feet of wire than they do for five-barred oak gates, and I never could trace entrance or exit. They came always by night, and I suppose if I or a gardener had sat up through a spring or summer night we might between us have got a shot at one—there was a March morning in which before dawn I once caught sight of a grey form among azaleas—but neither of us chanced the loss of a night's sleep that way. As for setting a trap, I would sooner lose lawns, and the flowers round them too for that matter, than hurt the air and the memories of a garden with that hideous instrument, the steel gin. So badgers had their way with turf and Joe Bassett for three years and more, when, of a sudden, damage came to an end. Spring came in 1943, and no badger woke from sleep to climb wire netting and dig. What was the end of him, or of his wife, or the two of them, or others beside them, I never heard or knew. There are still badgers on the hills and in the woods near. They may return.

Of another animal I write not in doubt or uncertainty, but with sadness. I am afraid there are no hares to-day in my part of Surrey. There were few when I first came to live at

Hambledon, and wisely or unwisely I tried to add to their numbers. In those days—they belonged to a time of life when I used to shoot—you could buy hares in Norfolk and set them at large in other woods, so I bought a small number for a few shillings apiece, and put them out in an enclosure of wire netting I had made in the woods. I had tried the same experiment with some success years before in Sussex and I hoped for the same result. And I succeeded for a time. The hares I let loose bred and increased, so that actually one day I counted six full-grown hares in the same field, my favourite field, Great Bettams by name, close to the house. More than that, hares actually chose my garden as a place in which to add to their numbers, so that I had the experience more than once of being able to pick up a couple of leverets only a few days old—surely the loveliest little blue-eyed creatures in the world—and to look at them in the palm of my hand. And then, how and when exactly I never knew, the whole story ended. There were no more hares anywhere to be seen. I suspected gipsies, and I was probably right; it was a gipsy, I believe, as I have already said, who snared a fallow fawn in the same woods where my hares had been. At all events, there is not a hare to be seen to-day for miles around. Gardeners are not displeased, for hares prefer carnations to plainer food. But I miss the leverets.

Other animals there are whom I should never miss. Young rabbits, I admit, are pretty little creatures, to be dropped the other side of wire netting if you can catch them rather than put out of reach of wire netting for ever. But rabbits full grown who is to tolerate? Not a gardener, of all men. Even in a field, even in a hedgerow, a rabbit destroys and befouls all he touches; in a garden he is beyond any other pest execrable. He scratches holes in lawns, five or six in a night, not with the object of making a burrow, for that would mean purpose, of which he has none; he just scratches little holes, and by the side of each hole shows it was he. In the kitchen garden he swallows lettuces, cabbages, broccoli, peas; in the flower border he gnaws pinks to the ground. And you cannot catch him. That is to say if you have a gardener who is also a countryman, and who can see rabbits' "jumps" in long grass (if you have any long grass), your gardener may be able to snare a rabbit, or two, or three; but he will never be able to snare the last rabbit in the garden, or, if he does, another one, or two or three, will take its place. Probably there is only one possible way of catching a rabbit in a garden, and that is by setting a gin, which is the one trap I would never set, not even for a rabbit.

I think that I must have had more experience of rabbits than anyone else living in Surrey. When I first came to live in Hambledon, when it first became my good fortune to spend day and night in the happiest garden and in sight of the most wonderful view in south-east England, I used to drive in a cab once a week, perhaps, along a little lane near where the house I live in was being built. I remember those drives for the strangest sight of rabbits I could imagine. Cobbett in *Rural Rides* writes of a farm on Salisbury Plain on which he saw "an acre of hares." Well, on a field to the left of the lane along which I used to drive, I saw not an acre, but more, of rabbits. On an old map which I possess (see p. 144) there are three fields, named Upper High Field, Lower High Field and Crowledge Field. Upper High Field when I first knew it was a plantation of larches mounting to a hilltop named from time beyond memory the Tolt. Lower High Field and Crowledge Field had then been merged into one, an area in all of twenty-three acres, and when I first set eyes on those acres they were brown with rabbits. So was the side of the lane brown with their burrows. I had never before, and I have never since, seen such a sight. There was no question of farming those fields; nothing could have grown in them; so far as I know, indeed, there was no attempt to farm them, and until the golf links were laid out on the other side of the lane, and houses came gradually into the neighbourhood, they were derelict.

That was thirty-five years ago and more. Since I first drove down that lane with its lining of burrows, county council cottages have sprung up by the side of a tar-smooth road, a great sanatorium, twin to another two miles away, has spread wide its wards, St. Thomas's Hospital has fled from the Thames in London into what used to be bluebells and bracken in Surrey, and with doctors, surgeons, nurses, chapels, cottages and cars the countryside has gone. But still the burrows run deep into the flank of the Tolt, and still the County War Agricultural Executive Committee, with gas or any other contrivance, cannot get rid of the rabbits.

I wish moles would not hunt in rock gardens. I ought to wish, I supose, that they would not dig their runs in hayfields or anywhere else, but it is only in the rock garden that to me, personally, moles are a nuisance and have to be stopped from damage. Otherwise they are creatures as fascinating in their shape and their coats as in the problems of their lives to which nobody knows the answer. For silkiness and texture of fur the mole is unlike any other animal, and of the questions which it sets you could only get a solution by following it underground. I have written in *The Gardener's England* about the length of a mole run, the only one I have tried to measure; I can get as far as four hundred and thirty yards in garden, field and wood adjoining, but that is leaving out the measurements of the side galleries. And in particular there is one measurement which I do not know how to attempt—the length of the run here and there underground. On one patch of a small lawn at the back of the house there appears now and then a mole heap, or there may be two or three. But how far the heap or heaps may be from other runs with which they are connected I cannot even guess. There is no other mole heap within a hundred yards, and I am left wondering whether there is an underground run between the two. If so, it has been there undisturbed for at least thirty years, and for all I know for three hundred.

In the *Victoria County History* the editors mention a collection of mole skins made by Mr Reeves of Reigate, twenty-seven in different colours, orange, white, buff, grey, even pink. In my own experience, orange is the commonest variant, perhaps local and possibly peculiar to a family; at all events two have been brought to me in recent years taken in the same few yards of run. But orange has not been the full description of the fur that would be given by a taxidermist. One of the two shown to me was partly orange and partly cream, its nose was olive and its tail was banded with grey.

Of the four other insectivora, the hedgehog, common,

166

pigmy and water-shrew, the first two are doubtless common enough, but it is odd how seldom one sees a hedgehog. Years ago, when I lived at Weybridge, there was a hedgehog that came now and then into the house and drank from a saucer set before him, and Miss Martineau, designer of the bird-bath which bears her name, who was a Weybridge neighbour, used to attract hedgehogs nightly across her lawn with milk. But at Hambledon, for whatever reason, hedgehogs seem to be scarce. It was some ten years ago that a gardener called me to look at a family he had found as he was clearing some rough undergrowth : the mother had chosen a bird's nest, a chiff-chaff's or willow-wren's, as a nursery, and there were the three little ones in their pale, soft spines. But I have not seen a hedgehog since, and if it were not for occasional droppings I should not know there was one in the garden.

"So few persons are aware of the existence of this species" —the water-shrew—"that it has been found difficult to gauge its distribution in Surrey." Thus I read in the *Victoria History*. I think it must be fairly common. True, I have only once come across it at close quarters, and that was ten years ago, but if it were rare it is unlikely that I should have seen it at all. In my rock garden I have a number of small pools, and one morning I was summoned to watch a mysterious creature which was attacking frogs. I found a partly eaten frog on a ledge of stone, and there in the water among lily leaves I watched a dark, glistening creature not only battling with frogs, but catching hold when and where it could of young golden orfe, tenants of the pond, frog or orfe one after the other. At last we marked him down into a hole, and between us we set a run-through trap at the mouth and kept watch. Within half an hour he was in it, and biting furiously at the perforated zinc that closed it. I gave him the remains of the frog he had half-eaten, and he finished it ; then I put him back into the pool.

What are the colours of a water-shrew's fur and paws? In an extraordinarily interesting account of a mass migration of water-shrews in Upper Teesdale, sent by Lady Seton to the May 1945 number of the *Journal of the Society for the Preservation of the Fauna of the Empire,* she writes of a solid stream of shrews swimming up against the stream in hundreds, possibly thousands. "They followed along in a solid procession, pressed closely together. I saw no white ears, the fur coats were a pale, dull brown, but the outstanding thing was the long pointed snout and paws of a brilliant rose red." In a subsequent letter she adds : "As to the colour of the fur, I have wished ever since that I had expressed it differently. They were almost exactly the colour of the rock under them. Browns are so difficult to describe—not *black* certainly—but the dark wet rock is a deep brown. My impression of the rose colour was that it was skin, and that their fur stopped short of the long pointed noses, and of the forepaws, showing the pink skin." And in a postscript—"One word more about the colour of the fur on their backs— Philip Gosse writes of water-shrews dressed in black velvet. He, you, and others are describing the shrews on land and dry. I watched them *through* water."

In the same number that talented writer Phyllis Kelway, whose early death a few weeks before the *Journal* was published saddened all her readers, describes the colouring thus : "Many of the water-shrews I have caught have had white ear-tufts. From my notes I would suggest one in twelve. Often, too, there is a small cluster of white hairs above the tiny eyes. Generally the back is blue-black and the belly dirty white or very white. The feet are lightly covered with hairs of a whitish grey or clerical grey."

From notes I kept at the time, when I watched my water-shrew hunting frogs, I find that my gardener described the coat as black. My own remembrance of it is of a creature the colour of shining lead under water, and dull, dark grey in the air. As for the feet, I can remember nothing of pink. Except for short, light hairs, I should have said they were like the feet of a house mouse.

But water-shrews cannot be rare in south-west Surrey. Until I made my rock garden there was no water nearer than a mile from the hill on which the house stands. How this particular shrew discovered that there was a tiny stream with frogs in the pool it is hard to guess, but there must surely be others in the ponds and tributaries of the Wey not far off. Water-shrews are tiny creatures, and not often noticed; that must be why "few persons are aware" of them.

There is one animal which used to be common and which to-day I believe does not exist in Surrey. That is the red squirrel. I have written in another chapter of my first introduction to Surrey squirrels, and I have only one sad memory of the years I spent at Weybridge, and that is of the day when we left the house and garden we had lived in for nine years, and I knew I should not see again the squirrel I had come to know so well. I filled a bowl of nuts for him, and left it on the windowsill of my study; that was all I could do. But I hoped even then for other squirrels at Hambledon, and for a year or two I used to see them in the new garden we were making. And then? War came in 1914, and squirrels were forgotten with other things. I do not know when it was that we realized what had happened; perhaps about 1930, for I find I was writing in *English Wild Life* a couple of years before, of grey squirrels as a menace, but of red squirrels as still existent. Then in 1930 came the resolve of the *Field* to institute a movement from which developed the National Anti-Grey Squirrel Campaign, with its long list of supporting societies and no less a personage as its president than the Marquess of Salisbury. A second war has not helped matters; indeed, I suppose that nothing has added to the numbers of the pest more than the absence during years of war than its natural enemy the gamekeeper and the difficulty of plain people such as gardeners in getting small-bore cartridges. At all events, the grey squirrel, introduced by the Duke of Bedford at the beginning of the century, and let loose from Regent's Park into the countryside by the Zoological Society, has to-day completely exterminated our native red squirrel wherever the two have met, and to-day is recognized as the arch-enemy of bird life, the thief of the orchard and kitchen garden, and an introduction from abroad of danger to English fauna of which the half is not yet guessed.

One of the animals on which war has brought an unhappy fate in Surrey, as in other counties, has been the fox. Ten years in the present century during which hunting has been carried on with difficulty have meant that foxes have had to be kept down by processes which everybody hates. If they had been left alone what would have happened? Poultry-keepers would have suffered, doubtless; though, for that matter, Government during the war did not greatly encourage poultry-keeping. And against losses of poultry we could certainly have put to the foxes' credit the destruction of large quantities of rabbits and rats, both of which in the absence of their natural enemies were left to breed at large. But in any case—and this is a question which hunting in years of peace deprives of an answer—what is the average length of a fox's life? When does a fox die a natural death? I have only known one case which could be described in that way. Years ago, walking in the woods near my home, I used sometimes to hear near me a queer sort of half-cough, half-choke in the brambles or the young hazel; once, I remember, a spaniel who was with me stopped and went into the hazel, but nothing more happened. Then, one day, I heard the sound so close that I myself went into the hazel to look, but I could see nothing. And a few days afterwards there was found, close by the kitchen door of a neighbour's house the thin, wasted body of a fox. Examination showed that it had died of consumption; both lungs were gone. I thought again of the coughing I had heard near me in the woods; I thought of the place where the fox had lain down to die; it was as if in its suffering the wild creature was somehow asking for help.

I have written in another chapter of a polecat which I saw one day during the time when I was stationed with the guard over the powder factory at Chilworth during the war of 1914. It was during those same years that another polecat appeared in the woods near my house, leaving behind him the unmistakable evidence of two rabbits killed per day, polecat fashion, with holes torn in the back of the neck. I had hoped to be able to catch sight of this visitor, but he timed his depredations in periods when I was away from home, and so far as I know no polecat has been seen in Surrey since. Of a much rarer animal I first heard news in the winter of 1935. It was a pine-marten, stuffed and in a glass case, which I was invited to look at in a gamekeeper's cottage, and its story belongs partly to the history of Surrey road-making—the laying-out of the bypass that runs from Guildford to Milford, an invasion of machinery into Surrey woodland for centuries inviolate.

There, perhaps, lies the secret of so rare an animal's survival. It was caught in a tunnel-trap in May 1934, when some old trees were being cut in a wood belonging to the Peper Harow estate of Lord Midleton—an out-of-the-way part of a large area of quiet countryside. The keeper's boy who found it in the trap thought it was a young fox cub, but luckily it was shown to a neighbouring farmer who happens to be a good naturalist, and he gave it its name at once. Questions were asked in likely quarters, but obviously it was unlikely that it had escaped from captivity, so in due course it was set up in a case, and a very fine animal it looks with its bare teeth and a paw on its prey.

How it had escaped notice for so long remained a problem, for it was an old creature, as you could see by its worn-down teeth. But pine-martens in captivity have been known to reach seventeen years, and after all a gamekeeper does not sow every acre of his woods with traps. My mind went back when I saw it to a pine-marten I had watched once in the London Zoo, a creature that seemed happy enough, perfectly tame and dancing about in its cage. At all events, it was the first pine-marten to be recorded in Surrey for thirty years. In his *Mammals of Great Britain and Ireland* J. G. Millais mentions that Mr George Lodge, that talented naturalist and painter of game birds, saw a single marten in a wood near Dorking in 1904.

I pass to reptiles. I do not repeat here what I have written elsewhere of Hundred Acre, that noble expanse of ploughland edged with downland turf, thyme, bramble, birches, heather and known far and near as an abode of adders. Some day, perhaps, I shall see another adder as handsome as the orange and black captive which I released on Hundred Acre from a schoolboy's butterfly net, and there may come a time when I shall set eyes on a second grass-snake to compare with the six-foot wanderer in my orchard, which I was able to measure as it crossed a path, head in the hedge and tail still touching the grass the other side. Those are memories of summer days gone.

Memories of winter are fewer. One, perhaps, is worth a note here, since it was in a Surrey garden that there began the chronicling of a new theory of the life of frogs in winter. I have written the story in full in *Oddities of Natural History,* and I do not repeat it here except, so to speak, for the date of birth. It was in the winter of 1929 that, working in my rock garden, I heard a frog croaking near me. I was surprised, for I had been brought up on the statement of Robert Bell, author of the *History of British Reptiles and Amphibians* (1792–1880), who writes of frogs spending the winter in a state of absolute torpidity, generally in mud under water. I was led to question Bell's accuracy, and did so in the *Field,* which led to the publication of various letters on the subject, proving conclusively that whatever may have been the facts which led Bell a hundred years ago to his belief, stated in print and copied and adopted by writer after writer ever since, frogs at the present day do not as a rule hibernate under water.

This way of putting the case—"not as a rule"—may be regarded as an understatement. But a full and careful exposition of the life of frogs is needed. I cannot doubt that it will some day be made. Meanwhile, as a very small individual contribution to such a study, I add to the records of a Surrey garden that in winter after winter I have heard frogs croaking, and that in the bitter cold of January 1942 after nineteen days of hard frost I saw, in a pond in which there is no mud but a cement floor and sides built up with bargate stone on which they could get access to the open air, two frogs swimming under thick ice.

One experience I am not likely to repeat. It belongs to a year before the war, when I was broadcasting talks on natural history subjects to schools. A lady in Kingston wrote to tell me that she had in a pond in her garden a white frog with pink eyes. I wrote asking her if she could catch it. She caught it, and added to her kindness by packing it in a basket and taking it to Guildford, so that in due course it found its way to me. When I opened the basket I found not a white but a pale lemon-coloured frog, medium size, with pink eyes. In every other respect it seemed to be quite normal, and I decided to consult that hospitable institution, the Haslemere Educational Museum, with regard to its future. They solved all difficulties by inviting it as a guest, where soon afterwards I saw it comfortably established in a case and supplied with food and water in company with some locally collected natterjack toads.

CHAPTER XIV

BIRDS IN GARDEN AND WILD

March Missel Thrush

Out of the mists of time, this month of March,
Over wide fields, over a river flowing,
From elm-tops crimson-clustering rings out
To cloud and blue a wild, high clarion,
Waking, as once it woke in a wandering boy,
Visions tumultuous as stream or song,
Hope, wonder, welcome, beckoning to new worlds.

I T is not for a plain writer to hope that he may add anything new, of fact or theory, to the study of birds. But he may
set down things of his own experience for others to compare
with theirs; and such comparison, perhaps, might help to
further knowledge. I have never been able to spend hour
after hour, from dawn to dusk, day after day, in watching a
single species; and I have had no remarkable opportunities
of time or place for observing this or that bird's habits of
nesting or feeding or song. But I have thought about birds
and listened to them through many years, and I have lived in
Surrey for the greater part of my life; so that if I write of
what I have seen and known, others coming after me may
think it worth while here or there to set their experience side
by side with mine.

Here, then, I attempt nothing scientific in order or grouping, and if I begin with nuthatches it is because they have
been close to me ever since I came to live in Surrey, in the
two gardens one after another in which I have watched
them; because they are birds of individual habits, unlike any
other of our native birds, and because they offer a problem
to which I know no answer. First, then, for their friendliness.
You are to see it, as a newcomer to places which have been
their family home for generations, within a few days of your

invasion. At Weybridge, where I began my life in Surrey in a garden which had been untouched for months, nuthatches were the beginners in an acquaintance which has grown through the years. Their cheerful greetings asked for an answer, and when the answer took the form of nuts thrown down on the lawn for them, the greetings and the answering nuts became a conversation, so that they would call to me to come out into the garden. We talked to each other in this way all the years I was at Weybridge, and when at last the time came for the change to Hambledon it was only a few weeks before I heard the familiar greeting from the treetops and a new friendship began, with nuts asked for and given in the old way.

And then came the nesting. At Hambledon there were new chances of knowledge. We began making a garden in what had been partly hazel coppice and partly larch wood, and we cut down the larches only gradually, so that on their stems and those of the oaks with which the larch wood was framed there were many sites waiting for nesting-boxes. With the nesting-boxes followed new knowledge. I had hoped for increasing numbers in all the birds which we found when we came, and in particular for more than one or two pairs of nuthatches. We were disappointed. In thirty-five years we have never had more than two pairs nesting in the garden, and in most seasons there has only been one. I know no better example, not even among robins, of the marking out by birds of a territory which a pair will keep to themselves.

Next, for the making of the nest. There are few more curious habits among birds than the nuthatches' treatment of the entrance to the hole in which they build. To the uninitiated in nuthatch architecture it might appear that a nesting-box, comfortably fastened on the north-east side of a stout treetrunk, warm, secure alike from south-westerly gales and the heat of midday sun, free from draughts, entered by a single aperture just larger than a nuthatch's body and even furnished with a strong perch just outside the entrance, would offer the attractions of an ideal home. That is never the view of the nuthatch. He, or she, glances at what is offered them and the reaction is immediate and invariable.

"This is *all* wrong." The entrance hole is far too small. It must be altered at once.

And at once they begin to alter it. The first thing to do is to make the hole larger. This they do by pecking the wood all round the rim until they have made the diameter of the hole perhaps a third wider. Then they contemplate their work, and after due consideration decide that the hole is much too large. So they proceed to make it smaller with a mud plaster. How they make the mud plaster I have been unable to discover. It looks like a sort of mud, but it is not plain mud, which on the sandy hill where my house is built is unobtainable in a dry spring, as swallows discovered the first summer we had beams in a shed. It will last from one nesting season to the next, as I have seen it year after year, stuck round the entrance. It is composed of plain fine sand, as you can see if you take a cake of it off the rim of the hole, but it is of almost bricklike hardness which only crumbles with a good hard pinch. They make this sand plaster, I have come to think, with saliva. It does not yield to the rains of autumn and winter, but sticks firmly in and round the closely pecked wood of the entrance to the box.

After the entrance the next thing to look for is cracks. Nesting-boxes are sometimes made with lids, properly sloped like a roof so as to let the rain run off, but they may not fit to a hundredth of an inch, or perhaps they warp with sun or wet, and possibly the tiniest slit might admit air or light. These slits must be plastered up. More plaster is stuck on the box, under and along the sides of the roof-lid—more plaster even than around the entrance, till the very shape, it may be, of the box is altered here and there almost to that of a mud hut. Only at long last is the shaping, the altering, the plastering and the replastering brought to an end.

So to the building—or should I call it the making, or the lining?—of the nest itself. I have described this at length elsewhere, in *World of Birds,* and here I merely give bare detail. In the summer of 1940 a pair of nuthatches nested in a box in my garden and the hen laid five eggs; then the pair deserted the nest, for what reason I never discovered. At all events, in August I decided to look into the box and there I found a thing which I have never seen before and am not

likely—at least I hope not—to see again. The nest was in perfect condition, clean and dry, and the eggs were clear. They had not been sat upon, so the material of which the nest was made had never felt the warm damp of the hen's body and was exactly as the parent birds had put it together in the spring. It was entirely composed of the laminae of Scots pine with a slight mixture of birchbark. I decided to count the fragments—it took me three spells of counting on three separate summer mornings, and I shall always remember the monotony of it—but at last I could set down the number of fragments, 6,695. They had been brought from birch trees distant from the nesting-box forty-five yards and Scots pine thirty yards further, and there my sums in arithmetic ended. I could not tell the distance the parent birds had flown, for I had not counted the pieces of birchbark and the laminae of Scots pine separately, and I did not know whether they had carried the fragments one by one or several at a time. But that pair of birds had left their record in their nesting-box that summer, and in my mind and memory for all seasons to come.

In watching and listening to nuthatches I have spent much time and have been given much happiness; never greater than in the few moments when, year after year, I have heard their spring call through the new leaves of the larches. But they have set me a puzzle as separate and as individual as their song; a puzzle to which I have found no answer in any book and can only with doubt guess at an answer for myself.

Here is the beginning of the story. On a day in November 1942 I was looking, idly enough, at the bird-table outside my study window when I caught sight of a nuthatch hanging head downwards from a hazel bough I had bent over the bird-table to carry a wire coil for nuts. There the bird hung, its head and neck stretched straight out, motionless. I looked at it wondering; it remained still, grey and brown; it might have been part of the hazel bough. I watched it for perhaps two minutes. Then I was aware of another bird. On the terrace wall a few yards away crouched a form like a large hen blackbird. For a moment I was puzzled, and then saw that it was a young sparrowhawk, in its immature plumage, dark brown and buff. The form stretched, shook itself and

N

North Downs, looking to Ranmore
Ockley

flew off. I looked at the nuthatch, still motionless, then at my watch. For five minutes more it hung without moving, then there was a tiny twitch of the head, a glance right and left, and it flew away.

I had seen, then, a thing new to me, a little bird motionless, its mortal enemy the bird of prey within a few feet. Were the two sights connected? Was the stillness of the nuthatch its means of defence against the sparrowhawk? Grey and brown against the hazel bough, could it be part of the bough? And was the hawk deceived? I had seen a new thing; was what I had seen unseen by the sparrowhawk?

Two years passed, and in 1944, again in November, I was standing at my window and saw that there was a nuthatch, this time on the side of a small log of wood which lay on the bird-table, perfectly still, head downwards. Once more the thought crossed my mind, was there a hawk somewhere about? I could not see one. Suddenly something seemed to startle the nuthatch and it flew away. I was left again with my riddle asking for its answer.

Then the post brought me a letter. I get many letters from correspondents known and unknown, on many subjects, but this one happened to be on the subject of nuthatches. My correspondent was Mr W. Ernest Chard, writing from an address in Kent, and this was his message:

"For years nuthatches have come to a feeder I have within twelve feet of my window overlooking the garden at the back, and I have frequently noticed their habit of remaining quite still while hanging on the feeder or perched on the rail that holds it. On two occasions I carefully timed these periods of immobility, and they were seven minutes on the first occasion and nine minutes on the second, and in each case there were two birds, presumably a pair, and both remained quite still the whole of the time and each case one was head down on the feeder. Both these observations were made in April this year, 1944."

In all the books I have searched I have found no reference to this habit of nuthatches. Macgillivray, in his *History of British Birds,* writes that "all its actions are abrupt and lively; it climbs by short jerks, perches with ease on the twigs, throws itself into various postures, and is often seen with its head downwards, in which position it is even said at times to sleep." Macgillivray was a careful observer, and quotes from letters from many correspondents, but a man who writes of a bird that "all its actions are abrupt and lively" has obviously never seen one motionless, head downwards for seven minutes at a time, and when he says that "it is said" to sleep head downwards, he cannot have seen it sleeping in that way himself. And certainly the birds which Mr Chard watched, and which I saw in the same way, were not sleeping. Mr Chard on this point writes :

"Emphatically, no ! Eyes were open and there were fractional movements which, however, did not affect the posture. The whole appearance of the birds was one of alertness. Your suggestion that it may have been the presence of danger of which we were quite unaware [that was my guess. E.P.] seems highly probable. The demeanour of the birds suggests one of intense *listening*."

There I leave the problem. One of the strangest points is that it has never, apparently, been noticed in print before now.

Now for another disputed question. If in these pages I do not repeat in detail the story of its discussion, it is because I have already dealt with it at length in another book, *World of Birds*. It is the question of the "drumming" of the greater spotted woodpecker—briefly, the way in which the sound is produced. There are those who hold that the method is mechanical, others that it is vocal. I believe I was the first, at all events among modern writers—for the older naturalists do not seem to have raised or noticed difficulties as the production of the sound—to argue that the so-called drumming is a vocal sound, like the singing or calls of other birds. Of those who hold the opposite opinion, that the drumming is produced mechanically by the hammering of the woodpecker's beak on the bark or dead branches of trees, perhaps I may take as protagonists the editors of the *Handbook of British Birds,* who put their case thus :

"Persistent claims by a few writers that the sound is vocal are difficult to treat seriously, as little attempt is made to meet the overwhelming evidence to the contrary. The subject cannot be discussed at length here, but the difference in sound on different drumming-places and above all the *metallic* sound produced when the birds drum on metal—as happens exceptionally in the British Isles, but regularly (on corrugated iron roofs, etc.) in the case of certain American species —should alone be conclusive."

Well, I am not conscious of having failed to read, or shirked the task of answering, the contentions of those who hold that the noise of drumming is produced mechanically. My difficulty has always been the same; I have never heard or read any argument or array of facts designed to *prove* that the noise is produced mechanically; all that I have heard or read is the assertion that it is so produced. If, for example, the reader turns to the pages of *The Handbook* he will find the following:

"A few circumstantial accounts of woodpeckers drumming without the beak touching the wood are probably due to the drumming of a second and unseen individual close by or to other errors of observation, and must be set against the scores, if not hundreds, of observations by many careful and critical ornithologists who have found the contact of the beak with the wood unmistakable. At close range the dependence of the sound on the blows is so obvious that it is difficult to see how it can be seriously disputed, and the conclusion has been verified in captivity at even closer range than is possible in nature. It may be readily admitted, however, that the precise physical conditions under which the sound is produced require further scientific investigation. Under favourable conditions the head movements give a strong impression of actual rebound from the wood, the elasticity of which is probably an important factor."

As I have said, I do not propose to repeat here the arguments I have arrayed in *World of Birds* in my contention that the sound is produced vocally. But I may perhaps reinforce what arguments I have put forward by including here part of an article on the subject from the pen of a distinguished observer of bird habits, recently editor of the *Field,* Mr Brian Vesey-FitzGerald. His article, "The Problem of the Drumming Woodpecker: Is the Sound Vocal or Mechanical?" appeared in the *Field* of 2 June 1934, and here is the gist of it:

"This 'drumming' has been attributed to the bird hammering the tree with its beak. This mechanical theory is widely supported by ornithologists, including such competent men as Dr A. L. Thomson and the late Mr T. A. Coward, while it would not be too much to say that almost every layman believes it implicitly.

"The explanation, according to them, is simple. The bird places his beak against the tree—preferably against a hollow bough—and then hammers away so quickly that it is impossible to follow the movements of his head. The result is the 'drum' that can be heard half a mile away, perhaps a mile on a clear still day.

"But is there such a thing as a hollow bough? And surely it is a very powerful bird?

"And yet it is not the green woodpecker, which is a large bird, that we hear drumming regularly, but the great spotted, which is no bigger than a starling, and the lesser spotted, which is a little bird some five inches in length. It is difficult to believe that such small birds can produce so great a sound just by hammering with their beaks. Nor is the beak of the lesser spotted woodpecker noticeably different in construction from that of the nuthatch, a bird of almost identical size. One would suppose that the sound of their beaks, employed in hammering, would be something similar.

"Yet the woodpecker produces a sound that can be heard half a mile away, while the nuthatch, when hammering a nut wedged in a tree, produces a thin sound audible at a distance of no more than a few yards."

Next, arguing that a bird capable of producing a sound audible half a mile away by hammering its beak on wood would leave on the wood some mark, Mr FitzGerald examined with a magnifying-glass a piece of wood just vacated by a great spotted woodpecker, who had drummed for fifteen to twenty seconds at a time over a period of five minutes. But he could find no mark whatsoever. He goes on :

"The beak and head of the great spotted woodpecker weigh about an ounce. Experiment with a wooden instrument of that weight, fitted to a shaft in the manner of a hammer and used on the same section of wood as that 'used' by the bird, failed (before it broke, which was almost at once) to produce any noticeable sound at a distance of thirty yards. While it is admitted that the wooden instrument could not to any degree resemble the beak of the woodpecker, it would seem that the force applied by the muscular arm of a grown man would be sufficiently in excess of that applied by the neck of the bird to ensure a sound carrying at least as far as that produced by the bird were both sounds produced by the same process. Further, while the bird's beak left no mark on the wood, the wooden hammer could be clearly traced."

That was written in 1934. In December 1937 a fresh impetus was given to argument on the question by a series of photographs of a great spotted woodpecker taken in the act of drumming by Major Anthony Buxton, who in March 1938 was invited to sum-up the whole question with the correspondence elicited by his photographs. I have referred to these photographs in *World of Birds*. But in a letter resulting from the publication of these photographs Mr Vesey-FitzGerald himself, summing-up the correspondence in a sentence, adds further comment and suggestion of his own. His summing up is in twenty-two words :

"No one has disproved Mr Parker's contention that the sound is vocal, and no one has proved that the sound is mechanical."

His comment :

"I believe the sound to be vocal. But I think it possible that the wood forms a sounding-box, on the same principle that water adds volume to the tone of the human voice, at least to the ear of the householder, during his matutinal ablutions."

This, as it seems to me, is the best if not the only explanation of the fact attested by various witnesses that a woodpecker drumming in certain positions, for example in the neighbourhood of metal such as a corrugated tin roof, produces a ringing sound. As an instance I take a letter written to the *Field* of 18 December 1937, from Abbots Ann, Andover, by Mrs Duncombe Anderson :

"One day last year my husband was on his way from house to garage and heard what he thought was the ringing of the electric bell on the garage. When he reached it he discovered that the sound came from behind him, and he eventually traced it to a lesser spotted woodpecker which was drumming on the tin cap of the wireless pole. He called to me to come, and I also saw and heard the tiny bird hammering away. It sounded exactly like an electric bell ringing in the distance, and was absolutely distinct from the hollow sound produced by the drum on wood. To my mind there is no question that the sound is produced by the hammer strokes of the beak on a resonant surface. If it were produced by the throat there would surely be no difference in the sound, wherever the bird happened to be calling."

Well, that *is* the question. To my mind, Mr Vesey-Fitz-Gerald's sounding-box theory answers it. One more quotation may be set beside Mrs Duncombe Anderson's account of her lesser woodpecker's drumming. From Salcombe House, Sidmouth, in the same issue of the *Field*, the Rev J. G. Cornish writes :

"I think that the spotted woodpeckers, large and small, when calling for mates with their voices, long ago discovered the use of a sounding-box to assist them, and have several to which they resort each spring. Their call makes their head vibrate, but it does not drive their beak against the sounding-board, for it remains unmarked."

Add to Mr Cornish's letter another in the same issue, from Mr A. E. Barton, 26 Lytton Grove, Putney Hill :

"On looking closely at the beautiful photographs by Major Anthony Buxton it will be seen quite plainly, in Nos. 1 and 2 of the first series, that the beak is open, and therefore it is impossible for the bird to make the sound by contact with the wood."

Last, a word of hope from Mr FitzGerald :

"Finally, sir, could we have just a little co-operation? I have talked to many scientific ornithologists, some famous, on this question. Almost invariably they say dogmatically, 'Well, you're wrong.' They do not say how or why. And that is neither scientific nor convincing."

I would like to be hopeful. Of another problem of woodpeckers it is possible to write with certainty, and I can find happiness in the writing. It is, or rather was, for we know the answer, a question of the habits not of spotted woodpeckers, but of green, and the habit is not one to be noticed only in

the springtime, as is the process of drumming, but one of all
the year round—of food. For many years I have been fortunate in being able day after day to look out from my windows over a stretch of garden lawn bordered by oaks and
larch. Green woodpeckers in the trees and on the grass are
my companions through the seasons, and one of the riddles
which they set me through a period of some thirty years was
framed in their habit of boring in the turf, obviously in search
of something which they found and ate. I think it was ten
years ago, in the autumn of 1935, that I decided to find out
what they were finding. Morning after morning I sat with
glasses beside me, waiting for the moment when those sudden
quiet wings should set a lean, red-naped head probing among
the daisies, and leaving its mark in two-inch conical hollows
in the sand. I never found what I hoped to find, the tiny
supply of food that had drawn them to the lawn. That was a
reward kept for better eyes than mine. It was in the spring
of 1937 that my son Christopher, then a schoolboy at Eton,
set himself to find the answer to my riddle, and found it—
a discovery rewarding many hours spent in different ways
watching birds. His was a life of bird-watching, always from
a point of view separate and his own. I remember a letter
he wrote as a boy at a preparatory school, St. Andrew's, at
Eastbourne. Some one had found a nest in the school grounds.
"A boy actually put his hand into the nest—can you think of
anything so cruel?" As he grew older he took to photography
and built himself hides in the garden at home and in the
woods near. I have still the props which he used for a hide
from which to photograph drumming woodpeckers. On
Thursley Common he and his sister spent many hours; he
found a Dartford warbler's nest, but it never held eggs. We
listened there to curlews calling, that cry that is of the heart
of wild places. And in the garden, from one of his hides, he
took a photograph of a spotted woodpecker that afterwards
was hung on the walls of the exhibition in London in January
1938 which followed the International Sporting Exhibition
held in Berlin in the preceding autumn. The photograph
gained a special award.

But the achievement of his bird-watching which will last
is his discovery of the food for which the great spotted wood-

pecker probes turf. In the conical holes dug by the bird he found a number of tiny grubs, which we took for identification to two friends in the Haslemere Educational Museum, Mr E. D. Swanton, the curator, and his assistant, Mr Robert Blockey. In turn they referred the grubs to entomologists in the Natural History Museum, who identified them as larvae, one of an insect known as a fungus gnat—one of the *sciarinæ* —and the other of a small copper-coloured, black-spotted beetle, *Aphodius contaminatus*. These insects had not previously been identified as food of the green woodpecker, which doubtless is led to probe for them attracted by the strong smell which gives the beetle its name. And so it happened that to a schoolboy aged seventeen came the fortune and the reward of adding to the history of the birds which were his chief interest in the world, a fact new to science. Seven years later that short life ended in Italy, but he had left his name.

And for me, too, the birds which provide questions, perhaps unanswered, remain the great attraction. I have often wondered when we shall know more than we know to-day about crossbills. For theirs is a problem, as I see it, differing in essentials from that of other birds vaguely known as occasional visitors, or summer immigrants. It differs mainly in this, that we do not yet know the premises. Those who have watched crossbills differ in their accounts of what they have seen, and perhaps as to the deductions to be drawn from their records.

According to the *Handbook of British Birds,* crossbills are late-summer immigrants arriving in mid-June to August, arriving periodically (every three to ten years) in great numbers, frequently staying over the following spring into summer. Take the records given in the *Handbook* of the nesting of crossbills in the four southern counties of England during the years 1930 onwards. These are given as : Kent, 1930, probable but not positive record; Sussex, 1926 to 1936; Hampshire, from 1910, probably regularly to 1932, 1936, 1937; Surrey, 1930, 1931, 1936. If, then, there is any regular consequence of nesting after immigration, you would suppose the main years of immigration to have been the dates preceding these records of nesting. But how would these dates fit in with a period of immigration of every three to ten years?

Another point. The four counties Kent, Sussex, Hampshire and Surrey are the four counties nearest to the Continent. Apparently, then, the tide of immigration misses Kent, and if we look further at the *Handbook* records of nesting we find none for Essex since 1910, while since 1910 crossbills have bred regularly in Norfolk and Suffolk. It would seem, therefore, that of late years there have been two main routes of immigration, one arriving from France, perhaps, on the south coast, and another arriving from Germany, perhaps, on the east coast. But the period of three to ten years' influx is not easy to follow.

So far as my personal record is concerned—it is of a Surrey garden four miles from Sussex and eight from Hampshire—the great crossbill season of late years was the summer of 1935. I should guess, therefore, that my Surrey crossbills of that summer came in through Sussex.

One day I remember in particular—20 July. We had arranged a fête in aid of the Waifs and Strays, and I was to talk to the meeting on garden creatures in general. I had been watching crossbills on and off for days past, trying to see exactly what they did with the cones of the larches, which they treated in a curiously haphazard way : sometimes they would hold a cone carefully with a foot against the branch, stripping it open to get at the seed, and sometimes just biting or twisting the cone off as if it were no use—but I could see no difference between the rejected cones and the cones they held and fed from. At all events, I had noticed early in the morning of 20 July that underneath the larches at the side of the lawn there was an enormous number of cones bitten off, and I had it in my mind to ask the audience to look at the litter on the grass under the trees to realize something of the habits of the most casual of visitors. As the morning went on the weather became threatening, and soon after midday turned to rain, so that the Waifs and Strays' gathering assembled indoors, and it was not until past four o'clock that we were able to go out into the garden, where I was to talk about beasts and birds, especially about the habits of crossbills, which the day before had thronged the larches making

their meal. But the crossbills, incalculable as ever, were nowhere to be seen, and as for the traces of them, the larch
cones littered under the trees so that they had almost
hidden the grass, during the morning the gardeners, to make
the lawn tidy for the party, had swept up and removed
every one.

Perhaps that single afternoon—with Waifs and Strays—
sums up the crossbill. You never know what he will do next.
There is no calculating on any of his movements, from the
great or small exodus—as it must be from his home, wherever that may be—to the small or great influx into the country he decides or happens to visit. As to numbers, they vary
from day to day, hour to hour : two hundred, perhaps, in
the morning and parties of five to fifteen, or two hundred, in
the afternoon. And the length of his stay, in the garden or
in any of its trees, from larches full of solid cones to Canadian poplars and their naked leaves laughing at him, may last
from half an hour to half a minute, and then he goes off in
any direction. They look like wild birds, when flocks of crossbills flit in their sudden, happy-go-lucky flight from one tree-
top to another; and then, when you are standing near a bird-
bath, and six or seven come and settle close by you to drink,
they are the most confidingly tame of would-be companions.
That is one of the happiest visions of all my memories of
crossbills in the garden, the little company that is no longer
—for the moment—a band of nomads, but a contented group
of friends quietly sipping water a few feet away at a pool in
the rock garden or stooping from the stone edge of a lily
pond to dip their beaks among the leaves and flowers. And
then, a ray, a vibration that touches their bird brain, and
they are gone.

All of the crossbills that I have seen in Surrey—mine, I
must own, is only a limited experience, for during a lifetime
I have only been able to watch them since 1931, when I saw
them for the first time—have been bachelor birds, perhaps in
their first season. I have never had the luck to see a nesting
pair, though the Witherby *Handbook* shows a record of nests
in the year 1936, following the big influx of the year before.
What I have known is the song of the male crossbill, which
may or may not have been the song of a nesting bird to his

mate. That was in April 1931, and it is the only time I have heard it, a melodious, gentle warble, with here and there a higher note pitched rather crookedly, so to speak, into the tune. But I doubt if the singer was a nesting bird, for one reason that April is late for pairing crossbills, and for another that his plumage was merely chocolate brown, without the bright reds showing which are said to go with the adult plumage. For myself, I have never seen this bright plumage, though I have watched scores of birds. Of those that I have seen you could call the plumage rufous, but never red, much less scarlet, and olive-brown rather than olive-green or yellow has been the main colour of the female.

Now for a problem of another bird, the bullfinch. As with the crossbill, bullfinches vary in numbers in different years. In my part of Surrey, and, as far as my experience goes, in other parts of the country, bullfinches are birds which are to be seen mainly in winter and early spring, and when I see them they are generally doing mischief. In what may be called an average winter and spring, say during January to April, they are to be seen destroying fruit buds, cherry and plum, and the buds of flowering trees and shrubs, almond and forsythia, leaving the ground littered with buds, some of them chewed for the sake of the sweet centre, others merely bitten off in sheer careless destruction, thousands together. Then come winters in which hardly a bullfinch is to be seen —those were the winters, in my garden, of 1940 and 1945— and then a single season in which they are not merely a nuisance but a plague. I have only known one really bad plague year. In that year bullfinches were in all the orchards near in hundreds. I have tried, ever since I came to live in south-west Surrey, to keep my garden as a bird sanctuary, and my gardener knew what I hoped for, but in that January he came to see me in despair. Could he not shoot the bullfinches? If not we should have no fruit. There could be only one answer. So I told him he might shoot bullfinches on one condition—that I should never see a dead bird. And I never did see one, and the plague went on; and at the end, when the buds that remained had broken into blossom and I could see no difference in the numbers of the plague, I asked him how many he had shot. He told me sixty-six.

Here, it seems to me, we have an unexplained fact in the natural history of bullfinches. I can find little in any book to account for such a gathering of bullfinches. Macgillivray, with all his letters from correspondents all over the kingdom, has nothing to say of winter gatherings. Beach Thomas and Collett, in *Birds Throughout the Year,* which contains the experience of two of the best observers, have very little to say about bullfinches. In Witherby's *Handbook of British Birds* two species of bullfinches are distinguished, the British Bullfinch and the Northern Bullfinch, the latter with the name *Pyrrhula pyrrhula pyrrhula,* characteristic of the school of naturalists who call a wren *Troglodytes troglodytes troglodytes.* According to the *Handbook* the Northern is slightly larger than the British, but otherwise there seems to be little difference, and as regards the latter it is stated that it goes "generally in pairs throughout the year or in family parties in summer and autumn, occasionally in early spring, but rarely at other times in considerable flocks (up to one hundred and twenty-six recorded, but this is quite exceptional)." That is the only reference I can find to a great gathering, and the number given—one hundred and twenty-six—is far smaller than the numbers, whatever they were, of the plague year in south-west Surrey. And the cause, or the explanation, of such numbers remains as obscure as ever. If they had been starlings or woodpigeons the answer would be easy; we have all seen huge winter concourses. But of immigrations from abroad of the so-called Northern bullfinches there seems to be no record, and of British bullfinches the *Handbook*'s record stands alone. We have more to learn.

Of another bird the problem of numbers is different. I wish I could ask for an explanation of the presence of wrynecks in large numbers. I am afraid the fact is that wrynecks to-day are disappearing. There was a time when the note of the wryneck, the cuckoo's mate, was a sound as familiar as any call of April, and the sight of that questing, twisting neck as common as any other sight of orchards. But to-day? I have not heard a wryneck call for years past, and I do not know where I could be sure of hearing it, or I would set aside a morning for the journey. In the spring of 1944, indeed, I did that very thing, and walked out to a lane a couple of miles away in hope, for a gardener friend assured me that he heard it there every year of his life. But that year of his life neither he nor I heard it.

I remember well the first time I heard the old Surrey countryman's name for the wryneck. It was in the spring of 1915, when I was stationed with the guard of the 2/5 Queen's Regiment at the powder factory at Chilworth, and I was talking to an old soldier when the cry came down the April wind from the wood above the Tillingbourne. We stood there listening. "Hear th'ole pea-bird?" That was the voice, pea-pea-pea, that told you to sow peas, so he told me. But is it pea-bird, or the bird that calls pee-pee-pee phonetically, or, as others hear it, dear-dear-dear-dear? Or is it the "peel-bird" that tells of the time of peeling the bark of the oaks, the "rinding-bird," as woodmen of the Weald know it? That is a dying industry, it may be to-day—is it to match the wry-neck's vanishing? Yet another variant of local names seems to belong to the Surrey/Hampshire border country, according to a correspondent of *The Times* writing from Rowledge, near Farnham, who had recently heard a bird unfamiliar to her calling in an oak on the border of the Alice Holt Forest. A man standing near said, "That's the barking-bird."

But the barking-bird, I fear, calls less often to-day of the need to sow peas or to rind oaks. If only there were some means by which we might hope to increase their numbers! I have sometimes wondered whether the reason why they are fewer to-day in districts here and there is that we refuse them their old nesting-sites. Wrynecks love old apple-trees and plum trees, with hollow stems and holes in decaying branches, and those do not belong to days when we must have young trees carrying so many shillings per branch, wnen the bent and lichened stocks must be grubbed for fire-wood, to make room for upright saplings and the sprayer in April. But could not something be done, perhaps, with bird-boxes?

And now for a bird whose story, so far as it concerns the Surrey that I know best, suggests a different question. There was a time when the woodlark to me was no more than a name; I had never seen the bird nor heard its song. In the years when I first knew that best of writers of birds' nests

and song, Anthony Collett, the woodlark was not a bird of
Surrey. In April 1906, when he and I were bringing out the
book to which he, as the author—for I merely painted some
illustrations of eggs—gave the name *A Handbook of British
Inland Birds,* it was a bird of which he wrote that it "is a
much more local species than its better-known relation, being
commonest on the hills which bound the Thames Valley and
on the chalk range which runs thence into Buckingham and
Hertfordshire. It is found in other scattered localities in the
more southerly parts of England." Of its preference in choice
of country he adds that "it keeps more to the neighbourhood
of copses and thickets on dry, sloping ground." Twenty years
later, in *The Heart of a Bird,* we find him writing that
"woodlarks for years have been growing rarer, until the last
few seasons; now they are notably increasing their range
again, so that their establishment is no longer very unlikely
on any heathy common or rough hillside, partly tree-clad, in
the southern half of England and Wales."

I wonder how he would put the situation to-day. I well
remember the pleasure with which, when he was staying with
me soon after the war of 1914, we listened to a woodlark on
the flank of Hydons Ball. I believe it was the first he had
seen—certainly it was the first I had seen—in Surrey. To-day
things are very different. It was in the autumn of 1941 that I
first realized that the woodlark was a neighbour who, as I
hoped, had come to stay, a neighbour of woods and a
garden intended as a home for birds. In that autumn a field
which lies below the garden on the lower slopes of Hydons
Ball was ploughed from top to bottom for the first time since
I had known it; up to that date the higher part of it had
been left untouched, to grow what weeds or seedling trees
could find life in hungry sand. And over those twenty-eight
acres of crops and ploughland woodlarks sang week after
week, spring, summer and autumn, as skylarks too sang, but
with a music of their own.

I had not guessed what a gift that field could hold. For
how separate and distinct is the song of the woodlark! It
has its own qualities, unshared by any other. Like the sky-
lark, the woodlark sings on the wing, but not mounting; he
sings floating on waves and curves of flight. And singing he

travels from place to place, from one tree to another, from one side of a field to the opposite, from near at hand to far away. For the song itself, in accent and phrase it is nearest to the nightingale's, if for passion and fire it distils only peace; yet so like is the sound that in the February when I first heard it a message was brought me of a nightingale having been heard, and without any doubt about the very bird itself, for it was in the dark. But best of all is the song answered by another singer, as I heard it first in that October of 1941. A woodlark began singing in the field; as I listened, the song was answered from a distance, and as the first singer floated past me that antiphon went on, to die away, both singers out of sight.

That was in 1941. And following that year there came a change, unexpected and hard to understand. I had hoped that the bird and its song had come to stay, to be numbered in a new chorus of dawn, a new diminuendo with blackbird and thrush at night, if indeed it was not to set me new questions to answer about nightingales in February and March. But the sight of the bird and the song of the singer were to be with me no longer. In April of 1944 I found a woodlark's nest, in just such a situation as I should have expected from Anthony Collett's description in his book : "on the ground, well concealed by the colour of the dry grass of which it is entirely made, even when it is set in a hollow depression." It was in a hollow of rough grass among the stumps of a recently felled larch plantation, and I looked at the five brown-speckled eggs hoping for the day when I might see five beaks pointing out into the brambles and fire-flower. But that day never came. Even when I found them the eggs had been deserted, and next morning they lay wet from the night's rain. And that was almost my last meeting, so to speak, with woodlarks that year. Once, in September, near the little village church half a mile away, I heard the song, just a quiet passage of music in the afternoon; that was all. Through the winter, and the spring and summer of 1945, Hydons Ball, where I had listened hour after hour to that sweet haunting melody, next only to the blackbird's in its power to take memory into Aprils forgotten—Hydons Ball heard woodlarks no more.

Box Hill
Almshouses from the porch of Godstone Church

Then what had happened? What does happen when a bird hitherto reckoned as belonging only to a particular stretch of country, say the Thames Valley and the Chilterns, suddenly appears in a county distant from its natural haunts, nests there for two or three seasons, and then as suddenly vanishes? When woodlarks first came to the Surrey fields and woods, I found myself thinking of comma butterflies. In the early years of the century, and, I believe, indeed, ever since butterflies were recognized as belonging to the country-side at large or only to particular localities, commas were set down as belonging to the valley of the Wye. And then, on a sudden, about the end of the 'twenties, commas began to appear in the southern and midland counties, and to-day can be reckoned as regular natives, the broods appearing in July and August, the second remaining on the wing till late autumn and hibernating, to mate on emergence in April and in due course produce the first brood. I hope we shall have them with us in Surrey through the years to come; but may it not be possible that they among butterflies and woodlarks among birds belong to some tribe of creatures whose habit is to appear and disappear at irregular intervals? That is a habit, if it is one, hitherto unexplained.

And now for one or two birds which belong to Surrey either of right, as to a county of furzy commons where they should find the shelter and quiet which is their need, or which still are to be seen and heard in parts of Surrey still wild enough to keep them where they would be. First, then, for the Dartford warbler. One of the stretches of open country in which it used to be possible to watch that shy and graceful little bird was Thursley Common; but Thursley Common is not what it was before the days of tanks. Those broad and devastating highways over roots of gorse and heather have in every sense laid waste the recesses of bloom over which those short wings and spreading tail used to float and flow. *Revocet si pax annos!*

Curlew, again—one of the sounds which used to belong to the stretch of common that lies to the north of the road from Milford to Hindhead. For six years following 1939 heather and gorse heard little but the drone of steel: I would like to think that another six years might restore what the canker

O

Brewer Street, Bletchingley
A Thames-side path, Ham

of war has eaten. I shall always remember the sudden delight
which came to me in a garden not far from Chobham one
morning when there came to me that note of wild places
beloved beyond others, and I looked up to catch sight of a
form unhoped-for flying over a near-to rough field, and learnt
that every spring curlew nested there. I had news of them
in the autumn of 1945. "They returned about 12 March," I
was told. "They nest elsewhere, but arrive in the fields
usually about 11 a.m. and leave in the evening. We don't see
much of them while they are actually nesting, which is some
time in late April, but towards the end of the summer they
appear with their young, and leave in August-September."

But I have heard the voice of the wilderness even in my
own garden. There come days every autumn when in mist and
darkness the world is without sky. One such afternoon I
remember when instead of the cawing of rooks on their way
home—that happy "good night" called from high over the
fields—there came to me the sound of rooks calling from
trees in the garden close to the house, rooks invisible, be-
wildered. On another evening of thick mist came sounds even
more unexpected. First, a strange rush of wings low overhead, a big flock of starlings flying anywhere, nowhere. And
then—a cry incredible, belonging to leagues distant. A curlew
was calling from a field next the garden, calling nearer and
nearer—was it settled or flying? Again came the call, and
again; I was back in thought to August heather, to braes
above salmon rivers, to shores of Kintyre. Suddenly the bird
rose and flew over in the mist; I saw the curved beak I knew
so well, I heard the cry of a lost bird.

Curlew belong to the wild, and I should not hope for them
in a garden, any more than I should think of nightingales on
a moor. But you may hope in vain for nightingales in a
southern garden. When we built our house it was on the site
of a Surrey larch wood, and year after year I used to listen
at night to nightingales far away. In some years they sang
nearer than others, but never close to the house, where the
woods are of hazel and chestnut, cut in rotation, and so never
a home of quiet. If I wanted to hear nightingales by day I
used to walk to woods and lanes where I knew I should find
them, woods with undergrowth as old as themselves, lanes

bordered by blackthorn, primrose, oak. But nightingales never nested nearer than a mile away.

And then happened the thing I had longed for. On 16 April 1945, thirty-five years after the house was built and the garden begun, I first heard the unforgettable notes close at hand, and listened hardly knowing what I was hearing. Then came the knowledge, and I stood still. And then, day after day, night after night, came those age-old sequences, ripple, twitter, trill, deep-found notes echoing from a bird's heart, in full song in sunshine, at dusk, midnight, dawn. Nightingales were singing—would they nest? And if they nested, would they return? If they returned, the garden would be their home, and the dream would have come true.

For that voice, and for that vision of a nightingale, I still hope. Another vision comes to me, of hawks. I have often wondered how many new records we might not be able to add to the list, were we to spend more time looking into the sky above us instead of at what lies around us on our own level. Of kestrels, for instance; we see those fairly often, and sparrowhawks at times, though their traces are frequent enough, in patches of feathers in orchard and garden. Even so, records are incomplete, for Witherby's *Handbook of British Birds* makes no mention of albino sparrowhawks, yet for two or three days together in 1933 my gardener and I watched a pure white sparrowhawk with an orange bill. Oddly enough, I never heard the end of that bird, though you would suppose, had it been shot, that it would have found its way into a glass case.

But in the autumn of 1945 I was able to add to my garden records. On a day in mid-September I caught sight of a number of rooks and jackdaws behaving in a queer way, swooping, turning and curving this way and that, as you may see starlings or knots. Then I saw why. They were mobbing a buzzard. Round them, above them soared in magnificent circles that great hawk, careless of their presence, journeying towards his own end. South-west he circled on his broad wings, fainter and fainter showed his pursuing company, and all were gone.

Twice only before that day, in all the years I have spent in this corner of Surrey, have I been able to watch a buzzard in flight through the arc of sky that stretches south-west over Hindhead and Blackdown, and each time the journey has been the same, perhaps, I have thought, to a home in Devon. But then, in all those years, how few are the minutes I have spent looking up. Whenever I have seen these great hawks it has been by accident.

And now for a commoner bird, but not, I think, a common nest. The story begins in moonlight, and the time is of war. On a hill facing south stands a house of brick, with tall chimneys, a white-pillared balcony, white-framed windows, and a white cornice. In the unquiet nights of the second year of the war of 1939 the moon lit it so that it became a landmark, and to tone down the whiteness of it the balcony and cornice were draped with canvas and Archangel mats. Part of the canvas was folded over the cornice above a big magnolia which clothes the house wall side by side with roses, clematis and wistaria. In pre-war days a pair of starlings had made the wistaria their home.

Early in the summer the starlings decided to change their quarters to the fold of canvas. So they began to build, and, writing on the terrace below, I watched them idly, not noticing what they gathered, but listening to their cheerful pipes and castanets on the chimney-tops. But for whatever reason the building stopped; the birds carried no more material to the canvas and went back to the wistaria.

Then came a later day when it was decided to undrape the balcony and the cornice; the mats and the canvas in wind and weather had become tattered and torn. So a ladder was brought and the canvas from the cornice was pulled down—with a sudden cry of surprise. For out of its folds fell a mass, a weight, a barrow-load of leaves, bough-prunings, canvas scraps, and a cushion of fibre of cloth and sacking. It was the starlings' nest of the summer. And I decided to count what had fallen. There were two hundred and seventeen separate magnolia leaves—a leaf measures seven inches by two—thirty-two ends of boughs that had been trimmed, carrying one hundred and sixty-four more leaves, and a mass of woolly debris of sacking fibre and clematis seeds in a heap measuring nine inches by eight by five. All this a pair of starlings in April had carried up for a nest they never used.

I realized how little I had known about the nesting habits of starlings.

I come last to the bird which to my mind is the finest of all our singers, the blackbird. I know no other bird with so individual a song, no other which can sing of home, of summer in England, as the blackbird can; and no other which sings its own song, a different song from other black-birds, and different one day from the next. That is the general truth, as I see it, of all blackbirds. But there is more than that to be written of individual blackbirds, which make friends with different gardeners, for instance, in different ways. I have known several, but one blackbird I have come to know as I have never known any other. I never thought that I could know a bird so well, and I like to think that he, too, looks on me as separate from other folk, and trusts me day by day as his friend.

It was in the early autumn of 1942 that I first made his acquaintance, when he first came to the table where I spread food for birds outside my study window, and I soon learned to recognize him for his fearlessness and because of his plumage and the marking of his bill. He was never afraid of me, and from early days would come and perch close to my hand as I put out the breadcrumbs and cheeseparings morn-ing after morning. But as the months went on I noticed a peculiarity in his plumage. Of all birds, I should have said that the blackbird could be set down as best deserving his name—"the ousel cock so black of hue with orange-tawny bill." In Witherby's *Handbook* his plumage is as tersely described as a bird's could be : "*Glossy black plumage* of male with *orange bill* and eye-rim are unmistakable." That is all. But that never described my bird. All through the autumn and winter of that year he remained part black and part brown, his tail and the primaries of his wings as dark as could be, but his throat and breast mottled and his bill with only a yellow tip. So he continued through the spring and summer; he had a nest of young in rhododendrons close to the table, and it was his engaging habit to carry a large beakful of food to his young before returning, confident and quiet as ever, to make his own breakfast.

And then in the late summer of 1943 he disappeared.

Exactly when I do not know; we do not notice a departure with the immediate certainty with which we chronicle arrivals. I feared he might have been killed by a sparrowhawk, but I could find no feathers. And then—he came back. On 6 November at 9 a.m. suddenly there flitted from a yew hedge my blackbird, settled by my hand, looked at me, and began feeding. There he was, in his black-and-brown suit, his mottled throat, his yellow-brown eye-rim, and his grey, yellow-tipped beak.

That ended what I may perhaps call the second chapter in my blackbird's story. The next chapter begins with his nesting period in 1944, when in April I noticed that while his plumage still remained mottled and blotchy, his beak seemed to be changing to yellow, and I wondered whether it would turn to full orange. His wife, in that April, joined him at the table, and once or twice they were feeding together. She was not so confiding as he, however, and hesitated to come up to me, but she would perch near enough for me to notice her plumage, which was odd like her husband's. She had a bib of dull yellow, and breast-feathers of reddish-brown. I remembered Macgillivray's remark, that "the female differs considerably in colour," which sums up the long list of different tints and hues carefully enumerated in Witherby's *Handbook*. And then, once more, in the late summer—I could not chronicle an exact date—my blackbird disappeared.

And once more he came back to me. At nine o'clock in the morning of 3 February 1945 he suddenly reappeared. As before, I had feared that he would never come back, and once more he seemed to put the question, why a human being should puzzle and worry over what was only natural and to be expected. True, his manner of return was this time a little different, for instead of settling close by my hand and beginning to feed at once he occupied himself that first morning and for several mornings afterwards in first chasing away a couple of brilliant-hued black-and-orange birds which tried to come first to the table, and which only desisted after persistent pursuit from the crumbs and cheese. I wondered if they were his sons of the April of the year before; he behaved just like a stern parent jealously guarding his privileges. But the interesting point this year was once again his plumage. It had changed in two respects. His beak was now yellow, except for the extreme tip, which was black. For the rest of him, he seemed to me to be black in larger patches than before, but his eye-rims remained unaltered; they had not even turned yellow like his beak. I think it had always been his eye-rims which gave him so gentle and quiet a look : he never stared as do his brightly hued fellows. In one single particular he had changed. An inch behind his left eye he had a single tiny patch of white feathers—just a minute mark that was not there in other years. Like a man's grey hairs ! I wondered.

So the story reached its third year in April 1945. It is a chronicle of small happenings in the life of a single bird, of no importance, doubtless, as regards species, and of no great interest as regards plumage, perhaps, except that I cannot find any reference in books to any instance of a cock blackbird mating in the ordinary way yet never developing adult plumage. But what to my mind my blackbird has done is to exemplify in one particular case, perhaps, the life of all blackbirds during the four seasons of the year, with periodical absences, or wanderings, or migrations, it may be.

In birds of ordinary plumage we do not notice these absences, as a rule, and so we are not led to chronicling exact dates of appearance and disappearance. It would be of intense interest, surely, to know where blackbirds travel, and how far, and in what direction, autumn after autumn, year after year, and my blackbird, perhaps, has asked the question if he cannot be said to have answered it.

CHAPTER XV

INSECTS IN A GARDEN

To few observers in gardens to-day can it be granted to chronicle anything new of insects. So much has been written already—Lord Avebury's *Ants, Bees and Wasps,* F. W. Frohawk's *British Butterflies,* and Edward Step's *British Insect Life,* to take only three books which might serve as a warning to the adventurous newcomer—that he would be a bold intruder on occupied ground who should think he could add anything to the common store. But there is still room for accidents. It may happen to the unlearned to meet with adventures which have not fallen to the lot of the teacher.

To take, for example, the story of the comma butterfly. In some ways it is paralleled in the life of other butterflies, in one respect it is I believe unique. It is a butterfly which is double-brooded, like many others, but it shares with a very common insect, the large garden white, a rare peculiarity in that its second brood is different in appearance from the first. That is a fact which has only been realized in the present century.

Years ago there were two acknowledged writers of text books on butterflies. One was the Rev F. O. Morris, whose big green volume carries on its cover a design of large white butterflies on trefoil stamped in gilt. The other was W. S. Coleman, whose *British Butterflies,* a cheap and delightful little handbook, every schoolboy knew. But to both writers the natural history of the large white was only known in part; they did not realize that the insects we see in spring are different in pattern from those of summer. In May their markings are faint and grey; in July the second brood, their children, have their wings tipped and spotted with deep black. True, Morris has seen that there is a difference somewhere. "Some have imagined a separate species under the name *Pontia chariclea,*" he writes. But that the children, year after year, were differently marked from their

200

parents was an idea nowhere in his mind. And that it should be so is indeed a fact strange enough.

And now for the parallel in the life of the comma—or rather the part-parallel, for the likeness is not exact. I believe it was Frohawk who first drew attention to the butterfly's two forms. On this point he writes : "Pairing takes place after hibernation. The females start depositing in April and continue throughout May; of the total number of eggs laid by a single specimen, between 30 and 40 per cent, and always the first eggs laid, produce butterflies of the aberration *Hutchinsoni,* while the whole of the remaining eggs produce the normal type. . . . It was always considered that the aberration *Hutchinsoni* belonged to a distinct brood and was called the summer brood, as it was the first form to emerge, until I disproved this by rearing a large number of both forms from the same parent."

And this is his description of the variety *Hutchinsoni* :

"Ab. *Hutchinsoni* differs greatly from the normal type both in the formation of the outer margins and in colouring. The outer margin of the fore-wing is much less hollowed out and the projections of both wings are shorter. The colour of the upper side is orange-ochreous, and the spots are more clearly defined; the outer marginal hollow is bordered by a black band."

That is Frohawk's account of his experience in breeding commas. He first gave his account of the appearance of *Hutchinsoni* in the early brood, in his *magnum opus, The Natural History of British Butterflies,* published in 1914, and he wrote rather more definitely on the subject in the smaller popular edition of 1934. I do not know whether he may have altered his conclusions in the light of later evidence, but it has certainly been my experience in Surrey, and I believe that of others interested in butterfly life—notably a collector of wide experience, Mr F. A. Oldaker, of Haslemere—that *Hutchinsoni* is not a variety belonging solely to the first brood of the year, but may be seen with the normal butterfly side by side on the wing at any time in the summer or autumn.

But the comma is a butterfly incalculable. Of its habits, its periodical appearances and disappearances, we can prophesy nothing. A hundred years ago, with its lovely, jagged orange-brown wings, it was a common sight on the wing in many parts of England. Then it disappeared from the country at large, and was only to be seen in the valleys of the Severn, Usk and Wye. And suddenly, a dozen years since, it appeared in Surrey, Sussex, Hampshire, Kent in profusion, and in lesser numbers elsewhere. And then, again, it disappeared from districts where it had been as common as the peacock or small tortoiseshell. In the spring of 1945 in my garden, where in the autumn of 1943 I had seen, and written to my friend Frohawk to give him the news of them, *Hutchinsoni* and the normal butterfly on the wing in numbers together, there was not one to be seen. Should I see that sight again? Who could say? The answer came that same year; in September there were more commas in the orchard than in any other year I remember. On 29 September I counted eight feeding on a single fallen pear, with two others within a few inches. And they were accompanied by red admirals, which were to be seen by hundreds in every garden in the neighbourhood. They were September migrants, I believe; perhaps the commas came with them.

Butterfly years come in turn—years in which this or that species occurs in much larger numbers than usual—clouded yellows, painted ladies, large tortoiseshells, and even common or garden cabbage whites. All of us who collected butterflies in our youth or have watched them in later days remember such seasons, visions of a world for a few hours suddenly bright with flowers and wings. A summer comes back to me from long ago when over acres of clover under the South Downs—those bare slopes see only villas to-day—clouded yellows, unheeded except for their beauty, danced in the wind. In a later year—was it 1903?—painted ladies filled Surrey gardens in uncounted hundreds, too many for the flowers in that strange September. And a rarer sight than those remains from a day in the first German war, when I walked on an April morning by a ride in a Surrey wood and watched large tortoiseshells here, there and everywhere drinking from primroses. And perhaps a more unusual record still belongs to my own garden—at all events my friend F. W. Frohawk has thought it worth mentioning in his *British*

Butterflies, that monumental work of a lifetime—which was the appearance of a large tortoiseshell on 7 October 1914. Large tortoiseshells are not often seen on the wing late in the year, and I saw this butterfly again on the following day.

Large tortoiseshells to-day for whatever reason are rare insects in England; I have not seen one for many years. And neither of the other two—clouded yellow or painted lady—can be called common, so that to see them in quantities in any season is a note for the diary. But it happens now and then, too, that a really common butterfly suddenly appears in immense numbers, again for a reason difficult to guess. That has been my experience in two years in particular with the large garden white, one of the two really common insects—the other being the small garden white—which do damage in the garden to cabbages. It was in the summer of 1918 that I first saw white butterflies in myriads over garden and field, near Faversham on the coast of Kent, and I have no more vivid memory of that place, which otherwise remains in my mind linked with thoughts of T.N.T. and other explosives, than the sight of clouds of white butterflies wavering over fields of green corn. It was a sight I had not seen before, and I wondered then, as I have wondered since, what was the attraction that drew those incredible numbers to spend their days over fields which held neither flowers for themselves nor food for their families.

And the same wonderful vision came in another year which ended war, in the summer of 1945. In July fields and gardens at Hambledon, just as before at Faversham and Oare, were alive with myriads of garden whites. As in Kent, so in Surrey, they danced, floated, quivered over acres of oats and barley; they changed the whole landscape from fields of corn to a ballroom of fairies. But for me the chief wonder of that summer belonged to the garden. There, from the first warmth of sun in the morning to the last living ray of evening butterflies were a wreathing pattern of white over lawn and trees and flowers. On a single clump of lavender I counted between forty and fifty; those were the flowers that drew them together even from phloxes and buddleia. But the lightest and happiest company of all were over the tops of the tall eucryphias, which that year were in flower a fortnight before their time. I have never seen in any other summer such a sight as the scores of butterflies that wove their dance all the morning, like very petals of the tree itself tossed in the blue above its white flowers. And a strange thing to see lay on the turf under and about the eucryphias, torn wings of the butterflies lying among the fallen petals of the flowers as they fell. How they came there, how they were torn off and by which birds I could not make out; I saw chaffinches in the top branches, but I think flycatchers must have been there. There was the same sight on the floor of a woodland ride nearby, but I saw no flycatchers at work.

These garden whites must have been immigrants. My daughter, in charge of a school treat, was at Bognor on 28 July, and while she and the children were bathing garden whites were coming inshore from the sea in numbers. I myself was at Felpham, just east of Bognor, on 31 July, and through the afternoon, when the tide was coming in, I saw many garden whites coming inshore in the same way. The sea was calm, but the wind was northerly, as indeed it had been for days past. It was during the previous week, 14–21 July, that I had first noticed the large numbers of white butterflies in the garden, so that if they all belonged to the same migrating swarm, the invasion must have been enormous. There was no preponderance of either sex in the numbers which I saw, and many of them were mating, so that if a corresponding number of eggs were laid, the damage to the cabbage crop seemed likely to be widespread. But as against that, immense numbers of the migrants, so far as I saw, spent all their time in the cornfields, through what attraction I cannot guess.

Garden whites are thought of by most of us, perhaps, as belonging to gardens. Moths are creatures of wider fields. And one moth of which I always hoped for news, and even expected news in these later days of potato-growing on the vast scale of wartime, was *Acherontia atropos,* the Death's Head. One day the thing hoped for happened. On a September evening in 1941 a telephone message reached me. Would I help to identify a creature that had been brought to the office of the *Daily Telegraph*? A curious-looking animal, I was told, yellowish in colour, almost as big as a snake.

A caterpillar, I guessed, possibly that of a goat moth. Did it smell? I asked, and heard the question repeated, apparently with some surprise. After a pause the answer came, No. Then had it got a horn? Yes. And transverse stripes on its side? Yes. Then, I thought, it must be a caterpillar of the Death's Head moth, and I asked that it might be sent me to make certain. But I asked one final question, thinking of the creature's feeding habits. Was it found on a potato plant? There was a rather longer pause, and I imagined the finder, who lived in Kent, being questioned. No, it was found on concrete.

In due course it reached me, very carefully packed in grass, and rather damp, poor creature, for the weather was warm. There was no doubt about it. Out of its tin it crawled, a full-grown caterpillar of *Acherontia atropos*. I gave it a big box filled with mould, and in three minutes or so it had buried itself. There I left it, and in a fortnight's time found what I had hoped for, a large brown pupa, alive and kicking. So I waited in hope. In May, perhaps, should I at long last set eyes on what I had never seen alive, the moth itself? Only twice before in my life had I possessed the caterpillar, brought me from a field where potatoes were being dug, and both caterpillars—one of them injured, as I saw—had died. This caterpillar, so far as I could tell, was perfect. Should I actually see in the living creature those wonderful markings, whose skull-and-crossbones likeness on its throat had given the moth its country name? Above all, should I hear its "squeak," that strange noise which is made, entomologists tell you, by the moth expelling air through its proboscis?

Alas, May came and no moth with it. My chrysalis had met with the fate which seems predestined for most of its kind; it died in the winter. But it brought me an unexpected reward. A note on the accident which brought it into my possession, published in a Sunday paper, resulted in my receiving from the Rev Arthur Crookshank a copy of an article in the *Entomologist* of October 1939, containing an account written by Mr Leonard G. Hulls of various pupae and caterpillars of *Acherontia* which had been through his hands. The article, which was beautifully illustrated from paintings made by Mr

Crookshank's sister, Mrs Hulls, was full of interesting information, of which the gist as regards keeping the chrysalis was that you could only expect the moth to emerge alive if you "forced" it in hot, damp air over a stove. But Mr Hulls's account of the squeaking noise made by the moth is the fullest detail of those which I have read. He says:

"It is usually written that the sound is made when the moth is irritated, and this appears to be true. It is, however, worthy of note that many of the moths make this noise for quite a time when they first emerge, especially those that run up and down the gauze cylinder before deciding just where they will rest. The moth is tremendously active at emergence and often seems literally to shoot out of the pupa case and start rushing about."

I live, then, in hope. I expect to be surrounded by potato fields for some years to come, and if fortune is kind, and once again a caterpillar comes into my possession, I shall know how to treat the pupa and shall hope to see the moth emerge from its steamy quarters. If it rushes about I shall even hope to see it fly.

And that, to me, is the supreme pleasure with all big moths. They are night-flying creatures, but it can happen that we may see one of them in flight in daytime. Some, of course, are day-fliers by nature, like their smaller companions, the orange underwing, that bright newcomer of March and April, and the rose and grey cinnabar of full summer, or the gamma or silver Y, as some books prefer to call that migrant to our autumn flowers from across the Channel. But I treasure the memory of a rarer vision.

On a day in April 1943 I found myself in the afternoon staring at grey-purple, rose-clouded wings eyed like a peacock butterfly, flitting round the budding stems of *Romneya Coulteri*—of all queer plants to choose—in a herbaceous border. Then, as it rose and flew fast away, returning to flit again about the green stems and leaves, I saw it for a moment settled. It was an Emperor moth, which I had thought of as an insect of upland heather. Had I seen it a few hundred yards away, on Hydons Ball, there would have been nothing to wonder at. But here? Then I caught sight of the attraction, and understood. At the foot of the stem was settled the lovely mauve-marbled consort. A moment, and she too rose, and the pair vanished.

That was on 18 April, and I thought I had seen all and had understood at least in part. But there was more to come. Next year, 1944, on 30 April, there was a male Emperor flitting round the same few inches of soil and stem where I had seen the Emperor the year before. There was no Empress. Last year's plant had been cut down, as we cut down *Romneya Coulteri* every year, for the plant to make its new growth for the year. It is a Californian plant and the new leaves have no scent that I can distinguish. So that for two years running, near the same date in spring, a moth of the English heather was seen haunting the young growth of a plant imported from America. I have never at any other time seen the moth in the garden.

These two springs, of 1943 and 1944, were days of coincidences. It falls to the lot of all who have bred and watched moths to see through the cycle of life year by year in full, but the supreme moment when what was once a crawling grub fares out on wings comes as a rule in the dark. We leave the perfect insect to take its free flight at night. But once or twice in a period of years we catch a glimpse of that glorious adventure in sunlight. On a day in May 1943 I was brought by a gardener a covered flowerpot and under the cover some live creature struggling eagerly for the light. I took off the cover, and out flew full-winged, sweeping and swooping as might a swallow, a privet hawkmoth. It turned the corner of the house and was gone. And the next year, in June, an elephant hawkmoth, which I had reared as a caterpillar, having left its chrysalis in the night, sat gently fanning its wings in sunlight. Suddenly the wings quivered, faster and faster, then, in a moment, it was gone—a flash of light, fifty yards down the lawn, out of sight. So in a second of time life was begun and, for the watcher, renewed. These were visions of days of war, and I have sometimes thought over the sights and sounds which I might not have seen and heard had I not been confined, during the six years of the second great war, to the same few acres of Surrey. To travel about the same fields day after day for months together is to notice small accidents and changes, as well as great and new, the tiny stick caterpillar, the slot of deer. And to find different creatures setting the same questions, answered and unanswered, or suggesting the same comparisons.

It is the accident of living on the side of a sandy hill, no doubt, that sets an inquirer pondering over such unlikely sharers of the same habits as dragonflies and toads. Both come to water for the breeding season; both live the beginnings of their lives in water, and some of the many species of dragonflies spend long hours in the driest places of the countryside. Over fields of stubble, for instance, I have often watched that fierce flyer, *Æschna cyanea*, gliding the length and back of a hillside terrace, or cruising up and down the sides of a larch plantation; and I have come upon him between the newly shocked sheaves of a field of wheat, as hot and dusty a hunting-ground as you could find—but flies like that and so do butterflies, and he would evidently know where to look for a meal, shedding the wings, unwanted beauty, of a small garden white as he flew. His is the perfection, surely, of a hunting insect's flight, the long gliding between the slightest flickers of invisible wings.

Yet it is to water that we go back to look for dragonflies, as happened to me at long intervals during that period of war hindrances, when I was able to look out over the light and shadow of a small south-country lake, and saw and heard sights and sounds I had half forgotten; the sharp sweet call of a kingfisher flitting from alder to bulrushes, the twitter of house martins, and the level surface suddenly broken by a dipping swallow. Above all, the sweeping angles of that glorious pirate in copper and bronze, *Æschna grandis,* twin of the blue *cyanea,* greatest of dragonflies of August : and beside him, or below him, rather, on weed and waterlilies, another dragonfly, oddly named in Latin *Calopteryx virgo* and in French *Demoiselle,* the male suitor in turquoise of an emerald bride, settling here and there on leaf or tendril, or circling with the flight of a hummingbird, round and round again, but always head to flower.

But there are lesser surfaces than those of a south-country lake. There are the tiny ponds of a rock garden—even the plainest and tiniest, lacking waterlily or forget-me-not, just water over an empty floor—that very emptiness which, for

Whitgift's Hospital, Croydon
Shere

SURREY

me, is the attraction. For in it and on it the insects of the
pond have room to move, and it is a movement which in sunlight comes alive. First, perhaps, that of the whirligig beetles,
whose rapid curvings and waltzings look as if they were just
the joy of life, which perhaps they are; and next to the
whirligigs—what else should they be called but *Gyrinidæ*?
—the water boatmen, shaped and working to suit their name,
a pair of legs outstretched like oars on either side of the keel,
backing water stern foremost for ever, and never home to a
raft. And third, those that I like best of all to watch, the
pond skaters, but for those you need sun always. In sunshine
fairyland multiplies. Each insect dints the surface of the
water with three pairs of feet; each dint holds a tiny star of
light, and on the floor of the pool each star throws its
shadow; then, as feet and dints and stars move about the
pool above, six dots of shadow move on the floor below.

These are incidents, or accidents, of a garden. I should
never have had the accidental pleasure of watching the
shadows of the feet of so small a creature as a pond skater
if it had not been for the laying of the cement floor of a tiny
pond on a sandy hillside. But gardens can provide, too,
riddles of nature which would not ask for an answer if it
were not for artificial surroundings—riddles, for example,
propounded by so common a creature as the cockchafer.

In my garden I have a small lilypond, about fifteen feet in
diameter, which is surrounded by a pavement of bargate
stone. The paving is of irregularly shaped flat slabs from a
neighbouring quarry, laid nearly touching each other in the
natural soil of the place, which is mainly sand. Altogether
the paving forms a square, with sides measuring ten yards,
and the square is bounded by a yew hedge, planted in 1927.
In that year the pavement was taken up and relaid, and it
was not moved again until the last week of November 1941,
when, the weather having made other work in the garden
impossible, it was decided to lift and relay the paving, which
had been invaded by bindweed.

I talked to the gardener at work, and he remarked that
he had dug up a number of Joe Bassetts, which is the local
Surrey name for the grub of the cockchafer. He added that
he had also dug up several cockchafers; these he had thrown

Old houses in Shere
Looking over the Devil's Punch Bowl, near Hindhead

away into the yew hedge. But, he asked me, how did they get where we had found them? They were fifteen inches below the surface in solid sand, in ground which (as I knew) had never been trenched, and they were alive and moving. I asked him, if he found any more, to keep them for me, and that same afternoon he brought me five perfect cockchafers in a flower pot. Never in forty years had he seen such a thing in winter, and look! he had put a stone in the bottom of the pot, and they were so strong that they had moved the stone.

That was the beginning of my cockchafer conundrum, but there was more to come. I put my five into a big flower-pot and filled it with leaf mould. On a day late in the following April it occurred to me to look for them, and I found the pot empty. If they had come out of their winter quarters, I wondered, would not others be doing the same thing? And I remembered having seen, in a path near the lilypond where the chafers had been found, a number of small holes at the side. I had always supposed them to have been made by cockchafers emerging for their winged life of summer— though, when I thought the matter over, I had never actually seen a chafer in the act of coming out from the ground. I went down to the garden path to look at the holes. It is a path about a hundred yards long by eight feet wide, of sand paved with ironstone—about as solid a piece of surface masonry as could be devised. I counted the holes; there were three hundred and ninety-six in that one path, and others in paths nearby.

There is my puzzle, and perhaps it is no greater than others of insect life. A cockchafer born from an egg laid on the root of a plant lives as a larva three or four—or is it more?—years underground, a soft-bodied, hard-mouthed creature which is able to push its way deep and far into solid sand, which changes first from the larval into the pupal state, and next into the perfect form of imago, all the time there in solid sand—how does it get the room, how does it breathe?— which remains underground all through the winter, and then in late spring pushes its way up into the air, through solid sand roofed over by slabs of bargate or platforms of iron-stone; which then, for a few weeks, lives in open air, sunshine and night, and lastly creeps once more into soil again, to lay its eggs on plant roots and die. Four years, perhaps, under-ground; a few weeks in air and then back into the dark. Perhaps it does more in its long life than destroy; perhaps, in its enormous numbers, its life is to supply other life, such as that of rooks following the plough, with food; and the rooks, in turn, do good by destroying the plant destroyer.

So much for the story of common garden insects. Now for the commonest of all—ants. I do not attempt here to write of ants in general; they belong to everywhere. This is merely a note of one species out of many. At the foot of my garden lawn stands an oak, which from the size of its bole I make out to be some two hundred and fifty years old. Its roots spread deep and far, and form the frame of a huge under-ground nest of black ants—*formica nigra,* I believe.

I have watched this nest in spring, summer and autumn for years. I cannot guess its numbers, but they must be prodi-gious. They have made two roads from the roots of the oak, one running eighteen yards west over lawn turf to a young oak which they climb, as they do their own oak, the other seven yards south to the top of a dry wall, where I lose sight of them. Sometimes they crowd one road, leaving the other almost deserted, sometimes both roads are crowded. But on both roads most of them seem to be doing—nothing. They just travel, travel all day long, both ways, sometimes collid-ing, sometimes stopping to talk—or it looks like that—and then travelling on again. Are they in search of food? That would seem to be natural, but, if so, why stick to two roads only? I thought I would test them. So one day I got three kinds of food, (i) a strip of bacon quarter of an inch by four inches, (ii) a scrap of cake, (iii) a tiny bit of bread covered with treacle, and put them down at intervals along the two roads.

Of (ii) and (iii) they took no notice. The bacon in a few minutes was black with ants; then I had to leave it for half an hour, and it had vanished—I think a bird must have taken it. So another day I put down another small strip of bacon, which in the same way was at once covered with ants, but after eight hours it was still much the same size though it had been nibbled. So I set myself to watch the roads to see what, if anything, the ants might be carrying. After an hour's watching I had seen seven ants with burdens, of which four were tiny fragments of what looked like the horny covering of some insect's abdomen, and three were the empty bodies of some sort of small fly. These burdens they carried, some towards, some away from, the nest, one, nowhere in particular.

But on a later day I was more fortunate, if it was only by accident. Near the dry wall to which one of the roads runs from the oak is a sandy garden path. Going down the path I caught sight of a worm, some four inches long, which had found its way on to the path and had become choked in the dry sand. It was covered with ants from the nest; I tried to count them and made the number near two hundred. By sundown all that was left was a strip of sandy skin. Those two hundred or more ants, then, had somehow found food which they liked better than my cooked fragments, but whether they had somehow been searching for it (why go by the same road day after day?) or whether it was a gift of fate, like the snake thrown into the "horse-emmets'" nest by my friend the countryman of whom I have told elsewhere, I do but guess. All the while, that day as on other days all through that summer, the ants, up and down their two roads from the oak tree, kept on travelling, travelling.

CHAPTER XVI

FOLK LORE

SOUTH and south-west Surrey are linked to Sussex and
Hampshire by ties of soil and race. Of soil, for from the
Kentish boundary near Oxted, through Reigate, Dorking,
Abinger, Godalming, Thursley and Hindhead to Bramshott,
Liphook and Liss runs a belt of the Lower Greensand; and
south of that belt, all along the Weald from Crowhurst to
Kirdford, Lurgashall and Linch, the villages lie on Wealden
clay. And the ties are of race, for the same country folk live
in the cottages all along the county boundaries, which are
marked on the maps but not in the fields and woods. And
ties of soil and race together are the stronger for links of a
common industry, the smelting and working of iron. Modern
machinery has ended the industry, but the links of country
talk and thought remain.

So that we should expect the folk lore of these parts of
Surrey, Sussex and Hampshire, with a common ancestry, to
be much the same in sayings and superstition. I know of no
chapter in the literature of the county dealing in particular
with the folk lore of Surrey, but there are passages in articles
which have appeared in the *Record* of the Folk-Lore Society
which, though listed as belonging to Sussex and Hampshire,
might equally well have been labelled Surrey. One is entitled
*Some West Sussex Superstitions lingering in 1868: collected
by Charlotte Latham at Fittleworth*. Well, Fittleworth lies
only a little way from Petworth, on the other side of the
Sussex border, and here is a Sussex story of "hollow ground"
which belongs, too, to a wooded hill close to my own home
at Hambledon in Surrey:

"It is a popular belief that immense wealth lies buried
underground in various localities, and that it is mysteriously
guarded from all interference. In a neighbouring parish the
spot adjoins a road that sounds 'awful hollow' as you walk
over it, and in this instance the buried treasure has a very

watchful guard, which instantly starts out of a ditch if it hears anyone approaching. A woman told the clergyman's wife that she had actually seen *it*, and that *it* was clad in brown. In our own parish we have a nightly watcher over some hidden treasures in a wood through which a public footpath passes, that certainly sounds hollow to the tread from the interlacement of the masses of roots below it. It is traversed by few after dark, from a dread of encountering this unearthly guardian."

My Hambledon story belongs in the same way to a hill, and the same dread is about the place, or was when I first came to live near. The hill is named the Tolt, and though in our old surveyor's map dated 1845, which I have, it is marked as arable, I think it must have been wooded in earlier days (as it is now), for I see that in *The Place Names of Surrey* the name is given as

"the dialect *toll* or *tolt*, a clump, a row, especially of trees. It is used 'of a solitary hill, usually somewhat conical. The idea behind all these words is probably something which is bluntly pointed.'"

That certainly describes the Tolt, which rises like a steep moleheap out of the flank of Hydons Ball. As for its being arable, I heard from a ninety-year-old countryman living in a cottage nearby that when as a young man he used to drive the plough over the ground it rattled as if it were hollow, and from another villager I learnt of the local belief that it was unsafe to go there at night. But of the Tolt and the ground near it, and of what may possibly be found if scientific excavators get to work, I have written in Chapter V.

Here, however, belongs a local superstition concerning the Tolt which has its counterpart in other Surrey parishes. One of the first stories I heard about the hill, accompanied by the saying that it was not safe to go there by night, was that there used to be a church there. In *Bygone Haslemere,* that valuable record of south-west Surrey, edited by E. W. Swanton, there is a reference to Aubrey's statement that tradition told of Haslemere once possessing seven churches, and the writer adds that

"Until quite recently there were folk tales associated with two churches here. In many parishes where the church is not in a central position its isolation is attributed to the malignity of the Evil One. It is so at Haslemere, where to this day (1914) old people believe that Town Meadow (in the neighbourhood of West Street, beyond the present post office) was originally selected as the site for the parish church, but the Devil came by night and pulled down what had been erected during the day, continuing to do so until the builders gave up in despair and erected it further to the north."

There is folk memory somewhere in these traditions of building, as there surely is when you find traces of bygone local activity such as fragments of ancient pottery. There are certain acres of the Haslemere upland, adjoining the parish of Haslemere, which used to be known as "Old Haslemere," and close by is a piece of ground with the old name of the Churchyard of Old Haslemere. Flint implements and pieces of pottery have been found in an adjoining field; and in the same way, on the Tolt, where the pottery of which I write elsewhere is to be found in such quantities, legend says there was once a church.

To how many centuries belong superstitions of the nightjar? It would be natural that country folk would come to associate queer notions with a bird that flies in the dusk and claps its wings as it takes flight. Gilbert White writes of the the villagers of Selborne and its neighbourhood that they "have a notion that the fern-owl, or churn-owl, or eve-jarr, which they also call a puckeridge, is very injurious to weanling calves by inflicting as it strikes at them the fatal distemper known to cow-leeches by the name of puckeridge." In the *Folk-Lore Record* Charlotte Latham writes that "the fern-owl is in the west of Sussex called the puck bird, or puck, which was an old Gothic word for Satan; and it probably received the name from a belief existing among the lower class of persons that it is a mischievous sprite, which inflicts on calves and heifers a disease here called the 'puck-complaint,' and in some parts of England the 'puckeridge.'" Here in Surrey I cannot hear of any evil effects supposed to follow visitations of the nightjar, which is the more curious in that the puckeridge is one of the local names for the bird. But of the queer ignorance of countrymen of the habits of birds, and of the ease with which superstition or fear even

to-day can infect the country mind, I had an interesting
example in the early days of the war of 1939, when a young
man of some thirty years of age was talking to me of his
experiences at night as a member of the Home Guard. His
turn of duty took him to Hydons Ball, where the shadowy
flittings of the nightjar at dusk set him and his companions
asking questions. "It won't do you any harm, will it?"

Of the doings of smugglers, and the roads or paths taken
by them in their passage from the coast inland, many records
belong to the South Country. Talk of their nightly errands
still survived in days of Queen Victoria. "Not many years
ago," Charlotte Latham tells us, "a farmer residing on the
western border of Sussex and Surrey seriously declared that
the witches were in the habit of riding his horses by night, as
they were often found by him in the morning covered with
dirt and perspiration, and in a state of great exhaustion.
This marvel, too, like many of our ghost stories, might probably be accounted for by the lawless practices of the gangs
of smugglers, who took the liberty of borrowing the farmer's
horses for the night work of bringing up their kegs of brandy
from the coast."

It was the fairies who helped the smugglers in the South
Country, according to Tom Shoesmith in Kipling's *Puck of
Pook's Hill.* "Dymchurch Flit," the Marsh men called it.
"I lay the Marsh men ought to know. They've been out after
dark, father an' son, smugglin' someone thing or t'other,
ever since wool grew to sheep's backs. They say there was
always a middlin' few Pharisees to be seen on the Marsh.
Impident as rabbits, they was. They'd dance on the nakid
roads in the nakid daytime; they'd flash their liddle green
lights along the diks, comin' an' goin', like honest smugglers.
Yes, an' times they'd lock the church doors against parson
an' clerk of Sundays."

That would be the smugglers "layin' in the lace or the
brandy," is the comment of Tom Shoesmith's listener, and
Charlotte Latham, writing of the vigilance of the Preventive
Service in such times, supplies her own explanation: "there
being very little doubt that the numerous ghosts seen wandering formerly in blue flames, near lonely houses on the
coast, were of an illicit class of spirits, raised by the smug-

glers in order to alarm and drive all others but their accomplices from their haunts."

So the lace and the brandy found their way up country, as the local Surrey tradition has it, and as you may see for yourself, following the Smugglers' Path by Hundred Acre and Hydons Ball.

Other tales of bewitchment are less easily traced to natural happenings. Charlotte Latham relates a story told her by a lady living at Westdean. People suffering from epilepsy are supposed to be bewitched, and are advised of a Surrey cure :

"She had observed, upon a cottage hearth, a quart bottle filled with pins; and on inquiring why they were put there was requested not to touch the bottle, as it was red hot, and because, if she did so, she would spoil the charm. 'What charm?' she asked, in some surprise. 'Why, ma'am,' replied the woman, 'it has pleased God to afflict my daughter here with falling-fits, and the doctors did her no good; so I was recommended to go to a wise woman, who lives on this side of Guildford, and she said, if she was well paid for it, she could tell me what ailed the girl and what would cure her. So I said I was agreeable, and she told me that people afflicted with falling-fits were bewitched, and that I must get as many pins as would fill a quart bottle, and put them into it and let it stand close to the fire upon the hearth till the pins were red hot; and when that came about, they would prick the heart of the witch who had brought this affliction on my poor girl, and she would then be glad enough to take it off."

But the pin cure belongs, too, to the countryside over the Surrey border. A doctor living at Pulborough told Mrs Latham that a few years before (i.e. in the 'fifties) when a house in Pulborough was being repaired, "on removing the hearthstone in one of the rooms a bottle containing upwards of two hundred pins was found; every pin being bent, and some of them nearly in a curve. A gentleman present took up the bottle, and expressed his surprise at its being there, and at its contents, when the workmen told him that they often found them and that they were deposited under the hearthstone (with certain ceremonies that, my informant said, were ludicrous but unfit for him to relate) for the purpose of protecting the house against witchcraft."

Side by side with human ailments due to witchcraft are the ailments of cattle. In *Bygone Haslemere* we read of farmers of the district who as late as the 'sixties used to consult a wizard, or "wise man," about such diseases. "It was thought that the wizard could change himself into a hare or a rabbit." A hare, perhaps, would be wounded by farmers shooting, and next day the wizard would be seen with his legs bandaged. In the same way with witches :

"An old woman living at Anstead Brook (two miles east of Haslemere) was accounted a witch. On one occasion some horses failing to move a wagon that had stuck in the clay the leading horse was purposely hit across the mane with a whip because it was thought that the witch was concealed there. The story goes that the old woman was seen next day with her arm in a sling."

It was at Anstead Brook where there survived till the middle of the last century the ceremony of wassailing the apple trees on New Year's Eve. According to accounts of the period the wassailers "met in the orchard, stood around a favourite tree, rapped it with sticks, and shouted

"Here stands a good old apple tree, stand fast root;
Every little twig bear an apple big.
Hats full, caps full and three-score sacks full,
Hip! hip! hurrah!"

A loud blast, three times repeated, was then blown at the base of the tree.

There are other safeguards, simpler in kind than witchcraft, against human ills. Cork and wood were at one time believed to prevent cramp—an idea of other parts of the country besides Haslemere. "As late as 1880 it was thought that a bung or large cork between the sheets at the bottom of the bed was a 'wonderful' preventive. An even better one was a cramp-ball—'cramble' in the vernacular. A cramble is a little tumour of the kind not infrequently seen on oak and beech trunks. Tumours from the former tree were the more highly prized." In the Educational Museum are specimens that were carried for many years in the waistcoat pockets of men still living in Haslemere in 1914.

There must be many local variants of the custom of throwing at "Jack-o'-Lents"—puppets set up for country folk to vent their ill will, or perhaps merely fun. A variation survived at Haslemere into the last years of the past century. An old inhabitant has described what he saw:

"One custom, purely local I think, was the Jack-o'-Lent. This was a figure representing some local person unpopular at the moment, which was mounted on an old horse or donkey and taken round the place on Easter Monday, with a placard fastened in front detailing the offence. The figure was shown at the different houses, and contributions towards expenses expected, and it was finally put to some end appropriate to his crime, such as hanging or burning. I can see them now—a crowd of men and boys running down over the rough ground of Shepherd's Hill, shouting and singing, and leading the donkey on which was seated the rocking figure. The custom naturally gave much umbrage, and was eventually put an end to; but I remember once the perpetrators were made ashamed. They had gibbeted in this way a harmless old gentleman for some fancied offence, and presented themselves after their usual rude custom before his house. He came out and walked round his effigy, examining it very carefully, and, perfectly unruffled, pronounced it 'Good, very good, and here's half a crown for you'—and like whipped curs they slunk away."

In *Old West Surrey* Miss Jekyll describes a like performance of "rough music." This was prepared in the case of a man who was known to beat his wife, by laying a train of chaff to his cottage door. This meant "We know that thrashing goes on here." If the hint was not taken, a din of kettles and pans followed.

But of witchcraft Miss Jekyll could hear little. In my own village of Hambledon at a Women's Institute meeting stories were invited from the "oldest inhabitants," but all that could be remembered was talk of an old woman who "was supposed to be a witch." She bewitched cattle, and all the children were afraid of her.

I am fortunate in being able to add to this chapter some

notes on folk lore in Surrey of to-day, which have been sent me by one who is known by his work and research to all Surrey Archæologists, Dr Eric Gardner. He writes:

"Soon after I went to Weybridge in 1906 I was just about to go out one afternoon, and as I opened the front door a woman arrived pushing a perambulator in which was a baby about a year old. It was in the midst of the most violent spasm of whooping-cough I had seen for a long time. I commented that there was not much doubt as to what was the matter with the child, and the mother said, 'Well, and what is it?' 'Why, whooping-cough, of course,' I told her. 'Listen to it.' She was a coarse, aggressive-looking woman, and she put her hands on her hips and retorted, 'Well, that's just what it isn't. I know it sounds like it, but I did the bridges yesterday, and it still goes on making that row, so it can't be whooping-cough, and I want to know what it is.' I gently enquired what she meant by 'doing the bridges,' and after looking at me with pitying scorn, she explained that if you took a child with whooping-cough over a river by one bridge and brought it back by another no whooping-cough that ever was could stand that. She went on to say the child had had the cough for a fortnight now, and that yesterday she had pushed it over the Thames by Chertsey Bridge, through Shepperton, and home over Walton Bridge, and as it still continued she wanted to know what was really the matter.

"I ventured to ask her if all this happened during the awful thunderstorm of the previous afternoon, and she said, 'Oh yes, the pram was pretty full by the time I got back.' I had to tell her there was no doubt about the whooping-cough, so she picked the child up, put it in the pram, and with a parting 'If that's all you know about whooping-cough, I'll find someone who knows a bit more,' disappeared down the drive.

"Many years ago Professor Eliot Smith, the anatomist, was excavating pre-Dynastic Egyptians of about 4000 B.C. buried in the desert sand. He found the bodies had just dried up and were so preserved that it was often possible to identify the last meal, and he frequently found in the stomachs of the children the bones of a mouse. He made enquiries and learnt that a skinned and fried mouse was frequently given to children *in extremis* from any disease throughout the East even at the present day. My own enquiries (because I once had to stop a mother giving her child a skinned and fried mouse for whooping-cough) showed that it was a well-known remedy at least in the South of England, and I personally ran across it again also as a remedy for whooping-cough, but this time I think it really was given though the mother denied it. The child's expression when the mother made the denial was something to be remembered."

Dr Gardner writes out of further local experience that "on the principle of using, as a remedy, a hair of the dog that bit him, Wisley cottagers boil the bodies of adders and obtain the oil which they use for adder bites." And he goes on :

"Now here is a puzzle of the past I have never solved, as the expression must now be quite dead. In 1904–5 I was working from the London Hospital in their Whitechapel maternity district. Except just at the end of my time all the help I ever had at a confinement was given by one of the terrible old Whitechapel 'Gamps.' Should one of them attend the birth of a run of boys she would say 'The lions have whelped.' I often used to play up to this and if a boy were born I would say quietly, 'Another boy, mother; the lions have whelped,' and she would reply, 'Aye, the lions have whelped, doctor. Always a lot of boys when the lions whelp.' I could never find out what lions, though I imagined those formerly at the Tower were referred to, for it was obviously an old saying, stereotyped—always 'whelped,' a single phrase, a quotation. No questions were answered or invited.

"I was surprised when I got to Weybridge in 1906 to find that the village Gamps were quite familiar with 'the lions,' and still thinking of the Tower I wondered if that thorough-paced rascal, George Payne of Bròoklands, who was 'Keeper of the Menagerie of the Tower of London,' and whose bear pits were found on the top of Members' Hill when the Brooklands Track was made, had anything to do with the survival of the legend. I have seen a letter Payne wrote to Warren Hastings, 'The tygres you have promised me are not yet come.' But the whelping lions were talked of in

Woking and other parts of Surrey, and were quite common-place in rural Essex, and I have heard of them elsewhere.

"Except certain common rites in connection with child-birth and death, I have not met very much folk lore in my practice, as I was not sufficiently deep in the country, but I have seen all the looking-glasses covered up in the death chamber—even in that of a President of the Law Society—against the possibility of the spirit of the dead being 'caught' in the mirror and held there till some demon entered the dead body.

"In my present work it always intrigues me to see the white stockings on a corpse, even among the very poor. They can be obtained for the purpose from any undertaker, even at this stage of the war. It is, I think, the last relic of the ceremonial dressing of the dead in white in an effort to counteract the dark influences."

Here is another Gamp reminiscence :

"The afterbirth is just disposed of in these days, but usually is still burnt. No doctor witnesses the ceremonial-burning of it, such as I have seen. The old Whitechapel women, no matter how poor the mother, always managed to acquire coal. I have known one collect lumps one by one from neighbours, and always as the child was born was there a big fire. In my early, inexperienced days, when I thought the baby would soon be here, I learnt to realize I was quite wrong if the fire had not been brought up to a bright heat. As soon as the child was born, or rather separated, you were almost pushed out of the way as the old dame gathered up the afterbirth, and I have seen her holding it high over her head, march solemnly across the room and place it on the fire. Then she would sit down and neighbours who had heard the baby cry would sit down with her, and as the after-birth crackled so she would count one crack for each child to be born."

Dr Gardner concludes :

"One final little story. A woman in Weybridge brought her child to me with a small nævus on its temple. She was a Catholic. I froze the nævus with carbon dioxide snow and warned her that she would see no change for a few days, but that then I expected it would rather suddenly change, dry up and disappear. 'Anyway, come back and show me in a week.'

"She did so, and all had happened as I had told her. I said, 'Well, that's all right.' 'Yes,' said the mother, 'but no thanks to you, doctor.' I asked her why, as everything seemed to have gone according to plan. So she told me 'As nothing happened after you treated it, I sent the monks at St. Winifred's Well in Wales a shilling postal-order and got a bottle of the Holy Water from the Well and put that on the place, and next morning it was all shrivelled and dried up.' Thus do miracles happen, for I am sure she wrote and told them."

CHAPTER XVII

THREE MUSEUMS

HASLEMERE Educational Museum was founded by Jonathan Hutchinson in 1888, and carries a world of history in its name. Its founder, a Fellow of the Royal Society, three years earlier had declared the object at which he aimed. "We have been content long enough that museums shall be used by a few, and simply gazed at by the many. It is time that we set ourselves earnestly to make them what they should be in our educational scheme." That was his gospel, and its fruits are to be seen in the faces of the thousands of visitors—especially the faces of the children—who spend happy hours in its corridors to-day.

Its beginnings were simple. For the first few years the contents of the museum were housed in a little building put up by the founder close to Inval, his home, about a mile from the town. Soon afterwards it overflowed. Talks and demonstrations given at week-ends became so popular that Mr Hutchinson decided in 1895 to build a much larger museum in the town itself. Further improvements and enlargements followed : the founder was knighted in 1908; and to-day the Museum has gained a name far beyond the boundaries of the county of Surrey.

And it fulfils the hope and the plans of its founder every day of its life. That is the right word for Haslemere; it is the most live museum I know. You are among living things the moment you enter the door. No matter what the month or the weather, you will find things breathing and growing at your side. Take, at random, a day in September. Opposite you as you go in is a table of wayside fruits—sweet briar, cuckoo-pint, hawthorn, elder, beechnuts, scarlet berries of lily of the valley. Other tables will be covered with trays, distinct and named, of growths which ask for the naming in woodland and garden—autumn fungi. There, in particular, the visitor will find many questions answered; he has been want-

224

Old water-mill at Elstead
Castle Gate, Guildford

ing to know the scientific name of the brown and yellow toadstools which decompose on his lawn, and which he has heard vaguely called *boletus,* but he wants to find out if there are different kinds; or he has been attracted by the lovely shades of a group of little fungi at the foot of a beech, and learns that in future he must think of *Clitocybe laccata* var. *amethystina.* Or to come nearer home in a wet autumn, he discovers that the brown rot in which his apples have dropped from the trees should be properly named *Monilia fructigena,* and that the grey scab disfiguring the green fruit is *Venturia inæqualis.* It is all so much simpler than looking the names out in books (which in wartime he has been unable to buy), and he is assured of the rightness of the labels by the knowledge that the curator of the Museum is one of the greatest living authorities on the subject of fungi, Mr E. D. Swanton.

Here, on side shelves, are glass tanks in which he can watch the life of tiny creatures of pond and marsh. He can look closely at the *Dytiscus* beetle, or at pond snails, the so-called cheese snail and the round-mouthed snail, both of them here feeding on lettuce; or at mosquitoes, their larvæ and pupæ, or at the whirligig beetles and water-boatmen, so much more easily observed within a few inches on a shelf than in dim waters of a pond. Frogs are plainly at home in little waterside places of their own under glass, and I was reminded, when I was last looking at tanks on these shelves, that it was to Haslemere that, on a day in December 1939, I sent my albino frog (of which a note belongs to another chapter), where it was provided with a home, and soon afterwards found its way into the newspapers. "The Lemon Frog with Pink Eyes," "One-in-Millions Freak," and so on, were the headlines in the evening newspapers, and the public were informed that the only other albino of which authenticated records existed was found in a pond in St. Lawrence County, and was sent to the American Museum of Natural History.

My albino frog was given a mate, but I never heard of any pink-eyed tadpoles. It shared a shelf, in its tank, with other exhibits common and rare. One uncommon addition came to the Museum in the same year, a swallow-tailed butterfly, of which the chrysalis was found near Tilford in July 1940. It emerged, to be properly described as a perfect insect, on

Q   225

Mediæval doorway in Quarry Street, Guildford
Through the lychgate at Shalford

4 August, and has lived next-door, or next-shelf, to some fine nests of common and Norwegian wasps ever since.

Of what I may call the fundamental features of the Museum, the *Guide,* written by the Curator, gives short descriptions. One of the founder's objects was to try to convey to the mind of youth—and in so doing he succeeded where others have failed with older minds—some idea of the spaces of geological time. Look at the space-for-time schedule on the south wall of the Geological Gallery. "It consists of twenty equal spaces, marked on the wall and front shelf by vertical black lines. To each space is allotted a hypothetical period of thirty million years." This time-chart is based upon astronomical grounds deduced in regard to the formation of certain rocks. "It indicates in a striking manner the brevity of the human period."

Another space-for-time schedule is to be studied in the Gallery of Human History. Here are forty equal spaces marked by vertical lines on a wall seventy feet long. Each space represents a century, and in the space and on the corresponding shelf fronting it are specimens, maps, and so on, belonging to that century; for instance, under the 11th century A.D. you find a facsimile reproduction of the Surrey part of the Domesday Survey.

Other galleries particularly attractive to children are the Zoological and the Gallery of British Birds. In the Zoological Gallery, beside a series of fossils, a collection of abnormal horns and antlers, and the complete skeleton of a moa, there is a big open cabinet of foreign butterflies. There are exhibits illustrating albinism, melanism, and changes of colour according to the season; foreign mammals, from the pink armadillo of Argentina to the flying phalanger of Victoria and specimens of British mammals, of which thirty-one out of the forty-two have been seen within six miles of Haslemere. Among them is the water-shrew, which I once had the luck to be able to watch through a whole morning in a rock-pool in my own garden.

We get all the British reptiles in south-west Surrey. Near Churt you may be able to set eyes on the smooth snake, and on the commons round Thursley there used to be natterjack toads, but whether they have survived the devastation of

the tanks of the last war I do not know—it may take years
to find out.

In the Gallery of British Birds there are three hundred
and thirty-three species, and I do not doubt that many visitors, looking at the cases, have been enabled to identify birds
seen in sunshine and shadow, in a moment of noon or dusk.
A green woodpecker in sudden sunlight is a different bird
from the same creature half-recognized in rain. But the large,
open-air exhibits are those I like best; the golden eagle on
the rock of a Scottish hill, and the view of Frensham Great
Pond as it used to be before the war, with its coot, its moorhens, its kingfishers and the widgeon of bright waters in
winter.

Records of old days of travel by road in Surrey have their
fascination. I have written in the chapter "An Old Farm
Account Book" of the tolls and tollgates of Surrey roads.
Here in the Museum, on the wall of a passage to the left of
the entrance, is the actual wooden table of tolls which once
stood by the Winterton Toll Gate, Chiddingfold. This was
erected, the label informs you, later than 1824 in the reign
of George IV and was in use until 1871. Here are some of
the charges :

A Table of the Tolls payable at this Turnpike . . . (Here
the wood of the board is broken)
For every Horse, Mule, Ass or other beast
(except dogs) drawing any Coach, Berlin, Landau,
Barouche, Chariot, Chaise, Chair, Whiskey,
Taxed Cart, Waggon, Wain, Timber-frame, Cart-
frame, Dray or other vehicle of whatsoever design
when drawn by more than one Horse or other
Beast the sum of Fourpence-halfpenny (such
waggon, wain, cart or other such carriage having
wheels of less breadth than four and a half inches.   4½d.

For every Dog drawing any Truck, Barrow or
other carriage for the space of One Hundred
Yards or upwards upon any part of the said Roads
the sum of One Penny.   1d.

For every carriage moved or propelled by Steam, or Machinery, or by other Power the sum of One Shilling for every wheel thereof.   1s.

For every Score of Oxen, Cows, or neat Cattle, the sum of Tenpence and so in proportion for any greater or less number.   10d.

All these and other charges for use of the road you may read on the board standing in the passage, with a note adding that the inscription is line for line the same as that on the older North Chapel toll-board, which is to be seen on the loggia of the Museum facing the garden lawn. North Chapel of course belongs to Sussex, and presumably these toll-boards are examples of boards which used to be found all over the country. He was a far-seeing man who rescued them from Fifth of November bonfires and other such natural ends for what must have seemed at the time the proper fate for useless and uninteresting pieces of wood. To-day they have the interest and charm that belong to relics of a day when motorcars were vehicles of a dream.

Other relics are of interest without charm. A badger-trap found at Whitwell Hatch near Haslemere, spring-guns warning gamekeepers of the presence of poachers, pole-traps for catching hawks, owls and other perching birds of prey; and a hideous man-trap—there used to be an even bigger and wickeder instrument to be seen at Peper Harow—some of these belong to days within recent memory and the man-trap to a period hardly a hundred years behind us. One relic is mentioned in a classic, Gilbert White's *Selborne*. "On Hindhead one of the bodies on the gibbet was beaten down to the ground," White writes in his *Diary*, 23 December 1790. Here is a fragment of the gibbet.

A happier memory is enshrined in a name belonging to the same period. Close by the Table of Tolls is an instrument labelled "Spade or graft used for land draining. The initials W.C. on the handle are those of William Clark, the grandson of William Clark who planted the chestnut tree in the High Street in 1792."

There at the side of the High Street in sun and rain the chestnut tree stands to-day.

And in sun or rain in Quarry Street, Guildford, you may stand at the door of the Museum—and pass inside to an age beyond thoughts of weather or life of to-day. Here, in the first room, you are back at work with palæolithic tools found in the neighbourhood of Farnham, or you pass on to days of bronze, with a hoard of metal hidden as his reserve by a smith at Coulsdon; and then through millenniums to the moulding of box-flue tiles for a Roman villa on Ashtead Common, to window-glass and tessellated pavements, and then—with sudden pleasure in the knowledge of what was living—the footprints of dogs and the claws of a wild cat in clay that was wet as the Roman builder spread it.

Stairs lead up to our own English iron age—to the days of wrought- and cast-iron work used on hearths and in kitchens; basket spits, idle-backs, lazy-backs, kettle tippers, kitchen hangers, "black cats" of crossed iron rods for plates of toast; iron ox-shoes or "ques"—two shoes on each foot, one on each "claw"; and to viler uses of iron, fox-traps and a large man-trap from Loseley Park. You are brought, in the next room, into close touch with those savage days—for man-traps were abolished by law only in 1826—looking at a cotton smock worn by an English peasant, William Daniels, who died on 10 December 1916, aged 101.

There are reminders of other uses of iron in what we may still call our own time. In the furthest room to which the visitor wanders he finds a case of various relics, among them the big key of the old Hog's Back turnpike gate, which was closed in 1876. Near to it are staves served out to special constables during the riots in Guildford between 1859 and 1865. A savage weapon is the bludgeon carried by the leader of the "Guys," with which an attempt was made to murder Police-constable Stent, and with which another constable was so seriously hurt that he died. It is a horrid weapon, two feet six inches long, heavily studded with nails and at the end a sharp spike.

It is pleasant to come back to peaceful uses of wood. There are many quaint household implements in the collection presented by Miss Jekyll; butter-scoops, wooden scales, punch ladles, trenchers, lemon-squeezers; huge mouse-traps, more like cages than traps, and dead-fall traps with wooden blocks which I should like to weigh; flails of ash bound with raw hide and with heads ingeniously held to swing as loose and heavily as possible—the flails were called frails and the heads swingels, pronounced as if the g were j. But to list the tools and other farm and household furniture would be to reprint the pages of Miss Jekyll's unique book *Old West Surrey*.

One delightful exhibit attracts children. In the corner of the end room but one stands a small carriage made of wood, with the body swung on leather straps and with wooden wheels with iron tyres. It was drawn by dogs, and was presented by the Misses Williamson; it was made about 1830, and used to take one of the donors, when she was a child, to school.

There are times when the Guildford Museum is free to visitors, but it would be worth an entrance fee at any time to be able to look at the Jekyll collection alone.

At Godalming there is another museum. At certain times it is open free to the public and is housed in the little building which stands on the site of the old Town Hall. It is not a large museum, as you may guess from outside, but it holds an interesting collection. On your left as you enter the room stands a rough-hewn block of stone which those who last used it—they were farm hands—probably would have been little the wiser had they been told what it was. Thirty years ago it served as a pig-trough; hundreds of years before that it was a Roman altar in the Wall, dedicated to the god Cocidius, a deity of the North Country, by the Birdoswald garrison, the First Ælian Cohort of Dacians. It was discovered, the label tells you, by the Rev H. M. Larner, rector of Busbridge, in 1923, in the farmyard of a house in North Munstead. It seems to have been obtained from the collection of a Recorder of Carlisle by R. Carteret Webb, M.P., who lived at Busbridge Hall at the end of the eighteenth century and brought the altar there.

In cases and standing about the walls of the museum are household implements and farm tools collected from houses near—rush-light holders, pulley wheels, sickles and so on;

clay pipes and a basket made to hold them, of straw bound and laced with thread. There is what used to be known as a sack jigger, a curious instrument with a long wooden handle and an iron ring with hooks made so as to hold a sack so that flour could be poured into it. There is a large cheese-press, and close by an instrument of a different ancestry, a key-bugle said to have been used in Godalming Church before there was an organ.

Other exhibits of interest are photographs and drawings. There is a view taken of Borough Road about 1870, showing the River Wey and not a house in sight. I should choose for its charm a sketch of the old Town Hall, with its oak beams and lath and plaster, and a bell tower, of which the modern building is a not very graceful copy. A photograph which doubtless will be scanned with interest a hundred years hence is of the strata laid bare when the reservoir was dug on the top of Hydons Ball. But if I am to pick out one specimen for its separate value, it is an exhibit which must be one of the latest additions to the cases in the middle of the room. It is a china bowl made by a well-known architect-citizen of the town, H. Thackeray Turner. Here is a graceful design in greens and browns, of birds, snakes and boughs, a worthy memorial of the artist-moulder.

These are Surrey's three museums, each with its charm, each with its character; but the museum with life and magnetism of its own in each of its sunlit rooms is Haslemere's.

CHAPTER XVIII

TALK WITH A COUNTRYMAN

ONE of the first books I read when I came to live in Surrey at the beginning of the century was *The Bettesworth Book: Talks with a Surrey Peasant,* by "George Bourne"—or George Strutt as we learnt to know his name later. I have read the talks many times since, and have heard in them the quiet voices of other Surrey peasants whom it has been my good fortune to know through the years; gardeners most of them, as Bettesworth was, with the same speech, as slow and deep-rooted as the plants they tended. It is a speech, a manner of speaking, rather than a dialect with broad differences of sound and accent; you do not hear consonants altered as in Zummerzet, nor vowels changing places in the alphabet as with the Sussex farm labourer who "wunt be druv." Yet it belongs undoubtedly to Surrey, with, as I hear it, a certain thinness of tone and short-syllabled quiet in sentence after sentence. Here is Bettesworth talking of a shovel :

"No, he en't like yourn. Yours is one o' they patent ones. Got a holler back. But this is a very nice shovel. Got such a good lift to 'un. I lent 'un to Jimmy Cook up 'ere at the gravel pits a week or two ago. A lot of 'en up there fell in love with 'n. I says, 'I don't care, so long's you brings 'n back.' He wanted to borry a peck too, but I en't got no peck now. The best shovel as ever I had—oh, he was a purty tool an' no mistake !—he was as big as this, but as light . . . ! Got wore reg'ler thin he was; an't last I lent 'n to a man, an' he got 'n on to some big stones, an' the edge of 'n chinked out. 'R else I never had a nicer shovel than what that was. I got 'n down 'ome, now."

And here, of a horse :

"When I was at work for old Frank Cooper the builder, he had a new 'orse come 'ome. I went into the stable at night to give 'n some feed and see's he was all right. He let me go in right enough. But as soon as I was in, then he come for me. There wa'n't no way out—I was up in the rack an' I couldn't git away no-where. I thinks to myself, 'I dunno how this is gwine to be, with he like this an' me here alone.' So I looked round an' catched up a short stick about two foot long—a bit o' the rack it was—as laid there; an' when he come for me I reached down an' give 'n one behind the knees an' brought 'un down. Then I gits down; but as soon as I was down he come for me again, snarkin' and blowin', tryin' to pen me in an' git me up agin the side. I didn't like the looks of it, so I ups with my bit o' wood again, an' just as he got up close I give 'n the end of it in his side. He sprung away, an' I slipped out an' shut the door. 'Come,' I thinks, 'this won't do neither. I got to master he somehow.' So I takes a prong and in I goes again. 'I'll knock you down,' I thinks, 'if you gets up to any o' your games wi' me.' Well, I had to give 'n another behind the knees."

That is one of the magnets of *The Bettesworth Book*—the magnet of easy, practised dealing with animals—horses, pigs, dogs—that draws the countryman from page to page. And when a man has to deal with himself and his own ailments? Bettesworth's remedies, you would say, belong to days even before doctors. He hears of toothache :

" 'Oh dear! That *is* a miserable thing, is toothache. You can't bide nowheres, an' you can't sleep, an' you can't eat. . . . There, 'tis a *miser*able thing. . . . I 'en't had it for years now, 'r else I 'ave had it terrible bad. I've put baccer in my teeth—I've even gone so fur 's to put it in my ears.' "

"I shrugged my shoulders. 'I shouldn't like to do that!'

" 'No; you can't bear 't long. But I've done it. Roll it up tight an' soak it in rum an' poke it into yer ear the side where the ache is. . . . 'T stops the pain for a bit, but it very soon makes yer head begin to jump. Tell ye what's another very good thing now, an' that's a 'orse-radish.'

" 'A horse-radish?'

" 'Yes; tied round yer wrist.'

" 'What's that for?'

" 'For *tooth*ache.'

" 'Well, but——'

" 'Yes, that's it, sir. Ye see that's where the nerve goes

233

to from yer wrist—up to yer teeth. . . . An' if you gets a horse-radish, and scrapes 'n ye know, and ties 'n tight round yer wrist, 't'll very soon drive the toothache away. But you can't stand it for very long. It doo give to ye. I dunno but what the pain's as bad as the toothache.'"

Bettesworth comes back again and again to the horses :

"In Sussex, the farmers don't stable their horses, same as they do up here. At night they jest shuts 'em into the farm-yard loose, and there's a crib stands in the middle o' the yard, for 'im to feed out of. . . .

"'I remember,' he continued, 'one night when we was away harvestin', we all slep' in a barn—thirty or forty of us, I dessay there was. The last man in was always supposed to see that everything was all fastened up and right. Well, this night we was all in but one; and he come in late an' left the gate undone, and these 'ere horses got out. . . . Oh, we could hear 'em as we laid there in the barn, gallopin' for miles ! 'Cause everything was so still, ye know—'twas in the dead o' the night—miles an' miles along the road we could hear they horses gallopin'. They was so pleased to be out. The carter he got up in a hurry, an' the shepherd too. . . .'"

It is not often given to the writer of a book so original in theme and handling as *The Bettesworth Book* to better his own production in a sequel. But I think that is what George Bourne succeeded in doing when, in 1907, he published a second series of recollections of Bettesworth's talk and doings in *Memoirs of a Surrey Labourer*. It is a book fuller of the living man, his speech and thought, even than its forerunner. Bettesworth's "mate" in the garden was a robin. "You may do anything you mind to with 'n, but yer mawn't handle 'im !" The bird worked with him wherever he was turning up the soil.

"And now on this gay morning, as we crossed the lawn together, he said, 'Little Bob bin 'long with me again this mornin', hoppin' about just in front o' my shovel, and twiddlin' and talkin' to me. . . .

"'Sweet little birds, I calls 'em,' said Bettesworth, using an epithet rare with him. 'And it's a funny thing,' he continued, 'wherever a man's at work there's sure to be a robin find him out. I've noticed it often. If I bin at work in the

woods, a robin 'd come, or in the harvest-field, jest the same.
. . . Hark at 'n twiddlin' ! And by-'n-by when his crop's full
he'll get up in a tree and *sing.* . . .'

"The old man did a stroke or two with his shovel, and
then : 'I don't hear no starlin's about. 'Relse, don't ye mind
last year they had a nest up in the shed?'

"Next year they had a nest.

" 'Hark at those starlings !' I said to Bettesworth. And he,
'Yes, I dunno who 'twas I was talkin' to this mornin', sayin'
how he liked to hear 'em. "So do our guv'nor," I says. I
likes 'em best when there's two of 'em gibberin' to one
another—jest like's if they was talkin'. An' they lifts up their
feet, an' flaps up their wings, an' they nods.' The old man's
words ran rhythmically to suit the action he was describing;
and then, dropping the rhythm, 'I likes to hear 'em very well.
And I don't think they be mischieful birds neither, like these
'ere sparrers and caffeys [chaffinches]. They beggars, I
shouldn't care so much if when they picked out the peas from
the ground they'd eat 'em. But they jest nips the little green
top off and leaves it. Sims as if they does it reg'lar for mischief.' "

The talk strays at intervals into unexpected channels—
ways with donkeys, for example. "Moost donkeys goes after
dirty clothes o' Monday mornin's"—that was doubtless true
of cottage laundress work in days before big laundries drove
cars. But his old mother-in-law's donkey, named Jane, whom
he once drove down into Sussex for harvesting, was a
creature of individual habits. "She drinked seven pints o'
beer 'tween this an' Chichester. Some policeman give her one
pint when we drove down into Singleton. There was three or
four policemen outside the public there," Goodwood races
being on at the time; and these policemen treated Jane, while
Bettesworth went within to refresh himself. "That an' some
bread was all she wanted. I'd took a peck o' corn for her,
but she didn't sim to care about it; and I give a feller thrup-
pence what'd got some clover-grass on a cart, but she only
had about a mouthful o' that." In short, Jane preferred
bread and beer. "Jest break a loaf o' bread in half an' put
it in a bowl an' pour about a pint o' beer over't. . . . But
she'd put her lips into a glass or a cup and soop it out.

Reg'lar coster's donkey, she was, and they'd learnt her. Not much bigger'n a good-sized dog—but trot!"

The Bettesworth Book was published in 1901, *Memoirs of a Surrey Labourer* followed six years later, and forty years bring changes. Perhaps the Surrey gardeners and farm hands whom I meet to-day have felt the change; they have most of them lived for years of their lives in Army camps and barracks, and for that time and to that extent have heard and spoken a common language, which chokes or smooths provincial accents. Most of them seem to me to talk in the same way as other Surrey neighbours; none of them broaden dialect as do—or did—the Sussex countryman whose language furnishes such a delightful closing chapter to E. V. Lucas's *Highways and Byways in Sussex*.

But some of them preserve in speech and memory their own words and phrases, their own ways of speaking of what they see or repeating what they have heard. I have had the good fortune to be able to talk to more than one Surrey labourer who might well have been numbered among Bettesworth's acquaintances had they happened to be working, harvesting or gardening, a few years earlier; men of the same quiet, modest way of thinking of themselves and friends, but men who have lived their own independent lives on a working-man's weekly wages, owing nothing, saving little, perhaps, but working year in year out in all weathers on the same few acres of Surrey soil. Among all of them one stands out best in my memory of all his calling, a gardener, whom I have known; a limited calling, no doubt, for he is just a "kitchen" gardener without experience of the less common flowers and shrubs. But of the plain growing of vegetables, of the day to day work of a farm, of the life of the kindly fruits of the earth, he has little to learn, and I owe him thanks for much that he has taught me. Above all, I have learnt something of the speech of the countryman —words that are in no dictionary though they belong to the language of Englishmen, phrases that might have been heard by Chaucer or echoed in the talk of Piers Plowman. I wish I could have set down more of what I have heard.

He was once describing, for instance, how he had watched

a partridge till he lost it in the distance. "I followed 'im me eyesight out." And of a thing he had witnessed over and over again : "I've seen it drags of times." Of a hazel hedge-row he had clipped : it had grown over a garden path and was "flickin' 'isself in your face." He gazed at part of a cabbage-bed which was robbed by the roots of a neighbouring birch. "That's what takes the mike out of our ground." Another day there had been rain, but not enough to prevent digging. " 'Tisn't puggy yet; if 'twere puggy we should have to go to some other work."

Not often do we see a new sight in a wood we have known for many years. But one day I found myself looking at a patch of ground which puzzled me. I had walked across to a strip of hazel which was being cut for pea-boughs, stakes, beansticks and the other uses to which hazel is put, and I was watching my Surrey gardener drawing a withe through the glowing ashes of his fire, before twisting and knotting it to bind up one of his bundles—for in frosty weather unless you heat withes they crack and break—when my eye fell on a heap of some unrecognized substance at the foot of a hazel stub. I stooped to examine it. "Ah," he said, "now that's a thing I never remember seeing before. D'you know what that is? That's the seed of they hazels, bit by they short-tailed mice." There it lay, a patch the size of a dinner-plate and an inch deep. The "seed" was hazel catkins, "lamb's-tails," chewed up into tiny sections. I looked about me, and there were other patches of the same torn flowers, each by a stub. "Like mangel-seed," he commented. "You couldn't tell it apart."

A few yards away the hazel bordered what had the year before been a larch wood. By a sawn stump lay a pile of stripped cones. "That's the squirrels. No, I never see a red one. They takes the conies and they tears them to get at the kernels. Like white kernels. That's what they eat." I spoke of the lack of food in what had been, that winter, a long frost. "Ah, and look at the rooks. Hundreds and hundreds of them there's been in that field. And what are they getting? You'd think wireworm, but how does the wireworm get to the surface? There they are, hundreds and hundreds." The rooks rose and circled round and round in higher rings. He gazed at them. "Haymaking, that's what we call that." And he drew a withe slowly through the red embers.

We were standing, one winter day, looking at a wood pile, mainly hazel; it had been built two winters before, when a larch plantation had been felled and the frith, not wanted for timber, telegraph poles, pit props or paper pulp, had been cut and stacked for firewood large and small. My companion glanced at the sky. "Ah, and d'you know what we used to do to keep wood like that dry?" He told me, seeking no answer, "Small stuff, trimmings, anything, fern, pile it on the top, spread it, leave it, and there you've got your wood dry when you want it—there you are, you've got it dry." He measured the pile with his eye, and his glance travelled to the end of it, where lay a heap of oak logs, tumbled as the lorry-driver had left them.

"Ah, that's good wood. What did you say that was? Two cord and a half? But that's more than four feet, why, that's five, six foot nearly that is. You bought it unsawn? Well!" His eye ran over the lorryload in silence. "What do you call a cord, then?" I asked. "A cord of wood? Well, there's two. One of them's four feet long, sixteen feet in length, and two foot high. You get three cords, and you measure them so"— he moved hands up and to the side, shaping piles in right-angles—"and you've got them six foot high; then you take what you want and you know where you are. Then there's the other, three foot by three foot, and twenty feet in length, that's the other cord. That's two cords you've got, six foot high by the side of the road. . . . Yes, in Surrey all my life. That's good wood, that is." He measured it again in silence. And I puzzled, remembering the measurements on the page of the dictionary, when I had first calculated what a cord would bring me—"a measure of wood, stone or rock (? originally measured with a cord); a pile of wood, usually 8 feet by 4, and 4 feet high." "Ah, in different parts of the country—I quite understand. But that's what a cord is." He repeated the measuremnts. "No, I don't know as ever I saw it in a book," he concluded, and picked up a log in the rain.

I have often thought over this mental arithmetic, these tables of figures in the mind by which through season after season a countryman sizes and values the crops of gardens large and small. One day in early autumn I was looking at an onion bed, and vaguely wondering what a really good crop meant, in weight as a salesman might think of it. I asked my companion, who could measure so exactly a cord of firewood, what he supposed the bed weighed. "I calculate," he said slowly, "that that lot weighs five hundredweight and a half." He had sown the bed, thinned it, watched it, and there he looked at the fruit of his work. I thought to weigh the crop for myself; there were ten rows of ninety onions apiece. I chose a large and an average onion; they weighed seventeen ounces and twelve ounces, so I did the sum and showed it him. "I generally can tell what a crop weighs," he said.

It is he and his fellows, through the centuries—how many, who shall say, or using how many of the words they speak to-day?—who have given us our country proverbs of earth and sky, of trees, months, crops. There are not many proverbs of trees, and I wonder sometimes whether we get them right, or their meaning. "Oak before ash, we shall have a splash, ash before oak, we shall have a soak"—that is one of the most familiar. Is it in its true form, or have we somehow altered it? For its truth, surely, is not of the future, but of the past. We have had, or are having, a splash or a soak, would be putting it better, for the oak being a deep-rooted tree feels the push of sap from rain long past, while the surface-rooting ash remains thirsty in drought.

Again, who made the rhyme of the walnut? "A woman, a dog and a walnut tree, the more you beat them the better they be"—that does not belong to the thought of English villagers. It cannot be old-English, for walnuts were not introduced into England until the sixteenth century. I should guess that the proverb came from abroad with the tree.

Two other trees set me wondering, for different reasons— one because it has no proverb, the other because the proverb, I think, will come to it in time—but in what form? Of the two trees, the one which has no proverb, or if it has I have never heard it, is the beech. Yet it is a native of England and a tree of character; its buds are of a shape unlike others, its roots are grasping, it holds pockets of water—armpits of

239

water you might call them—and nothing will grow under it. Surely the ancestors of my Surrey gardener noticed all these things, and yet they have said nothing about it.

But the tree of trees of which the proverb is in the making is the mulberry. To my gardener, looking at apple trees on a day in May, I said something about late frosts. "Yes, she's cold," he said of the north wind, "but d'you know what I look at? That old mulberry tree. If you see him waiting, there, you don't know what you may get. But if he's green, you won't have much—not enough to hurt."

That old mulberry tree at which he looked was not old in years, for it had not been much over thirty years in the ground, but it stood for him for all the mulberries he had known, and it had never played him false. And then came the May of 1945, opening with night after night of frost, the most disastrous in my garden memories, with azaleas, rhododendrons, magnolias withered in leaf and flower. I had never before seen such a sight as the magnolias, with every leaf on tall trees hanging limp and grey. I went to the mulberry, to find its new shoots as grey as the magnolia's. My gardener had been there before me. He looked up from his digging. "Ah," he said, "he's bit. He's bit. That's against the rules, I says to Jack, That's against the rules." So there it is. At the end of a gardener's lifetime, or near it, the mulberry tree breaks the rules. What rule can you lay down? That is why, perhaps, Englishmen since days beyond reckoning have looked every spring at the mulberry, a foreigner from Asia by way of Italy, but have made no proverb about it yet. The children have begun with the mulberry bush, but the men have not yet had time.

Or is it that I have not yet had time to learn the proverb? —to learn what the countryman knows but does not tell me? One thing I have learnt—that my gardener friend tells me what he knows, not by way of direct answer to a question, but by accident, so to say, when I have been talking to him about something else. About goldfinches, for instance—I learnt something of goldfinches from him on a day which began with rabbits. Of rabbits I had often spoken, but in the kitchen garden, where wire netting comes first in his mind. This was in the flower garden, to which wallflower

Colley Hill, Reigate

plants and other seedlings under his care were to be trans-
planted.

We talked of cornflowers. I had planted some seedlings in
a flower border, five small clumps far apart, and I had looked
at them one morning, thinking of the June day when blue
would come into the garden with convolvulus and del-
phiniums. And the next morning they were bitten flat. I had
not thought of them as needing netting, and spoke to him of
what, I realized, he knew already.

"Ah," he said, resting on his rake, "I thought about they
cornflowers when they was planted out. Yes, they've left the
cheeryanthus; they've not touched them. But there—I'll
tell you. You wait till they cornflowers seed, and then you'll
get the goldfinches. Down in my place we gets them—oh,
twenty, fifty, feeding on the seed. Four and five in a bunch,
heads down, close as that to you, and in th' old apple tree,
and in th' old roses, beautiful little birds they are, they little
goldies, chirping, chattering. Flocks of them. Yes, it's something in the soil, I think. You don't get them in this here sand
same as in my place, where it's loomy. But they little goldies
—I like to see them. Twenty, fifty at a time."

That is the picture and the thought I like best of my old
countryman, spade in hand, looking at goldies. They are
quiet eyes, and it is a quiet brain behind them, watching and
working among the everyday things of cottage life, rain and
sun, winter and summer, light and dark—beyond all, rain
and winter and dark. For in them he cannot be working in
his garden, and he is alone with his thoughts; he can read,
slowly I hope, for that would help to pass the time, and time
itself must go slowly for him in his cottage. It is there, or
in his garden or mine, that he spends his life; any other life
near him in his home is that of a cottager like himself. There
is no other society; the village inn is a mile away, and he
does not drink or smoke; he has what the villagers call bad
legs, which mean that from time to time he has to stop work
altogether, "work" being digging, and even when he digs it
is with his arms only, never with his feet.

So that his world is his garden and mine, and the road
between them, and in winter the daily paper under an oil
lamp. And beyond, behind the news in the paper? I do not

Wolsey's Tower, on the banks of the Mole, Esher Place

guess. Of his country in his father's time, his grandfather's, of time before that, of kings and queens of the past, of "the Romans"—it is perhaps a vision of things round him becoming less and less distinct, merging into an indefinite light which is "'istory time." That is an age, a far world, dimly outlined for me in those two words. Once in a hedgerow I found a queer-shaped piece of metal. He looked at it, but its make was not within his knowledge. "That belongs to 'istory time."

And 'istory time merges somewhere into our own, with the slowly read columns of the daily paper, and the mixing of its language with a speech unknown to Fleet Street. Once I complimented him on the straightness of his rows of plants, and thought I heard an echo of farming in print. "I like to grow them in rowtation." And on a day in summer he spoke to me of a neighbour who had killed "an adder three foot six inches long." "An *adder*?" I says to him, "that's a snake. You don't kill *snakes*. Ah, I says to 'im, Mr —— 'd be up-straps to us if we did a thing like that."

And in his vocabulary snake and adder are entirely different creatures. "You don't kill snakes," which are harmless and even to be protected. He spoke to me of a snake he had found in difficulties; he picked it up and set it down in grass at the side of the road. "There he was in the middle of the road, on asphalt. Slipping he was. Didn't seem able to get a bite." Hands circled this way and that. "All of a wangle, he was."

"Tell you what I was going to ask you," he said to me one day; we had been talking about the lives of men and dogs, and the idea that one year in a dog's life was about equal to seven in a man's—I was surprised to find—was new to him. "I said to myself, I'll ask if I think of it. What is the life of a snake?" I could not tell him; I knew no way in which the life of a snake in natural conditions could be measured. I had never seen a snake that had died a natural death. "No, no more haven't I," he said. "But I know what'll kill them. Magpies. I've seen them. Flying round and round, catter-catter-catter. Over a snake in the field. And then, come down they would. No, I've never seen them kill a snake. But catter-catter-catter, and fly round—you'd be surprised. Tell you what I have seen, though. When they've been felling trees, and the trees have fallen and killed a snake. Athol and me"—Athol was the Christian name of a gardener in past days—"when we was getting emmets for the young birds, and we'd find a snake killed like that, and put it in one of the emmets' nesties. Cor! In a minute, you wouldn't see the snake. Horse-emmets, they was. And in a couple of hours— there wasn't a fletch of him. Yes, you'd be surprised. Not a fletch of him."

But if I can sum up his talk, the talk of him and his neighbours, the speech I like best to hear day after day in my Surrey countryside, it would be in his use of just two words, "he" and "she." There was a rhyme in days gone by which some of us learnt at school. "Common are to either sex," it began, and went on with lists, *artifex* and *opifex* and the rest. No such rhyme can have been needed in south-west Surrey by village schoolmasters teaching English grammar. For the easy rule, surely, has always been that common to either sex are all animals, plants, fish, fruit, things animate and inanimate, he and she the same.

I should like to have spoken with George Bourne on this point. Readers of *The Bettesworth Book* and *Memoirs of a Surrey Labourer* may remember various talks about horses. Bettesworth's horses, I think, are all "he," and so, I fancy, are most Surrey horses to-day. My pony is "he." I bought her when the war made petrol for lawn-mowers impossible; she was four years old, and her name is Kitty. She is dark brown, strong and rough, with a beautiful head and quiet, happy eyes—they would be happier still, I think, if she had not been docked—and an untiring worker and feeder. But she is always "he." Kitty pulls the mowing-machine, and he is bothered by the flies. She is tethered while the gardeners are at lunch, and she eats unmown grass until he is harnessed again.

I was asking my and her gardener friend about birds. Had he heard a wryneck? "No, not yet. But you may hear him any day. Tell you what I did hear, though—a nightingale. Heard and saw. It was this morning. Mother, she brought me up a cup of tea, and I listened and I says to her, 'What's that?' I listened, and I looks out, and there she was, on top

of the hedge, singing—oh, beautiful. Singing all hidy-glee.
Yes, I looks out, and there she was singing. *That* was the
boy!"

If I could be sure how to write it down, and knew all the
other words that my Surrey countryman knows and uses, but
so seldom when I am there! But could he spell them to me?
Does he even know he uses them? I think often of a story
told by Brian Vesey-FitzGerald in that fascinating study of a
little-known side of country life, *Gypsies of Britain*. Once in
the New Forest he had been listening to a gipsy named Lee
recounting the tale of a poaching expedition. "He took his
listeners step by step through the night and then as he
approached the climax he suddenly said '*Disilo*.' I asked
him what it meant. 'Day comes,' he said impatiently, and
went on with the tale. . . . Yet when I asked him a week or
two later did he know the word *Disilo* he said 'No,' and was
obviously astounded to hear that he had ever used it."

And in the same way I ponder over "Hidy-glee." Or
"High-de-glee"—is that it? When I heard the word—I
have only heard it once—I remembered another. My country-
man-friend was describing a jovial gathering he had been at.
"They was all run-aglee." "High-de-glee"—"Run-aglee"—
those surely belong to merry England.

Chapter XIX

GRASSHOPPERS AND SCHOOL CRICKET

WHEN I look at a school cricket ground I find myself wondering what the school sees. For that is part of the game, though the schoolboy may not know it when he is playing. He thinks of the match, of his side and the part he takes in it, of his innings and the particular hits as he makes them, or the catches he makes, or the wickets he takes with this or that ball; and these each of them are different in each game he plays. But there is one thing that remains from every game beyond the boundary. He may not realize that he sees it at the time, or how much it means to him, and will mean in days to come; but it is there, the background, the frame of the game; trees, a hill, the school tower, the downs, and again the trees and blue sky above them. That remains, that is the abiding vision.

For those who play on the ground of St. John's School, Leatherhead, I will guess that the vision is of poplar trees. Ten Lombardy poplars line the west end of the ground, ten as noble trees as stand above any ground. And they serve a purpose of the game, or they served it, at all events, in a match I saw the school play against the Grasshoppers, for they held up the sight-screen, fastened by rope and wire. As school cricket grounds should be, St. John's School ground is framed with trees, sycamores down one side, and limes at the end opposite the Lombardy poplars. But I remember a Canadian poplar too, shining gold-green in the light of a stormy July afternoon, when there was the contrast of the copper-green spire of the school-building opposite. Who that played in that match, on 14 July 1945, will forget the all-night lightning and thunder that followed it? But the abiding vision, for me, is of those ten majestic Lombardy poplars, dark against cloud and sun.

And the memory, for a schoolboy, of another ground five miles away? Epsom College provides its visitor with as

gracious an introduction as could any group of school
buildings, an avenue of beeches leading from a garden past
the chapel to a wide vista of playing-fields. Of the cricket
ground I do not know the length, but the first thing that
strikes the newcomer is its length compared with its breadth;
then, perhaps, as with other grounds, he looks at the trees
that stand about it, sycamore, thorn, beech, but markedly
beech, for there are copper beeches among the green. But it
is not the trees, I think, which set themselves in a player's
memory so lastingly as what lies beyond them; not what he
sees, but what he cannot see far away, the blue distance of
Surrey open to the north. There are no houses. Higher than
the ground stand the school buildings, but you would not
guess there was a town near, the thought would be of Epsom
Downs.

Perhaps for some there would be another memory. Next
the chapel are laburnums, and may trees among beeches line
the mown turf of the cricket ground. But the ground alone
sets itself in a separate scorebook, so to speak, because of its
flowers. I have never seen so many daisies. Has the grounds-
man his own idea, I wonder, of what should be meant by a
daisy-cutter? I looked at them lying like a shower of snow,
on a July afternoon I shall always remember for a thrush
that sang through the hours; I thought of Andrew Lang
writing of the cricketers of Nyren and Broad Halfpenny:

> Beneath the daisies, there they lie . . .

But that afternoon and that ground will always be linked in
my memory with the wild flowers in profusion on its levels
and banks—bladderwort, yellow toadflax, ladies' bedstraw,
a common but local hawkbit (*murorum*, is it?), white-
flowered plantain, and succory by the pavilion to match the
distance in its blue. They are all of the aura of that Epsom
cricket ground; perhaps they will be part of a schoolboy's
memory with, I will hope, a red ball soaring into the air
beyond its trees.

I do not know how many schools play their matches on a
higher ground than Charterhouse: I know none which looks
out on a nobler view. I have thought sometimes of elevens
coming from other grounds to field for the first time with so

wide a horizon—Winchester, perhaps, journeying from
Meads and the Itchen, or Eton from the banks of the
Thames, or even Harrow; but Harrow plays on the flank,
not the crown of the Hill. No school side, I am sure, walks
out on that broad circle of Charterhouse turf without a new
knowledge of clean air blowing, of sunlight spread from the
horizon to the wicket. From west to south stretches blue
distance, Hindhead to Blackdown, Hydons Ball to Hascombe; oaks, old as the school and young as yesterday, stand
from cricket nets and scoring-boards to the steps of the
school buildings and the severe beauty of the chapel. But the
outstanding welcome of the ground is to a game in fresh air,
a field from which the cricket of youth looks out into space
of years to come.

If the records of Cranleigh School cricketers may not be as
long and as varied as those of other schools, they must be
full of happy memories. The school stands above the road
half a mile from the village, and the cricket ground to the
south-west of it, a noble stretch of turf. My first recollections
of the game there are of matches with the Grasshoppers in
the 'twenties and 'thirties, and they mingle with those of an
August day in 1945, when it was my good fortune to find the
school cricket coach, C. W. L. Parker, on the ground. Schoolboy batsmen are surely privileged beyond others, who have
had the experience of facing at the nets one of the greatest
bowlers of all time, the left-hander who first played for
Gloucestershire in 1905, and who thirty years later for the
sixteenth season in succession took more than a hundred
wickets in first-class cricket. He will leave his mark in the
minds, as he will lend his skill to the hands, of many elevens
of Cranleigh cricketers. But those memories will linger with
thoughts of the ground itself, its broad stretches of sunlight
ringed with oaks, and the quiet of its surrounding fields. To
each school ground its separate setting, and in years to come,
I do not doubt, there will remain in the mind's eye of those
who played on that ground in times past a vision beyond the
creases and the rolled wicket, of farmfields, hayfields, hedges,
maybe of cows lying head to summer airs, and beyond all to
the north the wooded outline of the Surrey hills.

Wimbledon Common, seven miles from Charing Cross,

can transport the traveller the longest distance in the shortest
time. You may step aside from an asphalt highway fifty yards
and you are in deep country. So with the common's neighbouring buildings. King's College School, which from the
south side of the common fronts spaces of sunshine, hears the
everyday traffic of its surrounding roads. But close at hand
the school plays cricket. It possesses two cricket grounds,
one of which, near to its main buildings, is a noble stretch of
turf with as wide and fast an outfield as any batsman or
fielder of a country side could desire. Bordered by elms old
and young, and screened from the road by a high holly hedge,
it hears to-day only happy sounds. But it has known the scars
of war. When I saw it first on a Sunday in that July that
followed peace in Europe, I looked beyond the level sunlit
turf to a wall with white roses, and in the quiet afternoon;
but under the school buildings in the distance was a shattered
gymnasium, and at my side the broken masonry of a garden
lodge. That was the contrast.

And with the second field came another contrast. It lies
beyond the railway, and before we crossed the bridge I stood
watching a game of cricket played in the distance. White
figures moving in sunshine, yellow broom in flower at my
elbow, Carter's garden-seed plots away to the right—it was
the Southern Railway ground, and a happy sight that Sunday
afternoon. But the unexpected thing was the school cricket
ground, away across the line. King's College School Playing
Fields, the announcement at the gate tells you, and the playing fields are well named in the plural. For there are three
Rugby football grounds there, side by side, and a cricket
ground in the middle of them, an almost unbelievable expanse of meadowland bordered by elm and oak and thorn,
away to meadow and woodland beyond. There we were,
London just away up the line, in the sunlight of acres of pure
countryside. And those playing fields are bordered, as playing fields surely should be, by a stream, the Pyl Brook, which
runs cool and bright over brown gravel under ten-foot banks;
beyond the brook, a rim of villas to the horizon; I looked at
the villas, and turned to the countryside behind me, to
measure the expanse of those playing fields. They are fields,
and that is a cricket ground which should hold memories, a

schoolboy's hat-trick perhaps, or his first six over the boun-
dary; not out of the ground—that has been done at the
Oval, but not, I think, in these playing fields over the Pyl
Brook.

But of all cricket grounds in the county one, in qualities
that seem sometimes to belong to a past age, stands out alone.
That is the wide square of turf in Busbridge Park, where the
owner, Mr Reginald Earle, for twenty years and more has
been the host of elevens ranging from village sides to a team
from South Africa facing England bowlers and batsmen for
the first time. If any ground could be picked out as offering
ideal conditions for country-house cricket it would be Busbridge Park. It stands high in Surrey air, above lakes on one
side and Godalming a mile away on the other. It is a
generous space separated by a fence from parkland and noble
trees, beech, elm, oak, lime, poplar, chestnut—there is a
beech by the entrance gate that would shade an Oval crowd.
Far away in the Park you get a glimpse of Busbridge Hall,
and in gaps between treetops the trees and hills above Witley
and the grey-blue outline of Hindhead. Two pavilions—if
you may call buildings of hospitable country simplicity by
such a name—offer space for spectators and players, luncheon
and tea, and above them a flagstaff invites colours to the
wind. It is all of the best of the South Country, with the Hall
and its farm the only buildings in sight; if anything could be
said to fill the picture, it would be the Jersey cows feeding
where a six might be hit to square leg.

I have been glancing at the score of the first big match
played at Busbridge since cricketers have been Mr Earle's
guests. The South Africans who toured England in 1929
played their first match there on 29 April, with all their chief
batsmen, Taylor, Siedle, Owen-Smith, Deane, Morkel,
Mitchell and Cameron, in the side, and Quinn and Ochse as
bowlers, while in the home side were such names as Mac-
Bryan, Tennyson, Twining, Miles Howell, Stanyforth and
Douglas—"Johnny Won't Hit To-day," that nickname of an
old England captain sums up memories of the side. The Busbridge Hall eleven made 138 and the South Africans 129 for
seven wickets, but nobody minded who won or lost; it was
just the best kind of country-house cricket, and there were

just as many first-class cricketers among the onlookers as in the teams.

I remember another match of a different kind on the ground; there were first-class players on both sides, but it was nothing important : one side came mainly from Hampshire and the other from Surrey—just school and country-house cricket. But I have never seen better. Hampshire won the toss and at four o'clock declared their innings closed with the score 265 for seven wickets. There was to be an interval of half an hour for tea, so that we were left (I was merely a spectator) to get 266 runs in two hours twenty minutes. We started at 4.12 and at 4.19 lost an opening batsman with 6 on the board. Soon afterwards came tea, and after tea fours, sixes and short runs; the winning hit was made with five wickets down at three minutes to seven. I have been looking back at the score-book; there were three main run-getters, with scores of 67, 47 and 96 not out—this by one who had made his name in the Winchester eleven. All who know the ground will remember that a hit for 6 means a long carry, but I am not sure that it was not the short singles that won the match. I have never enjoyed a match more.

But I write as an onlooker only. Cricket at Busbridge ought to be described by players; above all, by those who have played there for the Grasshoppers, that happy band of Surrey cricketers who came together to form their club soon after the war that ended in 1918. There were clubs of the same type in Kent and Sussex and Hampshire, why not in Surrey? The Grasshoppers were privileged from the beginning with the use of the Busbridge Hall ground and have played matches there ever since. I see from their fixture card that out of seventeen matches arranged in 1939 five were played at Busbridge, against United Services, Free Foresters, Uppingham Rovers, Charterhouse Friars and Hampshire Hogs, and I am sure that their generous host of Busbridge Hall likes to think that wherever the war of 1939 carried cricketers there were memories of the sunlight on that broad turf and of the shade under the great beeches next the pavilion—thoughts of mid-off drives to the huge tree by the entrance gate, perhaps, or of a square-leg hit towards the laughing leaves of a grey poplar, or of Hindhead far on the

horizon, or of a catch in the deep field lost sight of against
the leaves of that towering elm behind the screen, and of the
Grasshoppers' flag, brown and green and blue, floating out
high over all. Henley's ballade comes back with those
memories :

> And the winds are one with the clouds and beams—
> Midsummer days! Midsummer days!

INDEX

Abinger, 12, 89, 213
Account Book, Great House Farm, 137–49
Adder, 171; cure for bites, 221
Albury, 12, 88
Aldershot, 11
Ancient Britons, 11
Anstiebury, 10; ancient camp at, 33, 34, 36
Ants, 211–12
Apple tree, 1
Aubrey, John, 14

Badger, 161–2; in gardens, 162, 163
Bagshot Beds, 11; Heath, 11
Banstead, 11
Bartlett, William, 42
Beech trees, 239–40
Betchworth, 12, 89
Bettesworth Book, 110, 111, 232–6
Billingshurst, 80
Binyon, Laurence, 1
Birch seedlings, 123–4
Bisley, 11
Bittern, 19
Blackberries, 133–4
Blackbird, 197–9
Bletchingley, 12
Bluebell Wood, 120
Box Hill, 11
Bramley, 87
Bramshott, 213
Brighton coach, 2
Brooklands, 2–9; Automobile Racing Club, 5–6; aviation at, 7–8
Buckland, 89
Bucknill, Sir John, 19; writings of, 19–24, 61
Bullfinch, 188–9
Buried treasure, 213–14
Burney, Fanny, 109
Busbridge Park, 249; cricket at, 249, 250
Buzzard, 195–6
Byfleet, 2
Bypasses, 81–6

Cæsar's Camp, Aldershot, 33; Wimbledon, 33, 42, 43
Camp Hill, 33, 41
Campion, 127
Carshalton, 15

"Casualty sheep," 143
Caterham Common, 11
Chalk ridge, 11; pits, 13–15
Charterhouse, 246–7
Cherry tree, 1, 125–6
Chestnut tree, 1; struck by lightning, 135–6
Chichester, 80
Chiddingfold, 87; glass works at, 50; Hunt, 107; pageant at, 52–5
Chilworth, 55, 87–8; in gunpowder industry, 63–6; Powder Factory, 55, 87–8; guarding the factory, 55–61
Chobham Ridges, 11
Church Cobham, 11
Churches in folklore, 214–15
Clay, London, 11; Wealden, 10, 12
Cloth industry, 66–70
Clouded Yellow butterfly, 202
Cobham Fairmile, 86
Cockchafer, 162, 209–11
Coins, Roman, at Brooklands, 3–4
Collett, Anthony, 191
Comma butterfly, 193, 200–2; Ab. *Hutchinsoni*, 201
Compton, modern pottery at, 77–8
Cormorant, 19
Coulsdon, 11
Countryside, changes caused by war, 30
Cowey Stakes, 35
Cramp, safeguards against, 218
Cranleigh, 90; School, 247
Cricket, school, 245–51
Crooksbury Hill, ancient camp at, 33
Crossbill, 185–8
Crowhurst, 213
Croydon, 11
Curlew, 21, 193–4

Dartford warbler, 193
Death's Head hawkmoth, 204; caterpillar, 204–5; chrysalis, 205–6
Deer, fallow, 157–60; roe, 160–1
Denbies, 15
Dialect, 232–8, 243–4
Diver, Black-throated, 21, 28–9; Great Northern, 21; Red-throated, 21
Dorking, 12, 15, 89, 213
Downs, the, 12
Dragonflies, 208

Dry Hill Camp, 34; excavations at, 39–41
Dunsfold, 109

Early settlers in Surrey, 37, 39
Egerton family, 34
Egg-collectors, 24
Elephant hawkmoth, 207
Elstead, 30
Emperor moth, 206–7
Epilepsy, cure for, 217
Epsom, 11; College, 246–7; Downs, 11
Esher, 11, 86; Common, 11
Evelyn family, 62–3
Ewhurst, 90

Fairies, 216
Farm labourers' wages, 139
Farnham, 10, 11, 12; cloth industry at, 68; modern pottery at, 78
Field, names of, 13
Flying bomb, effects of, 129–30
Fold Country, 105; in war, 106–7
Forrard Oak, the, 121–2
Fox, 169–70
French, George Russel, 49
Frensham Ponds, 24–5, 29–32; birds at, 24–5; draining of, 25–6; overgrown by trees, 26; refilled, 30–1
Frogs, 172; in winter, 172; albino, 172

Gale uprooting trees, 126–7
Garden White butterfly, Large, 200, 203; Small, 203; migrating, 203–4
Gardner, Dr Eric, 34, 35, 36, 220
Gatton, 11
Gault, the, 12
Giuseppi, Montague, 14, 46, 65, 74, 78
Glass industry, 49–55
Godalming, 12, 213; bypass, 81; cloth industry at, 66–70; leather industry at, 70, 73; Museum, 230–1; Wharf, 145
Godstone, leather industry at, 72–3
Goldfinch, 240–1
Gomshall, 89
Gould, John, 29
Grass-snake, 171
Grebe, Great-Crested, 22–7
Greensand, Lower, 11, 213; Upper, 11
Greenshank, 20
Groundsel, 123
Guano, 145
Guildford, 11, 85; cloth industry at, 66–8; Museum, 229–30
Gunpowder industry, 55, 61–6

Hambledon, 13, 15, 87, 106, 219; Women's Institute at, 152–6

Hare, 163–4
Hascombe, 10; excavations at, 34, 37, 38–9
Haslemere, 214–15, 218–19; Educational Museum, 224–8
Hastings Beds, 12
Hazel, 134
Heath galium, 127
Hedgehog, 166–7
Hedges, destruction of, 117–19
Herb robert, 127
Hill, Sir George, 4
Hindhead, 10, 12, 213
Hog's Back, 11, 84
Holmbury, 10; ancient camp at, 33, 34, 36
Horley, leather industry at, 72–3
Hundred Acre Field, 13, 15, 115
Hut Pond, 85
Huxley, Julian, 25
Huxley, Leonard, 16
Hydon's Ball, 15, 16, 43, 44, 92; Top, 17

Iron industry, 45, 46–9; in placenames, 46
Ironwork in Crowhurst Church, 49
Ironstone, 12, 17, 45

Jack-o'-Lent, 219
Jekyll, Gertrude, 158, 219, 229
Jerusalem artichokes, 116
Joe Basset, see Cockchafer

Kestrel, 195
Kew, 11
King's College School, 248; playingfields, 248
Kingsley, Charles, 92
Kingston Bypass, 85
Kirdford, 213

Lambeth, pottery at, 74
Lanes, 90–2
Larch trees, felling of, 158; replanting, 123
Large Tortoiseshell butterfly, 202–3
Latham, Charlotte, 215, 216, 217
Leatherhead, 109; Mill Pool, 109–10
Leather industry, 70–3
Leith Hill, 12, 33
Lime, 13; cost of, 15; at Dorking, 15; kilns, 13–17; used in St. Paul's Cathedral, 14
Limestone, 15
Limpsfield, 12; ancient pottery at, 74–5
Linch, 213
Lincoln, Earl of, 35

Lingfield, 12
Liphook, 213
Liss, 213
Loganberries, 133
London Clay, 11
Lower, Mark Antony, 45
Lucas, E. V., 81
Lurgashall, 213

Malcolm, James, 15
Malden, H. E., 12; work of, 33, 34, 43, 48
Mechanized farming, changes caused by, 114–19
Memoirs of a Surrey Labourer, 128, 234–6
Merrow Down, 11
Merstham, 15
Milford, 29, 82
Mitford, Miss, 92
Mole, 166; length of run, 166; skins, 166
Mulberry tree, 240
Mullein, 84

Newark Priory, 2
Nightingale, 194–5
Nightjar in superstition, 215–16
North Downs, 80
Nuthatch, 175–9

Oatlands, ancient camp at, 33; Park, 2; Hotel, 35
Ockham, 11
Ockley, 80, 90; Common, 30
Onslow, Lord, 37
Oxted, 12

Painshill, 90
Painted Lady butterfly, 202
Parker, Christopher, 184–5
Parkhatch, 90
Paths, 92–3
Paulhan, aviator, 7–8
Peyto family, glass-makers, 51–2
Phalarope, Grey, 19
Pigeons, decoying of, 57
Pilgrims' Way, 83; history and literature of, 94–104
Pine-marten, 170–1
Polecat, 60, 170
Pond-skater, 209
Postford Pond, 60–1
Potters' Arts Guild, 77
Pottery, ancient, 74–7; modern, 77–9
Prior's Field School, 16
Privet hawkmoth, 207
Proverbs, 239–40
Pulborough, 80

Queen's West Surrey Regiment, 56

Rabbit, 164–5
Rawlinson, Richard, 14
Ray, John, 46
Red Admiral butterfly, 202
Redshank, 20
Redstart, Black, 61
Reigate, 12, 213; leather industry at, 72
Ripley, 11, 85
Road, Roman, 80, 81
Robertson, Graham, 52
Rusper, 12

St. Anne's Hill, 11
St. Catherine's Hill, 11
St. George's Hill, 2, 11; ancient camp at, 33, 34–6
St. James's Church, Dorking, 90
St. John's School, Leatherhead, 245
St. Martha's Church, Albury, 88
Saltpetre, making of, 61–2
Sandhills, 122
Sandown, 86
Sandpiper, Common, 20; Green, 20
Shere, 89
Silent Pool, 89
Slinfold, 80
Smallfield, 14
Smew, 60
Smith, Reginald, 16
Smugglers, 92–3, 216–17
Snipe, 60, 88
Snowdrops, 131
South Downs, 80
Southwark, 11
Sparrowhawk, 195
Squirrel, Grey, 169; Red, 2, 169
Stane Street, *see* Roman Road
Starling, 106, 196
State ownership, 113, 118–19
Stoke by Guildford, 11
Sturt, George, *see Bettesworth Book*
Superstitions over birth and death, 221–2
Surrey Archæological Society, 33, 34, 36
Surrey, origin of name, 10
Sutton, 14, 15
Swift, 86–7

Tatsfield, 11
Terry, Ellen, 54
Thames, 10, 11
Thursley, 12, 29, 30, 213
Tilburstow Hill, 12
Tillingbourne, the, 55, 87
Tilsey, 11
Timber mill, 128

Tolt hill, the, 75; ancient pottery at, 75–6; in superstition, 214
Trees blown down in gale, 126–7; destroyed by flying bombs, 129–30
Turkey Oak, 132
Turnpikes, 148–9, 227–8

Vesey-FitzGerald, Brian, 180, 181, 183
Vine Cottage, Farnham, 111, 112
Virginia Water, draining of, 25; overgrown by trees, 27; refilled, 28; birds at, 28–9

War Agricultural Executive Committee, 113, 115, 117–18
War, changes caused by, 30–2, 105–8, 114–19
War Copse, ancient camp at, 33
Water-boatman, 209
Water shrew, 167, 168
Watts, G. F., 77
Weald, the, 13, 213
Wealden Clay, 10, 12, 213; Coal, 12
Westcott, 89
Weybridge, 2, 8, 91

Wey river, 2–3
Whirligig beetle, 209
White, Gilbert, 215
Whitechapel Gamps, 221–2
Whooping-cough, cures for, 220–1
Wild Birds Protection Acts, 19, 22
Willowherb, 122
Winbolt, S. E., 34; work of, 36, 37, 38, 39–41
Winterton Toll Gate, 227–8
Wisley Church, 2
Witchcraft, 217–18
Witley Common, 30
Woking, 2
Women's Institutes, history of, 150–1; to-day, 151–6; Produce Guilds, 155
Woodcock, 132–3
Woodcutters, 124–5
Woodland flowers, 134–5
Woodlark, 190–2
Woodpecker, Greater Spotted, 1; drumming, 179–83; Green, 183–5
Worms Heath, ancient camp at, 33
Wotton, 89
Wrecclesham, modern pottery at, 78
Wryneck, 189–90